HOW TO
LISTEN
to
GOD

HOW TO LISTEN to GOD

DISCOVERING *the* SIGNS *of* HIS LOVE *and* GUIDANCE

DOUG HILL

Guideposts.
New York, New York

How to Listen to God

ISBN-13: 978-0-8249-4735-4

Published by Guideposts
16 East 34th Street, New York, New York 10016
www.guidepostsbooks.com

Distributed by Ideals Publications, a Guideposts company
535 Metroplex Drive, Suite 250
Nashville, Tennessee 37211

Guideposts and *Ideals* are registered trademarks of Guideposts.

Acknowledgments

Every attempt has been made to credit the sources of copyrighted material used in this book. If any such acknowledgment has been inadvertently omitted or misattributed, receipt of such information would be appreciated.

All material that originally appeared in *Angels on Earth*, *Daily Guideposts* and *Guideposts* magazine is reprinted with permission. Scripture quotations marked (CEV) are taken from the *Contemporary English Version*. Copyright © American Bible Society, 1991. Scripture quotations marked (KJV) are taken from *The King James Version of the Bible*. Scripture quotations marked (NAS) are taken from the *New American Standard Bible*, © The Lockman Foundation, 1960, 1962, 1963, 1968, 1971, 1972, 1973, 1975, 1977. Used by permission. Scripture quotations marked (NIV) are taken from *The Holy Bible, New International Version*. Copyright © 1973, 1978, 1984 International Bible Society. Used by permission of Zondervan Bible Publishers. Scripture quotations marked (NRSV) are taken from the *New Revised Standard Version Bible*. Copyright © 1989 by the Division of Christian Education of the National Council of the Churches of Christ in the U.S.A. Used by permission. All rights reserved. Scripture quotations marked (RSV) are taken from the *Revised Standard Version of the Bible*. Copyright © 1946, 1952, 1971 by Division of Christian Education of the National Council of Churches of Christ in the U.S.A. Used by permission. "From Your Knees" copyright © 1999 by Leslie Satcher, EMI April Music Inc. "In My Hour of Darkness" by Gram Parsons and Emmylou Harris, copyright © Sixteen Stars Music/BMI. Reprinted with permission from HoriPro Entertainment Group, Inc. "Oh, my Lord, deliver us from darkness" and "Promised Land." Lyrics copyright © 1988 by George Fischoff Publishing Company, Rego Park, New York. All rights reserved.

Library of Congress Cataloging-in-Publication Data

Hill, Doug, 1950-
  How to listen to God : discovering the signs of His love and guidance / Doug Hill.
    p. cm.
  Originally published: Carmel, N.Y. : Guideposts, c2004.
  ISBN-13: 978-0-8249-4735-4
  1. Spiritual life—Christianity. 2. Listenings—Religious aspects—Christianity. I. Title.
  BV4501.3.H684 2008
  248.4—dc22
                          2007039733

Cover and interior design by Russ McIntosh/The Office of Bill Chiaravalle
Cover photo by Sanford/Agliolo/Corbis
Typeset by Nancy Tardi

Printed and bound in the United States of America

10 9 8 7 6 5 4 3 2 1

To Judy

CONTENTS

INTRODUCTION

You would think that if God wanted to speak with us, He could, and we'd know it when He did.

The first part of that statement is definitely true. God wants to speak to us, He can, and He does! All the time. The problem is we don't always hear what He's saying.

This book is aimed at helping you hear God's voice—or, more accurately, God's voices. For God, as we shall see, speaks in a multitude of tongues. Sometimes He whispers, other times He shouts. Seldom does He appear in a burning bush and speak to us directly. Our God is a God of nudges, signals and signs. Sometimes He sends angels to our doors, other times He plants ideas in our heads. He can push us in a direction He wants us to go or close off a pathway we feel sure we ought to take. He can reassure us with comfort as we kneel in prayer, inspire us with a strange but burning conviction, or strengthen us with confidence as we face a challenge.

The process of creating this book has been a marvelous experience for me. Each of its stories was chosen because it describes a true example of how God reaches out to His creatures. As I read them, I am astounded by how miraculous and varied God's messages truly are. Now I go about my daily business with my ears wide open. I pay attention in a way I never have before, listening more carefully for the myriad voices of the Holy Spirit. And I *hear* them—singing, swirling, sighing all around me!

My prayer is that you'll have the same experience.

—DOUG HILL—

How to
LISTEN
to
GOD

CHAPTER ONE

GOD SPEAKS TO US...
In Our Prayers

*I*t feels a bit odd starting this book with a chapter on prayer, since usually you're supposed to save the most important part for last. Still, because everything begins with prayer, prayer seems the most logical place to start.

There's no question that prayer is the *foundational tool for hearing God's voice,* and for learning *God's will for our lives.* The process is remarkably simple, really, considering that it's utterly miraculous. We ask God for guidance, and God answers. Both parts of this conversation occur in prayer. Prayer is the necessary and indispensable medium of any intimate relationship with God.

One of the glories of prayer is that it enables us to actively seek divine guidance. It's true that God often initiates conversation with us, using miracles both subtle and dramatic to attract our attention. But the surest way to learn God's will is the direct way: Ask.

Once we've asked, it's important to remember to listen for God's answer. Our prayers for guidance need to be two-way

*conversations—dialogues, not monologues. How do we listen? By being
quiet, by being patient, by being attentive. God's answers are not
always obvious, nor do they always come in the manner we expect.
"My thoughts are not your thoughts, neither are your ways my ways"
(Isaiah 55:8, NIV).*

*It's also important to make a habit of praying for God's guidance.
Doing so brings a double blessing. Our ability to hear and understand
the Lord's voice increases with practice. At the same time, we continually deepen our bond with our Creator. Each of these outcomes rein-
forces the other.*

*This is one of the points made beautifully in our first story, "The
Road I Travel." It was written by one of the wisest writers I know on
the subject of listening to God, Elizabeth Sherrill. A longtime
Guideposts contributor and editor, Sherrill has made spiritual discernment a special area of study and reflection for many years. Here she provides a sketch of how her confidence in asking through prayer for God's
guidance evolved.*

THE ROAD I TRAVEL
—BY ELIZABETH SHERRILL—

That dark Sunday night last August it was raining, and the needle on my
rental car's heat gauge was quivering at the top of the danger zone. I
took the next exit off Interstate 80—somewhere in Ohio—and stared
through slapping windshield wipers at the unfamiliar town names on the
signpost. *Turn left? Right? Where would I find a gas station open, and one
with a mechanic on duty at 9:00 PM on a Sunday?*

Then I did what I often do when in doubt: I asked God for guidance.

The prayer was so instinctive that it wasn't till later that the audacity
of it swept over me. Ask the God who had flung forth the galaxies to
concern Himself with my overheating engine? Expect, in other words, a
miracle-to-order for my benefit?

It was forty years ago that I first encountered people who believed in
divine guidance—and the experience was so off-putting that for a long
while afterward I shut my mind to the subject. My husband John and I
were taking our first stumbling steps toward faith when a couple whom

we had met while church-shopping asked if they could call on us. My cooking then was nearly as tentative as my religion, but we decided to invite them to dinner.

Things went wrong before the first bite. John said grace—as I had reminded him to do ("Remember, they're religious!")—and reached for his soup spoon. Our guests, however, continued to sit with bowed heads, while first one, then the other added their own long prayers as the sour cream slowly sank beneath the surface of the soup.

It was during the main course, however, that their behavior became incomprehensible to me. As the meat platter went around the table, both glanced swiftly at the ceiling before helping themselves. The same with the vegetable dishes—the momentary pause, that upward glance. Surreptitiously I too scanned the ceiling. *Peeling plaster? Cobwebs?*

The wife dipped the serving spoon into the scalloped potatoes, lifted her eyes, then passed the dish along untouched. Her husband took a helping of potatoes but, after checking the ceiling, turned down the next dish: "No peas."

So it went. Gravy, rolls, relish—till at last I understood. It wasn't the ceiling they were consulting; it was God. They were seeking his okay for every item of food.

I was not, as I say, a confident cook, but still! By the end of the dessert course (both said yes to peach cobbler) puzzlement had turned to indignation. This was at the time of the Suez Canal crisis; I remember thinking how incredibly self-centered those people had to be to imagine God would turn from a world on the brink of war to advise two individuals whether to put dressing on their salad.

From then on, whenever I heard the word *guidance*, I heard as a kind of echo: "No peas."

For four years I dismissed the matter as too trivial to bother with. Until, in 1961, John and I wrote a story for *Guideposts* about a young minister named David Wilkerson. David's work among New York City's street gangs was anything but trivial. Guidance was one of his favorite words: "I saw the knife in his hand and said a quick prayer for guidance," he said.

Without that element in his life, we soon saw, there would have been no story to tell. David had arrived in the city a country preacher with no idea how to contact the alienated kids he wanted to help. There was one gang leader in particular who David felt was the key to reaching all the rest. "So I asked God to lead me to him," he said. David started driving at random through the streets of Manhattan. Not really at random, apparently; in response to some inner prompting he turned the wheel first one way then another, until on a certain block he spotted a parking place. He got out of his car—and found himself in front of the gang leader's home.

What were we to make of stories like those? For that wasn't some once-in-a-lifetime coincidence. In David's life such mysterious leading was almost routine.

And not in his life only. The longer we worked at *Guideposts* the more we heard about guidance. Brother Andrew, a Dutchman ministering to Christians behind the Iron Curtain during the Cold War, would arrive in a strange city without a single lead to its underground church. Andrew would pray for guidance . . . be drawn to speak to a certain stranger on a crowded street . . . and discover that the stranger was the pastor of the local Christian cell.

At first we had trouble believing such stories. Yet time and again—where there were independent witnesses—the accounts checked out. Recording such experiences, I found my feelings about guidance had unconsciously swung to the opposite extreme. Instead of seeing guidance as too silly to concern me, I saw it as too important. Guidance was a provision for people engaged in major moves of God: for David, whose Teen Challenge Centers by then were redeeming young lives across the nation; for Andrew, whose Open Doors ministry was bringing hope to hundreds of thousands under totalitarian regimes around the globe.

I had become persuaded that guidance was real, but still had no inkling it could matter to ordinary people.

Then came a yearlong trip. In 1962 John and I, with our three children, ages six, eight and eleven, went to East Africa and found ourselves daily, even hourly, facing unfamiliar situations. I remember the first time we asked God to help us make a decision. John had stopped the car at a fork in the unmarked dirt track we had been following most of the day. Ten miles or so farther on was the village where we were expected. But down which of the two equally unpromising-looking paths did it lie?

"What do we do now?" I asked.

"I know what David Wilkerson would do," said John.

And so, awkwardly, feeling foolish and presumptuous, we bowed our heads—all five of us—and asked God which fork to take. Amazingly, in a family that an hour earlier hadn't been able to agree on where to eat our picnic lunch, every one of us promptly pointed to the right-hand fork.

Ten miles later the road brought us to the village. It "proved" nothing, of course; we had had a fifty-fifty chance of guessing right. Still . . .

We began to experiment regularly with this type of prayer, discovering that with it, more important than correct "guesses," came something harder to define: a strange new sense of connectedness. Between events. Between us and the people we "happened" to meet. Connectedness with God. As though in addition to the galaxies, He had on His mind one small family on one small errand.

Soon we were praying over many decisions. Where to settle down as the school year began. What stories to write. What water was safe to drink, what food to eat. Hesitating one day at a roadside market over a plucked chicken cradled in the market woman's lap, I found myself repenting of uncharitable thoughts toward a couple who had prayed over my peas. Perhaps they too had lived someplace where refrigeration was unknown. Perhaps those upward glances were unconscious mannerisms, left over from a time when praying over every food item mattered.

In Africa we learned to bring God into our uncertainties—and as we were uncertain about so much, our dialogue with Him became continuous. When we returned to our New York City suburb, those nudges to prayer came less often. We were back in the world of refrigeration and pasteurized milk. Guidance came in the "ordinary" form of street signs and weather forecasts. But the possibility of another kind of knowing, a new dimension of reality—both more mysterious and more meaningful —had broken through to us. A reality not only for heroes and leaders and doers of great deeds, but for us. To ask God into the moment-by-moment living of our lives is to act out the faith that He cares for us intimately, individually.

Three miles after turning left from the ramp off Interstate 80 that rainy night last summer, I pulled into a lit Shell station where a teenage boy, after a five-second glance underneath the hood, replaced my broken fan belt.

An open gas station doesn't qualify as a miracle, of course. Nor does the fact that a sixteen-year-old understood engines. The miracle was the calm of that three-mile drive from the highway before I got to the station, going I didn't know where, facing I didn't know what, but traveling in the company of the One who does know every road and every traveler. ❧

Ask and it will be given to you; seek and you will find; knock and the door will be opened to you.

— MATTHEW 7:7 (NIV)

Sometimes it seems a little glib to say that God answers our prayers. It's not often, if ever, that God literally speaks to us, in recognizable words and sentences. Many times we will "hear" the voice of God in our heads; more often we "hear" the Holy Spirit speaking in our hearts. But God does answer our prayers, frequently and quite clearly, in lots of different ways. All we have to do is to pay attention, as Mary Lou Carney reminds us below.

ABUNDANT ANSWERS
—BY MARY LOU CARNEY—

When our daughter Amy Jo's marriage ended, she moved back in with us. She enrolled in a full-time master's program at a nearby university, but was feeling restless and unsure about the future. "You know," she said one night as she was setting the table, "I used to talk about going to law school. Remember?"

I did remember. She had only been about ten when she first brought it up. And while she'd mentioned it a few times during the years, it somehow had fallen by the wayside as she got a degree in communications, took a job and got married. Now it was surfacing again. "I remember," I said, "but I'm not sure if that's what you should do now or not." Silently, I wondered where she would get the money. "Just pray about it, honey," I said, turning back to the stove. The words sounded frail. Wasn't there something else she should be doing?

A few minutes later, Amy Jo came back into the kitchen, beaming. She spread out the *Chicago Tribune* on the table and pointed to a classified ad: "Wondering if law school is right for you? Work for us and decide!" It was a large law firm in Chicago, an easy train ride from where we lived. So Amy Jo took the job, working for a year as a court runner. She loved it! Then she took her admissions test and enrolled in Valparaiso University, where she went on to law.

I've always believed in answered prayer. But these days I'm looking for those answers in lots of places. My Bible, of course. But also in the "thought for the day" that appears on my e-mail. Or in the overheard wisdom of an older woman in line at the grocery talking—on a cell phone—to her daughter. And, yes, maybe even in the newspaper. As for the financial problem of law school—Amy Jo is on full scholarship, which is something we *both* prayed about! ❧

"Does God speak to you in French?"

"I don't know, but I *hear* Him in French."

THE TRIAL OF JOAN OF ARC

Of all the decisions that must be made in the course of our lifetimes, certainly one of the most difficult can be the question of what we should do for work. At some point most of us wonder, "How can I best employ my talents and energies toward furthering God's plan? What is my calling?"

For so many of us, finding a vocation is a struggle. So many voices offer advice, so many paths seem to beckon. Which voice should we listen to? Which path should we choose? As Doris Christopher testifies powerfully in "Homemade," the right voice is the one that answers us in prayer, while the right path is the one that leads us closer to our own heart.

HOMEMADE

—By Doris Christopher—

Your daughter is a joy to have in the classroom, my parents were always pleased to hear my teachers report. Straight-A student. Smart. Hard worker. Puts her mind to a task and sticks with it. That was me. Until my junior year at Walther Lutheran High School in the Chicago suburbs, that is, when I found myself struggling with the one class everyone else seemed to breeze through—typing. Typing! I wasn't just struggling, I was failing. Failing miserably.

"You'll get the hang of it," my sweetheart Jay reassured me. "Relax. Don't worry so much." Easy for him to say. He was a senior. He'd passed the class and was already typing his college-application essays. Meanwhile, I couldn't seem to pass a single typing test, despite the extra practice I put in at the keyboard. Mama, who actually worked as a professional typist, would listen to my woes at dinner and patiently give me tips, and I'd put them to use the next day in class. I even begged God to help me get through typing, and prayed doubly hard in church on Sunday that I'd do well on the dreaded Monday morning test. But still my fingers kept hitting all the wrong keys.

The teacher tracked our progress on the bulletin board by using paper turtles emblazoned with our names, moving them along as we moved through the lessons in the typing workbook. Every time I looked up from the keyboard my failure stared me in the face. *God, how come my turtle's always dead last?* I lamented silently. *What's wrong with me?* Finally I got sick of feeling like a nervous wreck. *I can't take this anymore,* I decided one day, ripping another mangled typing-test sheet out of the roller.

That night after dinner, when Daddy got home from the service station he ran, I talked over my dilemma with him and Mama. "I don't want to be a quitter, but I just don't get typing." I hated to disappoint my parents because I knew how hard they worked so they could send me to the private school affiliated with our church. "You've tried your hardest, Doris," Daddy said. "There's no shame in realizing that there are certain things you're just not meant to do." Mama added, "Besides, I think people do best when they do what they love. Maybe it's time for you to explore what that might be."

I went to the school guidance counselor the next day. "Let's see what else meets that hour," she said. *I know it's six weeks into the school year. Please, God*, I prayed, *help me find another class I can take. I promise I'll do well.*

"There's only one class that has openings," the guidance counselor said, looking at me doubtfully. "Home economics."

Something inside me stirred, as if a puzzle piece had slipped into place. "That's perfect!" I exclaimed. My parents had given me a sewing machine for my Confirmation, and I'd been making my own clothes ever since. I loved trailing my mother around the kitchen. She'd come home from work, and I'd watch her speed from refrigerator to counter to stove, her hands a blur as she chopped, seasoned and stirred. Her wizardry fascinated me. Somehow she always managed to get a hearty dinner on the table by five-thirty for my older sisters and me. I looked forward to holiday mornings, when I'd put on one of Mama's aprons, and we'd knead dough on the Formica and make sweet, gooey cinnamon rolls. And Mama's famous Sunday dinners . . . they were a family ritual, almost an extension of church because they came right after.

My love for cooking must have just been waiting to be awakened because all it took was a simple recipe for mock apple pie in my new class, and I was hooked. Turning Ritz crackers and a few basic ingredients into something that tasted like real apple pie seemed almost magical to me. It hit me: This is what I'm meant to do. This is my calling—home ec!

For college, I chose the University of Illinois because of its excellent home economics department, even though that meant I would be able to see Jay, who was at Valparaiso University in Indiana, only when we were home on school breaks. I delighted in showing my mother what I'd learned in the college food lab. Being a working mom, she valued any tool or technique that made cooking quicker and easier, and that definitely rubbed off on me.

A few months after my college graduation in 1967, Jay and I got married and settled in Indiana. He worked in marketing. I taught high school home ec. A job opportunity for Jay soon took us back to the Chicago area. I found a job with the county cooperative extension service, leading workshops on homemaking. I'd never realized how much fun it was working with adult learners. It made me feel so good to share what I loved with other women, and to see them learn to love it too. I taught sewing, cooking, household budgeting and child development, which I'd studied in college. There was something spiritually gratifying about helping women make better homes.

Our daughter Julie was born in 1972, and I left the extension service to be a stay-at-home mom. Kelley came along in 1975. Raising my own family, I saw how remarkable my mother's achievement truly was, maintaining a healthy balance between her home life and her career.

I had the freedom to indulge my passions for family and homemaking. I invited folks over to taste-test new recipes. Guests would wander into my kitchen, and inevitably someone would ask me, "Doris, what's that doohickey you use to slice those cucumbers so evenly?" "That glass bowl with the handle and spout would be great for pouring pancake batter. Where can I get one?" Just as in my teaching days, it gave me great satisfaction to pass on the cooking tools and tricks I'd picked up.

The summer of 1980 I started thinking about returning to work. Both Julie and Kelley would be in school in the fall. The question was, What should I do? If I went back to teaching high school, I wouldn't have a flexible schedule to be the girls' room mother and Brownie leader. Catering? I enjoyed planning and cooking but not being away from my family on special occasions.

Many nights Jay and I stayed at the table after dinner, going over my career options. Was there some way I could combine my teaching experience and my love of cooking? Just like that day in my high school guidance counselor's office, I asked God for wisdom and guidance. *Help me find the career that's right for me*, I prayed. *And right for my family.* Jay and I kept coming back to my friends' always asking me about the tools and techniques I used in the kitchen, things that were new to them but second nature to me because of my home economics training. "There's definitely a need for good tools for home cooks," my marketer-husband observed. "And the key to marketing a product is finding a need and filling it."

We hit upon a concept for a business I could run from my house—I would sell professional-quality, reasonably priced kitchen products by bringing them right into people's homes, where I could give a hands-on demonstration of how to use them. I tossed out the idea to some friends over dinner one evening. "I want to show people how to make good food fast, and how to make life easier and better for the home cook," I said. "Hmm," someone remarked, "sounds like it's all about pampering the cook."

Cook became chef, and my business had a name! I took out a small loan and went to Chicago's Merchandise Mart to stock up on kitchen tools. Then I developed simple, delicious recipes using those tools, recipes that my busy working mom would have appreciated. My friend Ruth Niehaus volunteered her home for my first kitchen show and invited her neighbors, most of whom I didn't know.

Things were all set. At least, they were until I started thinking, *Am I just setting myself up for failure? I'm no businesswoman. I'm a teacher, not a salesperson.* I put off the kitchen show, making all kinds of excuses: I was waiting for one last product to come in, I needed more time to perfect the recipes. It was only because my friend had gone to all that trouble to help me that I finally decided to go through with it.

I drove to Ruth's that October night, windshield wipers whipping on high against the rain, doubts slashing at me in the same relentless rhythm. *Selling little gadgets to a bunch of strangers? What was I thinking?* Boxes full of kitchen tools rattled in the backseat of my Volare. *I'll give it my best shot, Lord, but I just don't know.* I pulled up at my friend's house, feeling the same terrible, sickening sense of dread that used to come over me in typing class in high school. I could almost see my turtle languishing on the bulletin board.

God, You've led me through failure before, I prayed as I carried my boxes into Ruth's kitchen, where the guests were gathered. *Guide me now, just as You always have.* I unpacked my peelers and graters and showed how to use them to make a tray of crudités, including garnishes for the dip. Then I put a frozen pizza on a baking stone, topped it with sliced vegetables and stuck it in the oven. The way everyone reacted when I served it reminded me of those workshops I'd led for the extension service. "I never knew all those fancy-looking garnishes were so easy to make," one guest remarked. "I can't wait to try this pizza at home," said another. "My kids will be begging to eat their vegetables!" The best thing was, I was having as much fun as these women were. Selling was teaching.

I left with a notepad full of orders, plus bookings for four kitchen shows. Most of all, I had a renewed appreciation for everything Mama taught me, not the least of which was that I had to look past failure because even if He had to use a pokey little turtle to do it, God would lead me to something better than I could imagine. To my calling—helping women make good meals and good homes, the kind that nourish their families' spirits, like the home my mother worked hard to give me. And all because I couldn't pass typing. ❧

> "I am satisfied that when the Almighty wants me to do, or not to do, any particular thing, He finds a way of letting me know it."
>
> ABRAHAM LINCOLN

Is That You, Lord?

It's one thing to say that God will answer our prayers for guidance. But how, exactly, should we ask?

There's no single answer to that question, of course. Our conversations with God are as individual and as varied as our personalities, our circumstances and our questions. Still, some practical guidelines for seeking God's will on a daily basis might help.

Guideposts contributor Pam Kidd suggests the direct approach. She sets aside some time each morning for prayer. She begins by centering herself on God, thanking Him for the miracles of His creation—"the way He grows trees and fluffs clouds and paints the sky." Then she tells God how much she wants to surrender her will to His, and she states her desire to turn over all her problems to Him. Then she listens.

"Is there anything You want to tell me, God?" she asks.

In the silence, Kidd says, her mind clears. She feels the breeze ruffle her hair; a sense of well-being comes in.

Next she asks specifically for direction. "Is there anything I can do for You today, Father?"

A list forms in her mind: people to check in on, notes to write, someone who needs encouragement. Sometimes more, sometimes less.

That's Kidd's recipe. Nothing dramatic. Just a consistent, conscious opening of herself in prayer to God's direction.

It works! D.H.

There's an old saying that we need to be careful about what we pray for—we might get it!

The point, of course, is that sometimes what we think would be best for us turns out to be mistaken. In that case an unanswered prayer turns out to be a blessing—and a form of guidance.

This is important to remember, because it's easy to feel disappointed in God for failing to come through when we don't get something we want.

What might God be telling us with His silence? Hanna Geshelin found out when God gave her a preview of the singing husband she'd prayed for.

SEND ME A SINGING HUSBAND
—By Hanna Geshelin—

For years I did everything I could to find a mate. I spent countless weekends at shabbatons, programs for Jewish singles centered on the Sabbath observance. I spent one New Year's at a singles event in Miami Beach. I even went to matchmakers. But it was all in vain.

When I was forty-five, a friend suggested I consult a rabbi who was known to help people overcome difficult problems. With a little urging I made an appointment. I poured my heart out to the rabbi, who listened carefully and then asked, "Did you give God a detailed list of everything you want in a husband?"

I stared at him. It seemed nervy to be so precise in a request to the Lord.

"Make a list," he directed. "Include everything you want in a life companion. If you are explicit, it is easier for God to answer your prayer. Remember, God is infinite, and He likes being asked. Every day after your prayers, read Him the list. I promise you that in time God will give you your perfect husband."

When I got home I wrote a list of what I desired in a mate: intelligence, kindness, good health, steady income. My list probably was similar to many other women's. But I added something else: sings well. The Hebrew prayers can all be sung and many of them—the kiddush recited over wine at the start of all Sabbath and holiday meals, the Sabbath table

14

hymns, the Passover seder service and the blessings over the Hanukkah lights—are intoned by the husband. I happen to have perfect pitch, and hearing music is a special pleasure. So I wanted a husband who would grace our home with beautifully sung prayers.

During the next three years I maintained the daily routine prescribed by the rabbi. I still hadn't met Mr. Right, but I had found a new peace within myself. As my younger friends married, and married friends had second and third babies, I turned to Psalm 119 and read, "I know, O Lord, that thy judgments are right. . . . Let, I pray thee, thy merciful kindness be for my comfort, according to thy word unto thy servant. Let thy tender mercies come unto me, that I may live; for thy law is my delight." Although I sometimes cried from loneliness, I was able to share my friends' happiness with complete and true joy.

Shortly after my forty-eighth birthday I decided to attend a weekend shabbaton in a nearby community. The organizer told me that most of those attending would be in their forties and fifties. On Friday afternoon, as I pulled into the synagogue's parking lot, I had second thoughts about the whole thing. *For twelve years I've been coming to these programs, yet nothing has happened. Should I turn around and go home?* Instead I pulled out my Book of Psalms from my purse and read a few verses for courage and guidance. Then I got out of the car and went inside to register for the weekend.

I probably won't meet anyone this time either, I thought as I opened the heavy door leading into the sanctuary. When the service started I was immediately attracted to the prayer leader's beautiful chanting. Later, at dinner, he sang the kiddush more exquisitely than I had ever heard it before. *Could he be the one, Lord?*

The next day I made sure to sit at the prayer leader's table for dinner. Excited, I struck up a conversation, but I discovered another side to him. As he sang prayers over our meal, he postured and posed as though he were performing rather than speaking to God. All talk at our table centered on him and how wonderful his voice was. I felt so let down.

Suddenly I knew why the Lord had brought me to this weekend! As soon as I got home, I pulled out my list of attributes for the ideal husband. None of them mentioned God. I crossed out "sings well" and wrote instead "prays with his heart directed to God."

Within two months I met Ira, the wonderful man who is now my husband. He can hardly carry a tune in a bucket. But he prays and sings the blessings with concentration and intensity, thinking of the meaning of each word and of the One to whom he is praying.

These days he's been practicing "A Woman of Valor" (Proverbs 31:10–31), a favorite of mine. The hours he has spent struggling with this simple song are a gift of love to me, and his off-key but deeply sincere prayers strike a note more true than any professional aria. When Ira sings he prays with his heart directed to God.

And that's exactly what I asked for. ❧

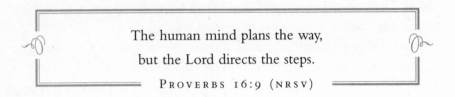

The human mind plans the way,
but the Lord directs the steps.

PROVERBS 16:9 (NRSV)

One of the messages I hope has come through in this chapter is that prayer can provide us with God-given clarity when we are confused. And these days, what a gift a little clarity can be! So many voices surround us, offering guidance and counsel—friends, professional advisors of every variety and stripe, TV and radio, and, yes, books. The clamor can be deafening.

It's all the more important to remember that we need to set aside time to simply ask God for His will and to listen for His answer. Linda Neukrug makes this point nicely.

GO TO THE SOURCE!
—BY LINDA NEUKRUG—

When I was traveling back east on Amtrak to see my parents, I thought I could get off the train at every one of the fifteen or so stations between Martinez, California, and Penn Station in New York City.

"How long do we stop in Albany?" I asked a woman in a gray skirt and blue blazer.

She shrugged. "About two hours, I'd guess."

You'd guess? I thought, annoyed at her vagueness.

"Can I get off the train there?" I persisted.

"I think so."

What kind of an answer is that? I wondered. Dissatisfied, I went off in search of another employee, who said confidently, "Twelve minutes. And if you're not back in time, you'll be looking at the train's caboose."

"But that other woman said about two hours!" I protested.

She looked in the direction of the woman I'd just asked, and then she started laughing. "She's wearing a blue blazer, all right, but she's not an employee! You need to go to the source!"

As I sat on the train in Albany (I didn't want to risk "looking at the train's caboose"!), I mulled over the times I'd made similar mistakes. I asked all my friends for advice about breaking up with a boyfriend, instead of praying about it. Their conflicting answers drove me crazy, and I just prolonged my decision-making time.

And when I was thinking about a career change to substitute teaching, I talked to co-workers and people at the temp agency where I was working, but I got no closer to making a decision. It wasn't till after I'd prayed and spoken to other substitute teachers that I decided to go ahead. ✒

 My sheep listen to my voice; I know them, and they follow me.

JOHN 10:27 (NIV)

Does it make sense to say that some answered prayers are more miraculous than others? Maybe not. If you consider the fact that we're talking about a direct communication from the Creator of the Universe to Joe or Janice Average, any answered prayer is pretty miraculous.

Still, when someone is willing to stake absolutely everything on prayer, and then succeeds against what appear to be insurmountable odds, one can't help but feel as if an especially miraculous event has occurred. Such is the case in "A Hatful of Miracles," a remarkable story that reminds me of the movie Casablanca.

A H A T F U L   O F   M I R A C L E S
— B Y   J O H N   G L E A S O N —

I had just graduated from Northwestern University and wanted to see something of the world before settling into a career. With three hundred and fifty dollars saved from a summer job—quite a lot in those days—I was heading for Puerto Rico and the Virgin Islands, places that seemed romantic to me. It was October 1938.

In New York I boarded a rusty old coal-burning freighter. At first there seemed to be just three passengers besides myself: a bright young civil engineer from Michigan; a worried-looking old man in a white linen suit; and a stately, charming woman who turned out to be Mrs. Charles Colmore, wife of the Episcopal bishop of Puerto Rico, who was returning there after a visit with relatives in the United States.

We made friends quickly, the way you do on a sea voyage. Then, two days out of New York, a young woman with dull blond hair appeared on deck for the first time. She was in her early twenties, much too thin. She looked so pale and wan that we instantly pitied her. She seemed a bit wary of the male passengers, but she accepted Mrs. Colmore's invitation for tea in her cabin.

"It's a strange story," the bishop's wife told us later. "She comes from a little town in Pennsylvania and she's on her way to the West Indies to look for her husband. He evidently left home several months ago after a violent quarrel with her mother over his drinking and his inability to find a job and support his wife properly. She finally heard a rumor that her husband had gone to the West Indies. She still loves him, so she left her 'old dragon' of a mother, and now she's on her way to find Billy— that's her husband's name: Billy Simpson."

"You mean," I said incredulously, "she's going to leave the ship when we get to San Juan and start looking? Why, that's crazy! There are hundreds of islands in the Caribbean."

"I told her that," the bishop's wife said, "but it didn't seem to make any impression. She just says she'll find him. How, I don't know. But she seems absolutely sure of it."

"It would take a miracle," the old man said, thin and intense in his white tropic suit and brown wool cap.

"It would take a whole hatful of miracles," I muttered.

"Does she have any friends where she's going?" asked the young engineer. "Does she have any money?"

"No friends," said the bishop's wife. "And almost no money. Ten dollars, I think she said. Not even enough to get her back to New York."

When we heard this, the rest of us dug into our pockets and raised twenty-five dollars to give to this strange waif of a woman.

"This will help you find a place to stay when we get to San Juan," the bishop's wife said when she presented the money in front of all of us. "And I'm sure our church there will help find enough for your return passage home."

The woman murmured her thanks. Then she said, "But I'm not going home. I'm going to find my husband."

"Where? How?" asked the old man. He had been fired from his bookkeeping job after thirty years with the same company. Now he was moving to Puerto Rico, where he hoped his experience would outweigh his age when it came to finding another job. I couldn't help thinking that he was seeking an answer to his own *where* and *how* as much as to the waiflike woman's.

The young woman shrugged, and smiled a little. She had the oddest smile—sad, fateful, dreamlike. "Prayers," she said. "My prayers. A few years ago I asked God to send me someone to love, and He did, and I married him. Now I'm asking God to help me find my husband again. That's all. Just asking. And I'm sure He will."

Time passed, trancelike, the way it does on shipboard, the young woman leaning against the rail watching the flying fish skitter across the cobalt sea, the engineer and I on the fantail, the old man asking the bishop's wife for ideas about getting a job in Puerto Rico.

We docked in San Juan early one morning. I was scheduled to catch another boat that afternoon for St. Thomas in the Virgin Islands, and so had a few hours to kill. The others were going to look for an inexpensive hotel where the young woman could stay while she figured out her next move, whatever that might be. The engineer and the old man needed a place to stay too. The bishop's wife had delayed her own trip to Ponce, where the bishop was, in order to give some reassurance to the young wife. "I've got to see her settled somewhere," she said to me privately. "And then I'll ask some people at the church to keep an eye on her."

In the smothering heat of midday we walked all over the old city of San Juan, finding the cheap hotels—all run-down establishments infested with fleas and bedbugs. Finally, the bishop's wife suggested that we get on a bus for the little neighboring town of San Terce. She thought accommodations might be more attractive and more available there.

So we clambered onto a bus for San Terce, but all the hotels we found in this pleasanter suburb were too expensive. Eventually, exhausted under the hot sun, the bishop's wife, the old man and the young woman sat down on a sidewalk bench. The engineer and I continued the search, and, amazingly, we found a pleasant, clean and inexpensive hotel within a block.

We tried to register for the group, but the clerk insisted that each person register individually. So the others lined up before the registration book. When it was the woman's turn to sign, she picked up the pen, glanced at the page, dropped the pen—and fainted.

The clerk dashed for some water. The engineer and I put her on a couch, and the bishop's wife bathed her forehead while the old man patted her hand. She came to slowly.

"Heat too much for you?" I asked.

She shook her head. "No . . . Billy."

"Billy?"

"He's in the book," she whispered.

We jumped up to take a look. There, scrawled after a date two days before, we read: "Billy Simpson."

"What room is he in?" I asked the clerk. I couldn't believe it.

"Simpson?" the clerk said, "Oh, he got a job. He come back after work. Not here now."

"This can't be," the old man said almost angrily. "She must have had some idea that he was here!"

The bishop's wife looked at us. "No, I'm sure she didn't," she said. "Otherwise she would have come directly to this hotel on her own, wouldn't she?"

Nobody could answer that. Now, I know that in a good story the narrator does not remove himself from the scene just when the climactic episode is coming up. But this is the way it all happened. Real life doesn't always write the script the way a good playwright would.

Anyway, I had to be on the boat that sailed to the Virgin Islands. The engineer shook my hand and wished me well. The bishop's wife gave me a letter of introduction to the Episcopal minister on St. Thomas, a Reverend Edwards. The old man said he would come and see me off.

The boat was belching smoke, more of a ferry than a ship. As we neared the gangway, the old man spoke.

"The real reason I wanted to come along was to ask you something. Do you think that prayer really led that woman to her husband?"

"I don't know," I replied uneasily. "There's always coincidence. But this is certainly a big coincidence."

"I wonder if prayer could help me?" he said. "I don't know much about it."

"Neither do I," I said. "Why don't you ask the bishop's wife?"

"Do you think I should? I've been a bit afraid to."

"Sure," I said. "Ask her. And if I hear of any jobs in the Virgin Islands, I'll write you at the hotel."

"Thanks," he said. "Have a good trip."

When I arrived, Reverend Edwards invited me to stay with him, charging only ten dollars a week for room and board. Settled in, I spent my time sightseeing, chatting with natives at the docks, writing, relaxing, learning all I could about the islands. I often visited with Reverend Edwards after dinner. One night I told him about the young woman on the boat and the missing husband and the prayers. I'm sure my tone indicated my doubts.

The old clergyman said, "Don't ever be afraid to believe, John. You're too young to have a closed mind."

With time, the woman and Billy Simpson almost slipped from memory. But one day I mentioned the incident to two new friends of mine, deaconesses who lived next door to the church.

"Why," said one of them, "that sounds like a Mr. Simpson we had here at the clinic. He came from Antigua with a bad case of the D.T.'s. We practically had to chain him to a bed."

"And then," said the other, "one day he suddenly became alert and insisted on getting up. Our Danish doctor said he'd better stay with us for a time, but Mr. Simpson was adamant. He said he had to get to San Juan to see someone. When we asked who, he said he didn't know. He just had to get to San Juan. That night he caught a small powerboat going to Puerto Rico. We gave him twenty dollars to get him there and maybe enough for a room. That's the last we heard of him."

We compared dates, and this Mr. Simpson would have landed in Puerto Rico three days before my group arrived. He could have reached that hotel before we had, as the register showed.

I had to find out. I wrote to the bishop's wife, gave her my news and asked for hers. In two weeks, her answer came: "Yes, it was the right Billy Simpson. His reunion with his wife was one of the most touching things I've ever seen. Now, there are several events to consider, miracles possibly. One, Mr. Simpson's sudden cure from alcoholism in St. Thomas, which he confirms; two, his strange compulsion to get to San Juan, which he couldn't understand at the time; three, the guidance that led him to that hotel; four, his finding a good job within twenty-four hours, after not being able to get a job for months; and five, the guidance that took our group to that hotel. For me, these events add up to a hatful of miracles that can be explained in only one word: *prayer*. The Simpsons are living happily in San Juan now. Not long ago they gave me fifty dollars to use for charity, and so I am enclosing twenty dollars for your friends who helped Mr. Simpson while he was ill."

A week later, I received a letter from the old man. He had gone to Ponce with the bishop's wife, found a good job, joined the church and become very happy in it. He wrote: "When we were at the hotel that day, Mrs. Colmore said that maybe there was a lesson in the experience we had shared. I believe there was. For me, the lesson was that some people instinctively know the power of prayer, but others have to learn it."

I couldn't argue with that. ❧

> Therefore I tell you, whatever you ask for in prayer, believe that you have received it, and it will be yours.
>
> MARK 11:24 (NIV)

JESUS' TEACHING ON PRAYER
LUKE 11:1–9 (NIV)

One day Jesus was praying in a certain place. When he finished, one of his disciples said to him, "Lord, teach us to pray, just as John taught his disciples."

He said to them, "When you pray, say:

"'Father, hallowed be your name, your kingdom come.

Give us each day our daily bread.

Forgive us our sins,

for we also forgive everyone who sins against us.

And lead us not into temptation.'"

Then he said to them, "Suppose one of you has a friend, and he goes to him at midnight and says, 'Friend, lend me three loaves of bread, a friend of mine on a journey has come to me, and I have nothing to set before him.'

"Then the one inside answers, 'Don't bother me. The door is already locked, and my children are with me in bed. I can't get up and give you anything.'

"I tell you, though he will not get up and give him the bread because he is his friend, yet because of the man's boldness he will get up and give him as much as he needs.

"So I say to you: Ask and it will be given to you; seek and you will find; knock and the door will be opened to you. For everyone who asks receives; he who seeks finds; and to him who knocks, the door will be opened." ❧

CHAPTER TWO

GOD SPEAKS TO US...
In the Bible

*T*he previous chapter illustrated the point that if we are to receive
God's guidance when we pray, we need to remember to listen
to God as well as to talk to Him. The miracle of the Bible is
that it so readily enables us to hear the voice of God speaking directly
to us.

"Praying the Scriptures"—reading the Bible and then praying on
what we've read—is one of the most powerful methods of spiritual discernment we have. When we stop to reflect on how a passage from the
Bible relates to our own spiritual journey, a self-reinforcing holy loop is
formed. God speaks through the Word to our hearts and our souls. As
we pray we bring ourselves, heart and soul, before God. Word, Holy
Spirit, and Soul are in communion with one another. A joyous synergy
results.

Another glory of Scripture as a tool of guidance is that it helps us
to sit back and allow God to set the agenda. We can focus when we
read on what God is trying to say to us, rather than on what we want
to say to God. Of course, we always bring our own thoughts and

concerns with us when we read Scripture. What we read often relates directly to those thoughts and concerns—often uncannily so. But Scripture can also take us, at any time, in directions we would not have considered by ourselves.

Our first story in this chapter demonstrates the rich gifts that regular Scripture reading can provide, especially in times of crisis. One detail to note in Betty Ulrich's testimony is how she came across a passage in her Bible that she had, at some forgotten moment in her past, already underlined. She couldn't remember the circumstances of that occasion, but no matter. The Word brings the counsel of the Holy Spirit to us where we are, at the moment we read it. Always fresh. Always alive. Always from God.

Drawing On a Rich Supply
—By Betty Garton Ulrich—

We thought my ninety-five-year-old mother was dying. Life became a nightmare of moving her from our home to the hospital, then to a nursing home, back to the hospital, then home, then back to the nursing home. So many decisions—I began to wonder if my husband and I were making the right choices. *How could we be sure?*

About that time, I began to notice something remarkable: Every day a verse of Scripture would be called to my attention, a special word that fit the day's crisis or uncertainty or low spot. Some days the verse stared out at me while I was doing my daily Bible reading; sometimes a verse just popped into my head.

Once, we were torn with indecision about the risk of surgery for Mother at her advanced age. There were so many factors to consider. Then in the midst of my vacillating I was reading Psalm 27. When I reached the end, the last verse almost leaped off the page and spoke to me directly: "Wait on the Lord: be of good courage, and He shall strengthen thine heart: wait, I say, on the Lord."

I quoted that verse all that day in my mind. It was as if God were saying, "Not all waiting is bad. You'll know the right answer in due time." I was at peace. The way would become clear—as indeed it did. A second medical opinion reassured us; Mother had the surgery and survived another three and a half years. The day after the surgery I was reading in Philippians, and there, in Verse 19 of Chapter 4, shone out my guidance for the day: "But my God shall supply all your need according to His riches in glory by Christ Jesus."

So it went, day after day. I still marvel, looking back, at how faithfully the right verse was there, either to be read from the Bible or just presenting itself in my mind.

Even more interesting, after the crisis was over, the "special" verses ceased. At first I wondered whether it was because I no longer needed special upholding, or whether I was not looking as hard!

I'm strongly inclined to think it was the former, because quite a while later, the verses began to appear again. I was in the midst of a serious emotional drain. I picked up my Bible and, because I was in a hurry to leave for an appointment, I just opened it and began reading Isaiah, Chapter 30, a chapter that had nothing to do with me. It was about Israel's making a treaty with Egypt against God's will. But suddenly the last part of Verse 15 stood out. I was reading from the *Good News for Modern Man*, which said, "Come back and quietly trust in Me. Then you will be strong and secure." That verse had been underlined. I'm the only one who uses that Bible, which meant that sometime in the past the verse had spoken to me so strongly I'd underlined it. Whatever need had prompted me to do so was not only long gone—I'd even forgotten what it was!

I received a double benefit that day from that verse: First it brought me back to the source of my serenity and peace of mind. I didn't need to indulge in hysterics or self-pity. I could quietly return to my trust in God; that would be the basis of my strength and security. And second, the underlining was a silent witness that "this too shall pass away." Just as I had forgotten whatever caused me to underline it in the first place, so also this present burden would depart, and in some future time the memory of a disturbing period in my life would fade.

I'm past wondering anymore whether God does or doesn't operate in this way or that. I just know that when we need divine help, it's there. The problem, as always, is from our side, not God's. It's really true that "my God shall supply all your need according to His riches in glory by Christ Jesus." We just have to stay tuned and to keep listening. ❧

> I will instruct you and teach you the way you should go;
> I will counsel you with my eye upon you.
>
> PSALM 32:8 (RSV)

Anyone who's read the Bible knows that Scripture is filled with sur-prising—sometimes shocking—images. The visions that open the Old Testament book of Ezekiel are a graphic case in point. Bizarre crea-tures appear amidst a cloud of fire and lightning. Then God tells the prophet that he is to take a message to the rebellious Israelites. To insure that he delivers this message faithfully, Ezekiel is commanded to eat the scroll on which God's word is written. "So I ate it," Ezekiel writes, "and it tasted as sweet as honey in my mouth."

Taken literally, eating Scripture is a pretty odd notion. Figuratively, it makes perfect sense. We are what we eat, after all. When we feed ourselves regularly on a diet of the Word, we glow with the Spirit that the Word contains.

Keith Miller comes at this issue from a slightly different metaphor-ical angle in the following commentary. As he points out, we are not the only ones nourished by the scriptural sustenance we consume.

FEEDING THE ANGELS
—BY KEITH MILLER—

A friend of mine seemed so serene in the face of the dragons (the prob-lems and pains) of life. "I quit feeding them!" she told me. "I quit nurs-ing the lizards (my doubts and fears) while they're small, and it keeps them from becoming those huge, fierce dragons."

I made a conscious effort to do the same, and it helped. But from time to time an emotional lizard would appear that I couldn't seem to avoid feeding. Finally, one sleepless night, I cried out to God, and a memory came into my mind. I was a boy, and my mother was telling me, "What you put in your mind on a regular basis is what you will become in a few years, or even a few months."

So I began to memorize Bible passages that would, if I really lived them, change me into a strong, confident man of God. One was Paul's admonition from Philippians 4:8. I added the Twenty-third Psalm, the thirteenth chapter of First Corinthians, the Beatitudes and others.

Yesterday someone in our prayer group asked me, "What are you feeding the lizards these days?"

I smiled and said, "You'll never believe it, but the 'food' I'm putting in my mind now is the Word of God."

"Do the lizards eat it?"

"Gosh, no, they *hate* it."

My friend smiled and asked, "Then to whom are you feeding the Word?"

"Um," I said, thinking about that, "I guess I'm feeding the angels God sent to free me from my fears." ✍

Finally, brethren, whatever is true, whatever is honorable, whatever is just, whatever is pure, whatever is lovely, whatever is gracious, if there is any excellence, if there is anything worthy of praise, think about these things.

PHILIPPIANS 4:8 (RSV)

We know that God works in mysterious ways, but the point bears repeating. When we're looking to discern His guidance, anything can happen.

I bring this up because in some respects this next story seems to hinge on a Scripture-reading practice that many spiritual leaders discourage. That's the one where you open up the Bible at random and stab your finger down at the page, figuring that God will lead you to exactly the passage that will answer the problem you're facing. This is known in some circles as playing "Bible roulette." The cautionary story is told of one believer who played the game and landed at

Matthew 27:5. There she found the passage describing how Judas hanged himself after betraying Jesus. She decided to try again, this time opening her Bible to Jesus' words: "Go and do likewise."

Never say never, though. God doesn't, as Peggy Mulligan-Cavallaro's story proves. Feeling desperate, Peggy looked in her Bible for help making one of the most fateful decisions of her life. She didn't like the advice she received one bit, but she obeyed. Blessings followed.

WHY DID WE GET MARRIED?
—BY PEGGY MULLIGAN-CAVALLARO—

It was the worst way to wander into marriage. I should have known from our first session of prenuptial counseling that things would be tough. That day when we met the priest in his book-lined study, he smiled and asked, "Chris and Peggy, do you love each other?"

Wind rustled the autumn leaves outside and the church organ bellowed next door. *He's marrying me because he feels trapped*, I wanted to tell the priest. *He doesn't really love me.* If Chris wasn't going to speak up, I wouldn't either. We were there because I was pregnant. Having grown up in good Catholic families, we both decided this was the right thing to do.

"Of course you love each other," the priest jumped in. "That's why you're here." It did nothing to appease my doubts.

After our wedding we moved from place to place, living with Chris's parents in New Jersey for a time, then finding a first-floor apartment in an old house. After the birth of Michaela we hardly saw each other. We had met in 1969 at an outdoor pop festival. Back then we were hippies in tie-dyed T-shirts and tattered jeans, with not a care in the world. But now life was different. Chris worked several low-paying day jobs so he could get together with fellow musicians and jam all night. When the baby cried at dawn he nudged me—"You get her"—rolled over and went back to sleep.

With the arrival of our second daughter, Erin, I had my hands full. Chris wasn't around to change diapers, warm bottles and shepherd the girls into baths and bed at night. He wasn't even sympathetic when I complained about how hard it was to keep shushing them in the mornings while he slept. "This marriage isn't working," I announced.

That night we found a baby-sitter and went to Mom's Kitchen, our favorite Italian restaurant. Over antipasto we mapped out terms for a divorce settlement, but in the crowded restaurant we moved closer together. We lowered our voices. Our knees touched under the table and our hands met across the tablecloth. We talked about music, books and movies—not about kids and money. Somehow by the time the check came, we had changed our minds. "Maybe we should give it another try," we said.

In a few weeks we were back to fighting. We were constantly scrimping for money. Eventually Chris started a recording studio with two partners and his hours away from the family grew even longer. I went to a regular Bible study and to worship services with the girls on Sundays, but church was one more thing that Chris didn't participate in.

Then one Saturday we planned to take a family outing. The girls were dressed and ready to go; I had packed a picnic lunch; the day was warm and sunny. But Chris simply wouldn't get out of bed. We three girls had to go on our own.

All day I stewed. I couldn't bear Chris's erratic behavior anymore. He was argumentative and easily irritated. When Michaela would ask him for help with her homework, he snapped that he was too tired. I decided I would be better off without him.

The next morning I threw clothes into suitcases for the girls and me. I called my parents, who agreed to let us stay with them. The car was running and the trunk packed when I realized I hadn't consulted God. I turned off the engine. "Mommy will be right back," I said to Michaela and Erin and scurried into the house. I sat down on my bed with my Bible.

"You know I've tried to be a good wife, Lord," I said. "I've done everything possible to save this marriage and nothing has worked. I can't go on anymore. My plan is to leave today, but I need to know from You that it's okay."

Opening the Scriptures, I half hoped I would read a verse that urged, "Let my people go." Instead, the words that leapt out at me warned of death "by the sword, by famine, and by pestilence" if I went where I wanted to go (Jeremiah 42:22, RSV).

Looking at those words ruefully, I sighed. There was no mistaking God's message.

I called the girls inside and put away the suitcases. On an index card I wrote: "What holds this happy couple together? Sword, famine and pestilence!" and taped the message above the kitchen sink. Time and again I glanced at that water-spattered card and felt reassured.

For weeks I prayed, trying to understand what else God wanted me to do. Then one day I discovered my bottle of prescription pain-relievers suddenly empty. Suspicious, I went to Chris's briefcase. Inside I discovered a dizzying array of pills, and white powder in a plastic bag. When confronted, Chris claimed that he didn't have a drug problem, but I saw how addicted he truly was. With little choice I moved with the girls to a trailer on my parents' property in Tennessee. Chris stayed behind, living in a rented basement room at a friend's house. I couldn't have my children around all those drugs.

That Christmas he visited us, assuring me he was no longer using cocaine. But later, when I put away his jacket, a plastic packet of white powder fell from his pocket.

I took it with me on what was supposed to be a romantic walk through the woods. After he told me how much the girls and I meant to him, I took the bag out of my pocket, hurled it to the ground and told him, "This is what you love. Not me, not your family." Back he went to New Jersey.

Chris started attending meetings of Narcotics Anonymous. While getting off drugs he gave his life over to God. Now I was sure everything would be all right. The girls and I returned to Chris in New Jersey. He closed the recording studio, got a job at a radio station with regular hours, and I took a full-time job in sales. We went to counseling and church together (although I loved to walk and he always wanted to drive).

But something was still missing. We treated each other politely, like perfect strangers, not like a couple who had been married for twenty years. I thought back to our first meeting with that priest. *Did Chris really love me?*

Then one night we were in the living room talking. I was telling him about a difficult situation at work when he abruptly stood up and walked across the room to change the TV channel.

"What are you doing?" I asked, livid.

"Changing the channel," he said.

Something inside me broke. All the pain that I had stored up. After all we had been through I had hoped things would be better. *He doesn't love me,* I thought. *He has never loved me. He never will. Lord, have I been wrong all along? Maybe we were not meant to be together after all.*

The next day was Sunday. When I went into the kitchen, he was there, drinking coffee. "Would you like to walk to church?" he asked.

A walk, something he doesn't even like to do. "Yes," I said.

This was his peace offering. We sauntered together side by side, neither of us speaking. With each step I dreaded facing the future.

At church I slipped into a pew, took off my sweater and leaned forward to bow my head. Suddenly my eye caught the church bulletin. There in bold letters were the words: Can You Save Your Marriage? The notice described a weekend retreat for couples in trouble. In our desperation we would have tried anything.

On the way to the retreat, Chris and I didn't say much in the car. "I'm not interested in any touchy-feely group therapy," he warned.

A first glance around the room at the center confirmed my worst fears. I had never seen such a motley group of angry husbands and wives. Some had faced substance abuse; others emotional and physical abuse. Most of us were worn raw after years of disappointment and pain.

"Marriages may be made in heaven," the priest said, "but they sure take a lot of work on earth." There was much cynical laughter.

We separated for our first exercise, answering a long series of questions about why we had gotten married in the first place. *Because we had to,* I wanted to say. *But, no,* I thought as I kept writing, *it wasn't that simple. We had been attracted to each other for good reasons.*

We came together and read what we had written down. At first our voices were timid, then stronger, louder, more confident.

"What I loved about you were your eyes," I told Chris. "They were so soulful."

"I liked the way you laughed," he said.

"I liked the way the muscles in your forearms moved when you played the guitar."

"I loved your voice."

"I loved your music."

There it was, in that litany of healing, what we had rediscovered in

Mom's Kitchen years ago and what came alive when we sat together in church and what had drawn us to each other in the beginning. The priest was right. Marriage took a lot of work here on earth, but that wasn't to discount the heavenly part. Our marriage had lasted because God had blessed it all along.

"I loved you from the start," Chris said.

"And I loved you."

We would never again forget to communicate that.

Last year Chris completed college, and in addition to his work at the radio station he teaches at a local university. We have finally bought our own home. Our daughters, Erin and Michaela, have grown into beautiful young women.

Today, looking back, we know we didn't wander into marriage after all. I believe we were called to be married by a God who has always wanted the best for us. ❧

O Lord, thou art my God; I will exalt thee, I will praise thy name; for thou hast done wonderful things; thy counsels of old are faithfulness and truth.

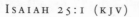

ISAIAH 25:1 (KJV)

The Bible is so many things—a book of history, a blueprint for salvation, and a manual for daily living, among others. With all the gifts Scripture brings us, we can easily forget its most basic quality of all: God's Word is a miracle!

Edward Grinnan reminds us of that knowledge with his lovely piece on the Book of Kells.

A WELL-LIGHTED ROOM
—BY EDWARD GRINNAN—

More than half a million visitors come annually to see the Book of Kells at Trinity College, Dublin, but my hotel's concierge assured me there would be no crowds this time of year. "Ah, 'tis a lovely thing to see, sir," he said, pointing me in the direction of Trinity.

The Book of Kells, dating from AD 800, is a copy of the four Gospels. It was painstakingly transcribed and illuminated—that is, illustrated—by the monks of St. Columba on the island of Iona before it was removed to Kells in County Meath to protect it from plundering Vikings.

My eyes took awhile adjusting to the dim lighting of the Old Library's East Pavilion where the manuscript is kept. Tourists were indeed in short supply, but there were several groups of Irish schoolchildren, and I kept bumping into them in the russet gloom. "It's so dark in here I can hardly see my own foot," I remarked to a studious-looking older gentleman bent over one of the display cases.

"Light can damage the paper," he remarked. "None at all would be best but then . . ." His words trailed off as he gestured to the milling children. My eyes followed his back to the fragile but magnificent pages beneath the glass, bathed in soft light. The breathtaking beauty of the manuscript shone through as if it had light of its own.

The monks labored over their manuscript during what we call the Dark Ages. Their rich and ornate embellishments emblazoned the pages of Scripture, the words of Jesus that lighted the way through the chaos and darkness that followed the fall of the Roman Empire. All these centuries later we are protecting the Light of the World from—literally—the light of the world.

We may not consider ourselves as living in a dark age, but you never know. One Light burns a path of beauty and brightness when all seems dark. And it burns brightest when the world seems darkest. ❧

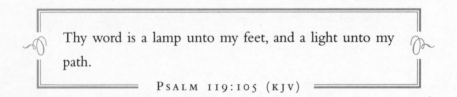

Thy word is a lamp unto my feet, and a light unto my path.

PSALM 119:105 (KJV)

I s T h a t Y o u , L o r d ?

What is the best way to read the Bible if the goal is understanding God's will?

Again, there's no single answer. As we've seen already in this chapter, rules about how the Holy Spirit does and doesn't work are made to be broken.

Certainly I can recommend starting by reading the Bible daily. Take it in small doses: It is better to savor a few verses a day than to skim a chapter. I also recommend following a set schedule rather than reading randomly. That way God can surprise you with passages you might otherwise skip.

Guideposts contributor Patricia Houck Sprinkle plans her Bible reading by periodically asking God in prayer, *What book would You have me study now?* When she feels she has an answer, she reads that book straight through, even if it takes several weeks. Each day she begins her reading with a prayerful question: *What would You show me in this today?*

Sprinkle also has an excellent word of advice for those of us (all of us!) who sometimes feel confused about what Scripture is saying: "Try asking the One who made you and Who wrote the Scriptures to help you find in them what He would teach you now." D.H.

Funny how much weight even a little Bible carries. The weight of two thousand years of belief, two thousand years worth of prayers, two thousand years of gratitude and awe. All of that seems to radiate from the pages of this Book, even when it's hidden beneath a prisoner's pillow in a crowded jail cell.

Larry Bolden seems to have a talent for understatement. His story, "Thirty-Two Men and One Good Book," doesn't make big claims. Having a Bible in jail "strengthened my faith and helped me stay straight," he concludes. It seemed to help some other people around him, too—at least one of them a convicted murderer.

That strikes me as a pretty big deal, although Larry's humility is appealing. In any event, his testimony says a great deal about how the Bible can help guide even the most obvious sinners back on the path toward redemption.

THIRTY-TWO MEN AND ONE GOOD BOOK
—BY LARRY BOLDEN—

As I walked through barbed-wire gates into the county jail, I was strip-searched and handed two blankets, a pillow, a brown uniform and a rolled-up sleeping mat. The only personal possession I was allowed to keep that day in April 1975 was a blue softcover Bible my wife had given me. We had both started attending church after I got busted for selling narcotics.

The steel door to the cell slammed shut and I looked around. Thirty-one men stood or lounged around the fifteen-by-thirty-foot cell. The air was hot and smelly. Cockroaches scurried up the cinder-block walls. At one end of the cell was a picnic table bolted to the floor; against the walls were sixteen cots, all of them claimed. My mat would have to join the others on the floor.

I couldn't sleep that night. I knew I had messed up bad, just like my father, who'd spent eighteen years in prison. I'd become filled with anger and I'd hurt a lot of people. I was facing five years.

I hid the Bible in my pillow for several days, but I couldn't stop thinking about it. There was a gnawing in my heart. Finally, a little nervous, I pulled the Bible out and held it close, so no one would see.

As I turned a page, a voice barked, "What are you doing?"

"Man, I'm just reading this book," I answered.

Duke, the head guy, rolled over in his cot and looked down at me. "Is that a Bible you got?" he demanded.

"Yeah," I answered, but I was thinking, *Oh, man, we're gonna have a fight*. Duke was a little crazy; he was waiting to be sentenced on a murder conviction.

"Get outta here," Duke shot back. "You ain't readin' no Bible."

"Look," I said, "I don't want any trouble."

"Let me see what you got," he grumbled, grabbing the Bible out of my hand and examining it. Then to my amazement he asked, "Would you read it to me?"

I looked at him to see if this was a trick.

"I ain't funning," Duke said. "I can't read." Then he ordered the man on the cot next to him to exchange places with me. That was the end of my sleeping on the floor. Every evening after that we huddled together while I read to Duke.

Gradually, other men joined us until we had a regular Bible study going. Duke ordered the rest to turn off the TV, which caused some hassles. After one inmate complained to the guards, Duke grabbed him by the throat and pinned him up against the wall. I ran over, pleading, "Let him go. That's not the way."

I got to know Duke. He'd spent most of his life in prison. But when he heard the Bible read, he became less fearsome and even smiled.

Other inmates were touched by the Scriptures, and there was less anger. We set up an exercise program to keep us from turning to mush and to offset the boredom that leads to fighting and other trouble.

Duke was eventually sentenced to two life terms and transferred to a maximum-security prison. I moved on to a work-release cell with four of the guys from the Bible study, and my sentence was cut to less than a year—I couldn't believe it!

The new cell, with only ten men, was near the kitchen and much quieter. I worked days driving cars for a local auto dealer. Back in the cell just about everyone became involved in Bible study; the cell became like a home. And when one of my cellmates, Bubba, asked, "How can I get to Jesus?" I was glad I knew.

"Just ask Him into your heart," I told him. "Tell Him you know that you have done wrong and want forgiveness."

Bubba did—and cried for about fifteen minutes.

In December I was released, five months early. I was so grateful to God. That was the beginning of the turnaround in my life.

Throughout my incarceration the Bible was my constant companion. It made me feel I was worth something. In spite of the bad things I had done, it told me God still loved me. It strengthened my faith and helped me stay straight. And it gave hope to a lot of others too. ❧

"Is not my word like fire," declares the Lord, "and like a hammer that breaks a rock in pieces?"

JEREMIAH 23:29 (NIV)

Anyone who's read the New Testament knows that Jesus' prescription for righteous relations with others is challenging, to say the least.

Love your enemies?

Judge not?

Forgive those who have sinned against you?

None of these teachings is easy to follow. Jesus called on us to be better than our human natures would normally lead us to be.

Fortunately, we don't have to accomplish this on our own: The Holy Spirit is there to assist us. And as Louise Majors testifies in "Bless Them That Curse You," Scripture is one of the primary places where we can claim that power.

"BLESS THEM THAT CURSE YOU"
—BY LOUISE MAJORS—

The summer of 1953, before our children went off to elementary school, I started looking for a job. I pounded the pavement unsuccessfully for weeks. Then I answered an ad placed in the *Los Angeles Times* by the California Institute of Technology.

The opening turned out to be for an accounting clerk at the Cooperative Wind Tunnel facility, which tested aircraft parts for strength and wind resistance. Carl Jorgensen, who headed the finance department, was a matter-of-fact man who peered kindly through his black-rimmed eyeglasses and said, "Louise, you have excellent qualifications. If you are willing to start at minimum wage, a dollar and nineteen cents an hour, you can begin next Monday."

I gulped. In my previous job, before I took years off to rear our children to school age, I'd made in a day almost as much as he was offering for a week. But I'd already been turned down for six other jobs. "Thank you, Mr. Jorgensen," I replied. "I want the job very much."

Come Monday morning I went directly to Carl Jorgensen's office. His cheeriness put me at ease, and I followed him as he introduced me to the office staff. "Everyone here goes by first names," he said. He stopped at the first desk. "Hildur is our payroll clerk. Hildur, this is Louise, our new accounting clerk."

I smiled, "I'm glad to meet you, Hildur."

She was grandmotherly with soft, wavy white hair, rimless eyeglasses, smooth fair complexion—pleasant looking. She looked me up and down, then her expression changed. Getting up, she railed, "We don't need an accounting clerk. I don't know why you were hired!" She slammed shut the record book she'd been posting, snatched up her purse and stomped out the door.

Everyone's mouth dropped open. I stood stupefied, feeling the blood surge to my neck and face. This was awful!

Carl Jorgensen was quick to regain his composure and started more introductions: "Bernice, Manna and Esther—the last desk on the right—are members of the steno pool. Joy is our mail clerk and relief switchboard-operator. Please welcome Louise."

It didn't take long to be welcomed. The "girls" (as even we called ourselves back in the forties and fifties) were very kind and helpful, and they asked me to have lunch with them later.

I'd just returned from Carl's office with my first assignment when Hildur reappeared. She ignored everyone, slammed drawers, and was testy on the telephone and to people stopping at her desk. There was no conversation in the office until shortly before noon.

"Did you bring your lunch today, Hildur?" Bernice asked.

Hildur looked up warily. "Is she going to lunch with you?"

"Yes."

"I'm working," Hildur snapped.

I liked the "girls"; they were relaxed and friendly. But I was troubled by Hildur. On the way back to the office, I mentioned I was going to bring my lunch and study in my car, starting tomorrow. I didn't want to be the reason for Hildur not eating with the others. She would soften up after a bit, I reckoned.

Meantime, I was enjoying the bustle of the Wind Tunnel facility—"the Tunnel" as we called it. Four or five times a day the warning bells would go off, and we'd hear the high whine of the turbines that generated the air flow in the test chamber. I loved the family atmosphere in the halls and offices. No matter whether you were greeting a hard hat or a world-famous scientist, it was "Hi, Ted" or "Hi, Fred," with a genuine friendliness and a shared sense of mission.

Yet Hildur didn't mellow. Weeks passed, and the tension only worsened. When I was out of the office, the other women said Hildur was congenial and talkative. The minute I walked in, she fell glaringly silent. Each morning she would ignore my cheery greeting.

I searched my Bible and ended up by pasting my mother's favorite Scripture in my middle desk drawer. As Hildur rebuffed each of my advances, I referred to it: "Bless them that curse you, do good to them that hate you, and pray for them which despitefully use you" (Matthew 5:44, KJV). I nearly wore out that drawer as the weeks went by.

A couple of months passed. One of the women I'd come to know in the next office was retiring. We all chipped in for a little afternoon send-off party that I was looking forward to. Maybe I could get an opportunity to talk with Hildur in this kind of a setting.

I was just getting ready to go when Bernice called over to Hildur, "Aren't you going to the party?"

Hildur glared over at me, then at Bernice. "Is she going?"

"Well, of course," Bernice said, "we're all going."

"Then I'm not."

I gritted my teeth and then said as evenly as I could, "Oh, Bernice, you all go on without me. I've got some catching up to do. Maybe I'll come in later."

But after they'd gone, I brooded. I pulled open my drawer, and there was the message. "Do good to them that hate you," I read aloud. Then I said, "Lord, You know I'm doing that. My question is: How long must this go on?"

As if by answer, I recalled a scene of twenty years before, when I'd had a falling-out with an adolescent friend. I was back in Mother's kitchen and she was telling me, "Seventy times seven, that's how often Jesus told us to forgive. Remember, Louise, the only way to destroy an enemy is to make a friend of him."

I shut my drawer gently. "Thank You, Lord," I whispered.

A couple of months later, on a windy March day, we had a torrential rainstorm. Creeping along in our old, green Pontiac coupe on my way home, windshield wipers batting furiously, I spotted Hildur standing at a bus stop, huddled under an umbrella. I stopped and flipped open the passenger door.

As kindly and firmly as I could, I said, "Hildur, get in." She hesitated a second and then lowered her umbrella and scrambled in. Water dripped from her hair and she looked soaked through. I turned up the heat. "Hildur, please give me directions as we go," I asked.

Except for directions, she was silent all the way to her apartment in East Pasadena. Before dropping her off, I asked her if there was anything I could do. She said, "No, but thank you very much."

After I had watched her disappear into her apartment, I exulted, "Well, praise the Lord, at least she talked to me!" All the way home I felt elated, singing the old hymn "Love Lifted Me." Hildur may not have changed, but at last I felt better.

The next morning was bright, crisp and clear. "Good morning, Hildur!" I said when I got to the office.

"Good morning, Louise," Hildur said with a shy smile. The whole office seemed to give a collective sigh of relief. The harmony was instant; it was as if someone had let the sunshine and singing birds right into the office.

That Friday Hildur and I went out to lunch. She admitted her job was her love, and that she had felt threatened when I was hired. She thought management intended to replace her with me. But over lunch we became friends.

On the way home from work I stopped in Pasadena, had my hair cut and styled, bought a geranium-red dress, patent leather shoes with a pocketbook that matched, and a nifty wide-brimmed straw hat. Mac and the kids went into shock when the "new me" walked in that night. "Wow," Mac said, "I thought your job was getting you down!"

"That was last week," I said. "Now it's getting me up!"

And it stayed that way. Making a friend of Hildur was one of the hardest things I ever did, yet one of the most rewarding. It was wonderful to have her as a friend, and I have Jesus to thank for that. ❧

And God is able to make all grace abound to you, so that in all things at all times, having all that you need, you will abound in every good work.

2 CORINTHIANS 9:8 (NIV)

I chose "A Piano for Noel" as the last story in this chapter partly because I liked the way it made me feel after I'd read it. But Amelia Reno's account also demonstrates how much can be accomplished when we hear God's Word—and then act on what He's told us!

A PIANO FOR NOEL
—BY AMELIA RENO—

I knew it was a crazy thing to do, but I did it anyway. I saw the advertisement for a piano teacher nearby. My seven-year-old daughter Noel was eager to learn and I didn't want to have to go too far for lessons. Impetuously I signed up Noel.

Now for the hard part. We didn't own a piano. We had recently moved, we were a one-income family, and our bills were piling up. "A piano is real far down on my priority list," my husband said. Over the next few days I contemplated canceling the lessons. But as I prayed about it, one particular Bible verse kept popping into my head: "Ye have not because ye ask not" (James 4:2, KJV).

Ask for what you need, the Lord seemed to be saying. Maybe there was someone in the neighborhood who would let Noel come to her house and practice. Halfheartedly I asked around. Nothing.

Two weeks passed. *Ye have not because ye ask not*, I kept hearing. But hadn't I asked everyone I could think of? Time was running out.

"Okay, God," I said finally, "Noel needs a piano. I'm asking you to provide one, if it is your will." Then in a last-ditch effort, I went downtown and placed a one-day-only ad in our local paper: "Wanted: To borrow in your house or mine a piano for my daughter to practice on." The lady who took the ad agreed it was a long shot, but I felt better knowing I had tried.

A few days later a woman called. "I just moved to a trailer," she said, "and had to put my piano in storage. I'd be glad to have it being used in your house instead."

We excitedly agreed to meet her at the storage place, and all piled into our van and drove over. The piano was in excellent condition! As Noel tried the keys, my husband said he'd be back with our pickup and some friends to help move the piano. The lady thought a minute, looking us over. "I'll tell you what," she said. "If you'll use your truck to move the rest of my things into my trailer, you can keep the piano—it's yours."

Noel jumped up and down. And I said a quiet thank-you to the kind woman, and to the One I had finally asked for what we needed, who provides even the wonderful nonessentials in our lives. In our house, we hear proof of that every day. ❧

I am reminded that one old saint was asked, "Which is the more important: reading God's Word or praying?" To which he replied, "Which is more important to a bird: the right wing or the left?"

A. W. TOZER

On the Road to Emmaus
Luke 24:13–29 (CEV)

That same day two of Jesus' disciples were going to the village of Emmaus, which was about seven miles from Jerusalem. As they were talking and thinking about what had happened, Jesus came near and started walking along beside them. But they did not know who he was. Jesus asked them, "What were you talking about as you walked along?"

The two of them stood there looking sad and gloomy. Then the one named Cleopas asked Jesus, "Are you the only person from Jerusalem who didn't know what was happening there these last few days?"

"What do you mean?" Jesus asked.

They answered:

Those things that happened to Jesus from Nazareth. By what he did and said he showed that he was a powerful prophet, who pleased God and all the people. Then the chief priests and our leaders had him arrested and sentenced to die on a cross. We had hoped that he would be the one to set Israel free! But it has already been three days since all this happened.

Some women in our group surprised us. They had gone to the tomb early in the morning, but did not find the body of Jesus. They came back, saying that they had seen a vision of angels who told them that he is alive. Some men from our group went to the tomb and found it just as the women had said. But they didn't see Jesus either.

Then Jesus asked the two disciples, "Why can't you understand? How can you be so slow to believe all that the prophets said? Didn't you know that the Messiah would have to suffer before he was given his glory?" Jesus then explained everything written about himself in the Scriptures, beginning with the Law of Moses and the Books of the Prophets.

When the two of them came near the village where they were going, Jesus seemed to be going farther. They begged him, "Stay with us! It's already late, and the sun is going down."

So Jesus went into the house to stay with them. ❧

CHAPTER THREE

GOD SPEAKS TO US...
Through Other People

"*H*ell is other people."

That is the best-known line from the best-known play by the best-known French existential philosopher, Jean-Paul Sartre (Huis Clos or No Exit). *Of course we know what he meant. Our relationships with the other people in our lives can be the source of untold misery and pain. That's not news. But it seems equally obvious that without other people around our lives would be pretty empty. Other people bring us love and companionship and support and joy and . . . the list could go on, ad infinitum.*

One particular gift we receive from other people—not only those we know, but also those whose paths intersect ours only briefly—is information. Information from God. Whether or not we're aware of it, we all serve as conduits of God's grace and direction for one another. This can happen in an endless number of ways, some as direct as the comforting touch of a mother's hand, some as indirect as a fragment of a conversation overheard on the street.

What's surprising is that we continue to be surprised when we recognize the work of the Spirit in some encounter or exchange we've had with another person. In fact, nothing could be more commonplace. This is an example of what theologians call an "ordinary" grace, although there's a built-in irony to that term. Grace might be common, but it is never ordinary. The same can be said about every person we meet. All are miracles, whether or not we have occasion to notice. Often it is when we realize that God has spoken through them that we do notice.

Each of the stories in this chapter describes an instance where God reached out through the voice, action or presence of another person. The first, Shirley Bard's "Prisoner of Silence," demonstrates how completely unpredictable this extraordinary, everyday miracle can be, and why it continues to catch us off guard.

P R I S O N E R   O F   S I L E N C E
— B Y   S H I R L E Y   B .   B A R D —

My husband Norval and I were sitting on the couch watching television. But my mind was on something else. I grabbed my pad and pencil and scrawled a quick, pleading note: "How much longer will I have to go on like this?" After months of living with a postoperative trachea tube in my windpipe, unable to say a single word out loud, I was beginning to give in to despair. Norval, no stranger to my impatience and frustration, could only pat my hand.

It's hard for anyone who's never been left voiceless to realize what it means to be reduced suddenly to writing down all your thoughts and feelings. Especially if you have three adolescent children who need you. You can't use the phone. Even Terri, our little fox terrier, looked baffled when I snapped my fingers for her to come inside. I lost my sense of smell. At restaurants I was embarrassed to have to point to what I wanted on the menu. My whole life was off-center.

This was not my first go-around with a trake tube. My throat trouble began with diphtheria at age two, when my life was saved by an emergency tracheostomy. A hole was cut in my windpipe at just about the spot where a top shirt button would be, and a short metal breathing tube was inserted. Again, when I was five, complications from measles made another trake necessary. Each time the tube was removed after a few weeks. But the pain and fear of being unable to speak or breathe naturally never left me, and as I grew up through years of hoarseness and recurring throat infections, I lived in dread of another tracheostomy. By the time I was forty-three, the scar tissue had so thickened that my breathing passage was reduced by sixty percent. And so it was that my last reconstructive surgery had been unavoidable. Now if all went well I would never need a trake again.

A few days later I was back in my surgeon's office for a follow-up. I knew by the look in Dr. Thawley's eyes after he'd examined me that all had not gone well.

"Shirley," he said gently but gravely, sitting on the edge of his cluttered desk, "the surgery has not been what we'd hoped."

My eyes widened. What did he mean? I wrote on my pad, "The trake will have to stay in longer?" underscoring "longer" and battling back tears.

"You have an infection. You'll have to go back in the hospital for a while," he told me. But then he went on to explain how my rebuilt trachea, made of grafted skin and bone splinters, had not healed properly. Dr. Thawley paused. "Shirley, I'm afraid you will have a trake for a long time—probably the rest of your life."

A verse from Job shot through my mind: The thing I greatly feared has come upon me. I wanted to scream, yet no sound could come out. I was a prisoner who, expecting a reprieve, had suddenly been handed a life sentence—in a dungeon of silence.

I spent the following days and nights doing jigsaw puzzles in my hospital room, as if I were trying to fit together the scattered pieces of my life. And I prayed, but the tone of these prayers had changed. They were tinged with bitterness.

I believe prayers are more than just thoughts. I feel prayer is fully formed communication with God, and so with the trake I'd gotten into the habit of not just thinking my prayers but actually writing them down. Now I found myself writing prayers like, *Lord, how could You do this to me? I thought You loved me. But You've taken away my voice so I can't even praise You! Why won't You heal me?*

Yet no answer came.

One night I looked up from my puzzle and watched listlessly as the other bed in my room was rolled out. Then a nurse pushed in a high-sided crib with a sleeping child in it. She explained that my new room-mate was a two-year-old girl who'd had a trake put in after surgery. "You two will get along fine," she said, smiling. "Her name's Amy."

I watched Amy sleeping before I drifted off myself. Her heavy, silent breathing soothed me. But it also dredged up memories of my childhood struggles with a trake. *At least hers will be coming out*, I thought.

The next morning Amy played forlornly with her toys. Every so often she'd stare into space. Finally she stood up in the crib, curled her small fingers around the bars and looked out at me. Big, sad tears rolled down her cheeks. Her little shoulders quaked and air sputtered through her trake tube. If ever I yearned to hear the wail of a child's cry it was at that moment.

I slipped from my bed and went over to the crib. Reaching through the bars I put my arms around Amy and pulled her close. I wanted to tell her that she would be all right, that her trake would come out in a few days. But we were two people trapped in silence.

I began to cry. Not just for little Amy but also for myself. Maybe mostly for myself. *God, how could You do this to me? How?* My arms fell away from Amy and my head leaned limply on the crib, as if a huge weight pushed me down. My tears splashed on Amy's bare feet.

Suddenly I felt the gentle touch of a hand on my head. Amy. With childish awkwardness she'd reached over the crib rail to soothe me. And all at once I knew that no words could ever have conveyed such tender comfort.

I went home not long after that, as did Amy. One day I was leafing through my notebooks when I came across some of the prayers I'd scrawled in the hospital. It's one thing to cry out to God. But my angry words were actually written down on a page in black and white: "God, how could You do this to me?" I wanted to tear it up. God had heard my prayer, and answered. He'd sent a little girl who showed me that some-times even words are inadequate to express our deepest human needs.

"Lord," I wrote hastily, "forgive me for blaming You. I give myself to You now, trake and all."

From then on, each day, God taught me a new language: how our marvelously expressive eyes can command attention, laugh, tease, cry, rebuke, empathize and sparkle with love. He showed me that my voice-lessness forced me to be a listener, to care about what people were saying. When I wrote down my words I measured them more carefully, more kindly. And I found that simple human touch can be the most powerfully reassuring communication of all.

One day about eight months after surgery I felt cool air in my throat. I placed my finger over the trake hole, forced air up through my vocal cords and discovered—I could speak. The next day in his office, Dr. Thawley shook his head in amazement. "I've never seen anything like it," he said. Contrary to the doctor's expectation, my trachea con-tinued to heal slowly and was eventually strong enough for me to breathe without the tube. Yet I knew that an even more amazing healing had taken place deep inside my soul.

Today I no longer need my pad, pencil or trake. But certain things—my children's eyes, my husband's touch, my friends' voices—all mean so much more to me now. I still write down one thing, though. My prayers. And every day I thank our loving, healing God, who always hears us, even when we can't speak. ❧

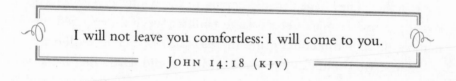

I will not leave you comfortless: I will come to you.

JOHN 14:18 (KJV)

God's primary surrogates on Earth aren't priests, they're parents. The Bible demonstrates that truth repeatedly by using the relationship between child and parent as a model to express the intimacy God wishes to share with his creatures. Jesus called God by the affectionate name for father, "Abba," and recommended that we direct our prayers to "Our Father, who art in heaven." Mary accepted the direction of the Holy Spirit with perfect humility and gave birth to the Messiah. Similarly, mothers and fathers have the opportunity to nurture the

Spirit of Christ within their children, until the time comes when their children can nurture that Spirit on their own.

It is a remarkable responsibility, fulfilled by countless parents around the world with miraculous grace and generosity. Among those whose circumstances demanded special determination and faith were Jack Kearney's parents, who picked cotton for a living and sent fifteen kids through college.

EXPECT THE BEST
—BY JACK KEARNEY—

For most of his life my father has been a sharecropper. Even though he and Mother worked from sunup to nightfall picking cotton here in the delta country of Arkansas, they were so poor they used to tie brown paper bags over the heads of their children to protect us from the sun.

And yet Dad and Mother inspired each of their seventeen children to seek a college degree. Fifteen out of the seventeen did just that—graduating from Harvard and Yale and Vanderbilt and UCLA and Stanford and Brown and Syracuse, and from our own University of Arkansas.

Dad and Mother told us over and over about the early days of their life together. They began sharecropping in the winter of 1936. In those days poor row-farmers needed large families; survival depended on the number of acres you could plant. In 1937 their first child was born.

"Maybe we could call her Jamie?" Mother said. Dad's first name was James, and he smiled, looking at the infant the midwife had just handed his young wife there in the unpainted farmhouse.

When Jamie was a week old Mom carried her to an open-sided shed in the middle of the forty-acre farm she and Dad were working. Mother put Jamie in the shade, then went back to chopping cotton. She returned frequently to nurse the baby, moving her as the shade moved. By the time Jamie was two she was "helping" with the work. Of course the small hands were really a hindrance, but Mother and Dad wanted their child nearby because they had another job to do, one that had nothing to do with field work.

By the time she was two, Jamie was already hearing about college.

"When you go to college, little baby," Dad would say, "you'll be our pioneer." He didn't say "if you go to college." At home in the evening too, Dad was preparing Jamie for a good education. It cost fifty cents a month to subscribe to the *Pine Bluff Commercial*, but even in winter when the food they'd put down from the garden was gone, and they were forced to accept rice and beans from the government, even in those bleak days, Dad kept up his subscription.

Dad started teaching Jamie through that paper, before his little girl could really understand what she was hearing. After working, he'd settle her into a chair at the kitchen table, and while Mother sang softly and fixed supper, he'd pull the kerosene lamp near him and spread out the newspaper. Then in the yellow light he'd point to pictures and para- phrase the news items, and when Jamie began to wiggle he switched to Bible stories, which were more interesting.

James was the next baby, followed by Jerrell and Janeva and John and Janetta and Joseph and Joyce and Jesse. I came along in 1951 and, of course, I went out into the fields as a nursling, just as my brothers and sisters had done. After me there came Julius, Janis, JoAnn, Jerome, Jude, Jeff and Judy.

By age two I was "helping." Dad didn't bend down to pick cotton the way most people did; he knelt, so he could get at hard-to-reach bolls— and so he could tell us stories while Mother sang in the adjacent row.

Dad's stories always made the same point, but it took us awhile to realize that because the tales were so lively. "Do you know how I found your mother?" Dad asked us once. "We met at a carnival. That's right, I found your mother at a carnival in Pine Bluff."

He told us how he had been asking God for just the right wife because he thought he could see a way for the next generation to escape the hand-to-mouth existence of the tenant farmer. Dad's hero was the great black educator, Booker T. Washington. Education, Dad believed, was the key. He needed a wife who shared his belief, and one night he got down on his knees and asked Jesus to help him find her. That night Dad had a dream. He saw a young woman wearing pointed, green-suede shoes and a plaid coat. In the dream the woman kept saying, "I'm your wife."

"Well," Dad told us, "since the Lord showed her to me, I expected I'd meet up with her."

When a carnival came to Pine Bluff, Dad scraped together enough money to go. There, sure enough, he met a pretty girl wearing pointed, green-suede shoes and a plaid coat. "When I asked her if she would be my wife, she agreed. Just like that."

The word "expect" always seemed to creep into Dad's stories. What you expect, he'd tell us, has everything to do with what you receive.

"Seems like some of our neighbors expect to be sharecropping forever," Dad pointed out. "But it doesn't have to be that way, now does it? Look at the boy Joseph, there in the Bible." Then he weaved the wondrous story about a young man thrown into a dark and slimy pit. "Joseph didn't stay in that hole," Dad said. "Joseph expected to be a leader, not a forgotten young man at the bottom of a pit. And do you know what happened to him? One day . . ."

Climbing out of a pit was hard—my parents never fooled us about that. I remember Mother crying as she sent the older children off to school with no breakfast. Her tears frightened me when I was very young but Mother didn't try to hide them. "Yes, I'm crying, Jack. Those children are trying to do good work on an empty stomach and I know how hard that is."

At planting and harvest time we didn't go to school at all. Still, Dad expected us to keep our grades up by studying at night. In the evening, before going inside, we would gather on the sagging front porch of the old farmhouse, with a pine knot smoldering nearby to ward off the mosquitoes. We didn't have good voices but we loved to harmonize. After we'd sung some songs, gospel and folk mostly, our talk usually turned to schoolwork. There was never a lot of pressure about school, just encouragement.

"That's a fine report card," Dad might say to Jerrell. "But maybe you and I could work on the math a little. I can stay up if you can."

As new children joined the family, the older ones began teaching the younger ones the lessons of expectation.

"By the time you go to college, Jack," Jamie said to me when I was four and she was leading me, barefoot, down a weed-choked row of cotton with my man-sized hoe dragging behind me, "I'll have my degree and I can help you get started."

It wasn't that simple.

When it came time to send Jamie off to college, Dad and Mother had the first setback in their goal of an education for all their children. Even setting aside every penny, Dad hadn't raised the tuition money, and to his dismay the local black college turned Jamie down for a scholarship.

That night Dad and Mother and Jamie and James and the other children —there were twelve of us by then—gathered in the kitchen and held a prayer meeting by lantern light. Dad reminded God of the way He rescued Joseph from the pit. "Was that just a one-time thing, Lord?" he asked.

The next day Dad set out, his old GMC pickup backfiring as he headed up the red-dirt road. He was going to call on a local landowner.

He came back honking his horn. "That good man was just waiting for me," he said breathlessly, holding up a piece of paper. "I said I was going to send you children to college and could he help us get started and he asked me how much we needed and when I told him twelve hundred dollars he went inside and came back holding this check!"

In her second year at Agricultural, Mechanical and Normal, the black college in Pine Bluff, Jamie finally got her scholarship, and Dad began paying off the loan. Jamie went on to do her graduate work at UCLA. She had set the pattern.

By the time I was seventeen and it came my turn to go to college, I thought I might get a football scholarship to play with the Razorbacks at the University of Arkansas. A knee injury ended that career before it started, but the coach saw to it that I got a scholarship anyway. Later I took my law degree at Syracuse.

One by one I watched as Julius and Janis and JoAnn and Jerome and Jude and Jeff and Judy followed me to school. Dad and Mother didn't make too much of our graduation ceremonies as they rolled around. I wondered about that until I remembered Dad's telling us the story of Samson.

"Samson was no great hero, not for me," he had told us out in the fields when we were small. "Samson stopped short of the best. He forgot about the other people counting on him and settled back to live in luxury. Don't be like Samson, children. Best means best for everyone!"

For Dad and Mom, graduation was one more step in each child's journey as we went on to become lawyers and publishers and teachers and doctors and businessmen.

Mother died eleven years ago, after standing by Dad for forty-five years. We children differ from our parents in having much smaller families—just two children, on average—but we value education as much as they did. Our children are graduating from college now. My brother James's son, for instance, is the sixth Kearney to earn a degree from Harvard.

My brother James himself is one of only two of us who still have some time to go before graduating. James continues his studies part-time, after a full schedule as a manager for United Parcel Service in California. He still has a semester to go, and I tease him that at age fifty-three he has become a professional student.

Jerrell is also in California, where he's a manager at the Goodyear Tire and Rubber Company plant. He left college in his junior year, but says he's now thinking of going back.

I'm doubtful about both of them, but Dad takes no such attitude.

"Oh, I expect James and Jerrell will graduate," Dad says. "Yes, I expect they will." ❧

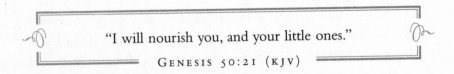

"I will nourish you, and your little ones."
GENESIS 50:21 (KJV)

IS THAT YOU, LORD?

Knowing that God speaks to us through other people, it makes sense to seek His will by consciously drawing on the human resources around us. In any matter of importance, asking the counsel of others should be considered a must.

One Christian denomination, the Quakers, has devised a formal method for just that purpose. It's called a "Clearness Committee," and it has been a part of Quaker spirituality for hundreds of years. Several hours are set aside to prayerfully help a person who is wrestling with some problem or decision. Members of the Clearness Committee are not to give advice, although they can ask questions. Mostly, though, the committee sits silently with the focus person as he or she listens for the guidance of the Holy Spirit. The purpose of this admittedly "shapeless" approach, as one Quaker described it, is to resist the notion that human beings ought to take charge of the situation. Instead, the goal is to create an environment of receptivity to the divine will.

Many of us may desire something more direct than this, although the cautions built into the Quaker method are good ones. We need to be aware that the advice we receive from other people unavoidably reflects their own biases. That's why the Bible says that in an *abundance* of counselors there is safety (Proverbs 11:14). Also make sure that those whose opinions you solicit represent a variety of perspectives. Don't be afraid to listen to someone who might tell you what you don't want to hear. D.H.

I'm a writer by trade, and like many writers, I tend to be something of a loner. If someone chooses to spend most of his working time alone with his hands on a keyboard, it's a pretty good bet he's ill at ease in crowds.

There was a time when my isolationist tendencies interfered with my faith. For years I struggled to connect in any meaningful fashion with a community of believers. That meant that whatever guidance I might have received from God through other people wasn't getting across.

Faith and community are inextricably intertwined. Although we can commune with God in solitary prayer, the Spirit is most distinctly manifested with and through other people. "Where two or three are gathered together in my name," Jesus said, "there am I in the midst of them" (Matthew 18:20, KJV).

Small groups—specifically, Bible study groups—saved me from my isolationist tendencies. They provided a focus that circumnavigated the necessity for small talk (which terrifies me!) while at the same time providing an opportunity for the warmth you can only get from sympathetic sharing with other human beings. The bonds I established in these small groups also helped ease me into communion with the wider church community.

In recent years there has been tremendous growth in small-group participation in churches around the world. That tells me that many others have learned, as I did, that such groups can be living megaphones for the voice of God. Our next story, "Small Group, Big Answers," by Florence Pert, describes the sorts of miracles that can happen when fellowship, Scripture and prayer are combined.

SMALL GROUP, BIG ANSWERS
—BY FLORENCE PERT—

My neighbor and friend Ev Kaiser was on the phone. "Florence," she asked, "could you and George come over for a while after dinner? Something has happened and Bob and I would like to talk to somebody."

During dinner George and I speculated over this "something." A problem in their marriage? The Kaisers, however, had impressed us as

being one of the happiest and in love couples in our suburban community of Scotch Plains, New Jersey.

Bob, a Phi Beta Kappa at Dartmouth, a champion golfer and a deco-
rated veteran of World War II, was now president of a small business.
Ev was a sparkling social leader in the community—and a devoted
mother of their four children. Bob's face was drawn and tense when he
greeted us. He came quickly to the point. "Our company has been
merged with another. I'm out of a job."

George and Bob went into the living room to talk while Ev and I
cleared off the dishes and sat at the kitchen table. "It's been quite a blow
to Bob," she said. "He's had to dismiss a number of his old employees
too. But I don't think losing the job is quite as bad as the loss of his self-
confidence. He is terribly depressed."

On several occasions Ev and I had talked about prayer and talked
about religion. The time had come to stop talking and begin praying.
And so, sitting on kitchen stools, we prayed for Bob's physical and
mental health in this crisis.

Meanwhile, in the living room, George and Bob were taking a somewhat different route. In his quiet way, George began suggesting to Bob
that perhaps he was trying too hard to run his own life, that he might do
better if he sought God's guidance and direction. We spent several
evenings with the Kaisers, trying to be helpful. One night Bob came to
a conclusion. "What you're telling me, George, is that there's a big difference between being the nominal Christian I've been for so long and
really offering my life to Jesus Christ."

That same evening Bob took what he called the gamble of an outright
transferral of his life and will to God. As George and I were leaving, Bob
said, "I think we'd be interested in that fellowship group you mentioned
to us one time."

George and I were delighted. Meeting regularly with a small group of
concerned Christians had meant spiritual lifeblood to both of us for
many years, both before we were married and after. Furthermore, many
of our ideas of what a marriage could really become resulted from spiritual fellowship with other married couples.

So it was that the negative fact of Bob's losing his job had a positive
result—the formation of a small fellowship group in Scotch Plains.

Being new in the community, George and I could not have brought this about without people like the Kaisers to spark it. The timing was perfect, for it was through this group that Bob was to learn how to receive God's guidance.

The first meeting was held in the Kaisers' living room. On hand were five married couples and one elderly widower.

Since George and I had already experienced sixteen years of leading small groups, we had learned certain pitfalls to avoid. George's opening statement went something like this:

"We're here tonight as a group of friends who want to grow spiritually. Many of us have felt a sense of vagueness about our religion. Here I hope we can get down to the nuts and bolts of trying to live out our Christian faith every day. We expect to learn from the experiences of one another, from the Bible and through prayer."

It was agreed that we would meet every Wednesday night in a different home. We decided to open each session by reading a chapter from the Gospel of Mark, then explore how that particular Scripture related to our personal lives. Our prayer period would be silent or vocal, as the Holy Spirit moved us.

At the first meeting Bob told about his effort to redirect his life. "All of you know what has happened to me and how I completely lost confidence in myself," he said. "There is no question in my mind that the decision to put my life in God's hands has already kept me from a serious breakdown. I still don't have a job, nor do I know what the future holds for me and my family. But I'm not as fearful as I was. I am seeking God's help and I would appreciate your prayers."

This kind of open request for God's guidance made before members of a group always seems to produce a chain-reaction effect. After the prayer petition—and a quiet-time to listen for answers—one person asked if Bob was sure he was in the right field. Another thought of a company that was looking for an executive director. In the days ahead, interviews and contacts multiplied. Bob was kept busy day and night seeing people.

He soon came to one conclusion about the quest for direction from God. It would be wrong to sit around waiting for it to explode in his face. He was to follow up every possibility. He was to be active.

Several weeks later Bob reported to the group as follows: "These interviews have given me a chance to rethink everything about my life. Perhaps God truly is trying to tell me that I belong in a different field, as was suggested in our first meeting. I've enjoyed my job in industry, but deep down I've often wondered if my real talent might not be in the field of education."

Weeks passed. Meanwhile, things were happening to other members of the group. One housewife healed a bad relationship with her neighbor. One of the men who had aimlessly stuck to a job he didn't like came to the clear decision to make a change—and did so. His wife became more reconciled to the loss of a loved one that had long kept her deeply depressed.

Meanwhile, Bob and Ev had the sudden impulse one day that they should visit his sister in Hanover, New Hampshire, where Dartmouth is located. While making arrangements on the phone, Bob's brother-in-law, also a Dartmouth graduate, jokingly asked, "Why not work for the College?" Bob took it seriously, however, and before they hung up, his brother-in-law had agreed to arrange an interview with Dartmouth's vice president of alumni affairs.

During this interview, and several more with other college officials, it turned out that the man holding an important job in the Development Office was retiring. It seemed that Bob had just the combination of qualities and experience Dartmouth was looking for in his replacement. Was he interested? He certainly was.

With excitement in his voice, Bob later told the group about the chain of events that had led to the New Hampshire trip. "You just have to believe that there is something to this matter of God's timing," he concluded.

But I noticed that Ev did not share Bob's enthusiasm for the Dartmouth job. She was silent at the meeting, unusual for her. Several days later I found Ev alone in her kitchen. She had been crying. We talked about recipes for a while, but finally she opened up her heart.

"It's no use trying to hold back my feelings," she said. "Hanover is a fine place, but I can't bear to leave our lovely home and the wonderful friends I have here in New Jersey. I've been so upset I didn't even want to go to that last group meeting. I don't want to pray. I don't even want to talk about these things to you, Florence."

She smiled ruefully. "I'm off base and I know it. I've tried to keep my feelings from Bob, but he knows something is wrong."

"You've been honest with me. Why don't you talk to God in the same way," I suggested.

So she did.

We learned something together that afternoon. So often when we ask God for help with a problem or in making a decision, we don't really want His guidance, we simply want His confirmation of a plan we already have worked out ourselves. Or we want God's help in a limited way. "Give me Your guidance, Lord, just as long as I don't have to do this—or that." God can't help us with these restrictions, for His Plan for our lives is often so much bigger and better than we could work out for ourselves.

Ev went through a period of agonizing struggle before she could say this prayer: "Lord, I want what You want for our family. I'll move any-where. I may not like it, but I'll trust in You that it will be best for us."

Bob's job offer from Dartmouth came several weeks later, and he took it.

Seeing such good friends move was sad for all of us. Yet there was a sense of jubilation at the way it had come about. A few weeks later we heard from the Kaisers. They were settled in a large, roomy house, had made new friends, loved the community. Bob was finding the job a great challenge and delighted in the fact that it combined two factors: use of the business experience he had accumulated over the years and work with young people in education, which he had always yearned to do.

"When we look back over the past months," wrote Ev, "it amazes us how God's hand was in everything—our first call to you for help, the starting of the group, the leads and contacts that changed Bob's thinking and steered him to Dartmouth, and even the way my attitude changed. I know you'll also be interested in learning that we have started a fellowship group here in Hanover that is meeting new needs. How great God is!" ❧

"I awoke this morning with devout thanksgiving for my friends, the old and the new. Shall I not call God the Beautiful, who daily showeth himself so to me in his gifts?"

RALPH WALDO EMERSON

Scarce though they may be, we still have heroes and heroines among us, men and women whose greatness of spirit gain them international renown. Their lives are testimonies of what God would have us be.

Mother Teresa was one such heroine. What an unlikely celebrity she was! Yet millions loved and admired her. If it is our job as Christians to embody the love of Christ, she showed us the way.

In an age of scandal and excess, her example seems to shine all the more brightly.

Here are recollections of Mother Teresa from four everyday Americans who were fortunate enough to have known her personally, in some small but significant way. All of them affirm that, despite her fame and the scope of her accomplishments, she still managed to touch people directly, heart to heart. That seems to have been one of the signs of her greatness.

"DO SMALL THINGS WITH GREAT LOVE"

RUBY STEED:

It was a fall day in 1968. I had just come off my nursing shift and was on my way to an orphanage in our suburban Dallas neighborhood, where I planned to meet the children I had volunteered to bring home for the holidays. I felt good about what I was doing, but frustrated too. There were so many people who needed help, and I could only do so much.

When I opened the front door of the orphanage I was stunned. A group of kids and several reporters crowded around a small woman in a nun's habit. Mother Teresa! I had just read an article about her. She reached out to touch the cheek of a little girl. *Now there's someone who truly makes a difference*, I thought. I moved closer, drawn in by the force of her personality. Just before she left she turned to me and smiled, her eyes crinkling at the corners. "You look like someone I would like to take back to Calcutta to help in my work."

I laughed and shook my head. "I'd miss my family too much," I said.

She handed me a small red card. "Then write me," she said, looking intently in my eyes.

At home, I didn't even change out of my nurse's uniform before sitting down at the dining room table with my stationery and a pen. I started a letter several times, only to crumple up the paper and toss it away. *What do you say to Mother Teresa?* Finally, I began by telling her how she reminded me of my own mother. Then the words flowed. I wrote about my married daughter, my job, even admitted something I had never really admitted to myself: Though I had gone to church regularly since I was a little girl, I had never really felt God's presence in my life. I didn't expect a response from her, but it was good to get those things down on paper. I mailed the letter the next day.

A few weeks later, after an exhausting day at work, I got the mail and listlessly shuffled through the letters. I saw one stamped "air mail" and tore it open. It was a simple note from Mother Teresa, thanking me for my letter and urging me to try to connect to God through prayer. "You can get so close to God that nothing can hurt you," she wrote.

A short while later I wrote back. And so it went. I babbled on about my joys, my troubles, my questions, and she sent short but powerful replies, always ending with "God bless you." Gradually I learned to share my thoughts with God as openly and comfortably as I shared them with Mother Teresa—a lesson I hadn't even known she was teaching me.

I asked what I could give her to show how grateful I was. She wrote that she needed nothing, but she knew some little girls who could use dresses. *Oh, how perfect*, I thought. One of my earliest memories was of my mother teaching me how to work a sewing machine. I filled several boxes with dresses, and mailed them to Mother Teresa, telling her I wished I could make hundreds more. Out of her next letter fell a picture of her with two little girls wearing my creations. She wrote, "It's not how much you do but how much love you put into what you are doing."

I thought often of those words after giving up nursing and moving back to Alabama. I focused on helping the elderly. I did their shopping, took them to church activities and administered their medication.

Years passed. I grew older; my grandchildren grew up. But Mother Teresa's letters continued, as dependable as the seasons. Often when I read her letters—typed on gray, grainy paper, with cross-outs and missed punctuation just like mine—it was hard to remember the woman was a larger-than-life figure for people around the world.

One day I needed more from her than words on paper. I felt overwhelmed by tragedy. My sister had recently died of cancer and another family member had just been diagnosed with a serious illness. All afternoon I cried, searching for the reassurance Mother Teresa said could always be found in God. At last I called her, not even realizing it was four in the morning there. But when she heard me crying Mother Teresa immediately began praying and continued until I calmed down. "Never be upset with God for what he takes away from you," she wrote me soon after. "There is a reason he takes anything away, and when he does he gives you something to fill that empty place."

Those words comforted me years later when I realized Mother Teresa's own health was worsening. In her last letter, a few months before her death, she asked me not to be upset if she didn't write anymore, saying, "We are all getting old." I knew that was her way of saying good-bye.

I still carry the card she gave me thirty years ago. Sometimes I open the mailbox expecting to see her familiar handwriting. She was right. The empty place in my heart is filled—by the reassuring words she once wrote me. "We don't die. We just get transferred to heaven and go to work there." I no longer despair over how little I'm able to do for others. I've learned that great impact can come from small gestures—like a simple invitation to write a letter.

RICHARD DICKENS:

During the summer of 1993, right in the middle of graduate school, I was a volunteer at Mother Teresa's Home of the Destitute Dying in Calcutta. I never thought it would be easy, but when I awoke in the oppressive heat each morning I wondered how I would get through the day. First I had to wash the patients' sarong-like garments (called *lungis*). Then I helped serve meals and clean up. I mopped the ward and helped patients with their personal hygiene. The work was unending. Soon I became sick. *This is horrible*, I thought. *I feel as weak as the patients I'm supposed to take care of.*

One morning after Mass, Sister JosMa came up to me. "Wait here," she said. "Mother will see you today. She likes to meet all of the volunteers herself." My pulse quickened. I couldn't believe she could find time for me.

Sitting on a balcony bench overlooking the clinic's walkways, I watched Mother Teresa as she hurried to her appointments. Finally, not wanting to intrude on her schedule, I got up to leave when suddenly she came over and asked how I was faring.

"I'm not handling India well, Mother," I confessed.

Reaching up with her strong hands, she pulled my head down to hers. "Yah. Yah. India can be very hard. But you must pray to Jesus for strength and you must come to Mass." There was compassion but no compromise in her voice. From her robe she pulled out a small metal crucifix, which she kissed. "You must put this on the chain around your neck," she said. She rested her hand on my chest for an instant, then left.

That cross remained around my neck through the rest of that long, hot summer in India, then through the rest of graduate school, a new career in social work and a bout with cancer. When I say my prayers at night I can still hear Mother's heavily accented English: "You must pray to Jesus for strength." Strength she shared with so many others.

CHARLES ZECH:

One night I was returning from a business trip, tired and a little home-sick. I finished my meeting notes just as the jet touched down in Detroit. Wearily, I stuffed the papers in my briefcase and shuffled off the plane and into the nearly deserted corridor, my footfalls echoing hollowly. My gaze fell on three nuns coming toward me. As they neared, I recognized Mother Teresa and called her name. She stopped and smiled. I put down my briefcase and walked up to her, my arm outstretched. She took my hand and held it in a friendly way.

"Will you please pray for me?" I asked.

She patted my hand, and surprised me by replying, "You pray for me."

While driving home, I did. I asked God's blessing on her ministry and thanked Him for the gift of meeting her.

Eight years have passed since Mother Teresa asked me to pray for her. I have pondered her words many times. At first I marveled that she thought I could help her. It occurred to me that not only did Mother Teresa want me to pray for her, but she knew that through prayer I would be closer to God.

VANCE THURSTON:

She'll probably never get the letter anyway, I reasoned. I had resisted the idea for three months. But I was home with the flu and the insistent urging wouldn't let up: *Write to Mother Teresa.*

Three years earlier, in 1994, I had parked in front of a small gift store called the Serenity Shop and looked inside. The owner had been easy to visit with, and I had surprised myself by confiding in her that I was so wrapped up with work I didn't feel I was being of much service to God. She'd smiled, then recommended a video entitled *Mother Teresa.*

Back home, I found myself drawn into scenes of Mother Teresa's Missionaries of Charity feeding starving children and caring for the sick and dying. A service was shown in an ancient church, where a young Indian novice in a blue-and-white sari stepped up to the altar. With quiet resolve she said, "I, Sister Mary, vow for life, chastity, poverty, obedience and wholehearted and free service to the poorest of the poor." The intensity of my feelings took me by surprise.

I had viewed the tape many times since, and could no longer ignore my urge to write. I told Mother Teresa how much her work moved me, and said that I had been many things—ranch hand, mechanic, carpenter and songwriter, but I wondered how I could serve God better.

When I recovered from the flu I took the letter to the post office. I had second thoughts as the clerk examined the incomplete address. "Let's go ahead and send this," he said. "I'm sure in Calcutta they know where Mother Teresa lives."

Spring came and went. Occasionally I wondered if Mother Teresa got my letter. Though I nurtured a secret hope she would write back, I knew Mother Teresa had bigger concerns than a carpenter in Montana.

In early August a simple envelope postmarked "Calcutta" arrived in the mail. I carefully opened the letter, took a deep breath and unfolded the sheet of rough paper. The words appeared to have been typed by an ancient typewriter. After a few kind personal references to my letter, she wrote, "Whatever you do—whether to carve a door or to write a song that God inspires you to write—do it all for his glory and the good of his people. Always do small things with great love, and be ready to take whatever he gives and give whatever he takes with a big smile. Let us pray." The letter was signed in blue ink, "God bless you, Mother Teresa."

Do small things with great love. What could have been a better demonstration of that belief than her letter? I had asked what I could do to serve God better and she had shown me.

Four weeks later I watched Mother Teresa's funeral on television. She had not tried to do great things. She did small things with such great love that it touched the hearts of millions. The gift of her letter might have seemed a small thing to Mother Teresa, but the love she shared has changed my life.

Christ plays in ten thousand places,
Lovely in limbs, lovely in eyes not his
To the Father through the features of men's faces.

GERARD MANLEY HOPKINS

One of the blessings of a hero or heroine is that he or she can inspire us to behave more heroically. Mother Teresa had that impact, as we have seen. So did Martin Luther King Jr. and Mohandas Gandhi. And, of course, so did Jesus.

Jesus left no doubt that it is our responsibility to be messengers of God to our neighbors, especially those less fortunate than ourselves. That means that while we are alert for the ways in which God may be speaking to us through other people, we also need to be aware that God may be trying to speak to other people through us.

To freely make ourselves available as God's messengers may well be our greatest responsibility as Christians—and also the source of our greatest joy. How odd that in the busyness of our lives we so often forget something so important! Marion Bond West gracefully reminds us of that in this chapter's closing reflection.

COMFORT, AND BE COMFORTED
—BY MARION BOND WEST—

For days I'd suffered with what I call "a rushing spirit." No matter how fast I thought or hurried, a nasty inner voice insisted, *You're still behind.* My list of things to do that spring Wednesday included going to our church at ten-thirty in the morning for one hour of solitary prayer. I entered the small, simple room in our trailer-church wishing I felt spiritual—like a real prayer warrior. I sat down in a metal folding chair and leaned hard against the heavy wooden table.

"You know my heart and mind are rushed," I told God. "I don't even know how to slow down and try to hear You, but I desperately need to."

I didn't really believe God would honor such a half-hearted prayer, but then thoughts began to glide into my troubled mind.

Remember the woman sitting alone on the bench outside the grocery store yesterday? You slowed down because she was reading from a small New Testament. You saw her defeated face, and I even allowed you to peek into her lonely heart. You understood that she was hurting. You almost stopped, but then you hurried on with your groceries to the car. I had placed her there just for you.

"Oh, Lord, Lord! Forgive me. Yes, of course I remember. I saw her all the way home in my mind. I still see her! It wouldn't have taken long. I...I..."

She was My plan to help you slow down and learn to be still, child. I often reach you through unlikely people. Just sit here for a bit now while I comfort you.

Why does God bring thunderclouds and disasters when we want green pastures and still waters? Bit by bit we find, behind the clouds, the Father's feet; behind the lightning, an abiding day that has no night; behind the thunder, a still, small voice that comforts with a comfort that is unspeakable.

OSWALD CHAMBERS

Elijah Taken Up to Heaven

2 Kings 2:1–9 (NIV)

When the Lord was about to take Elijah up to heaven in a whirlwind, Elijah and Elisha were on their way from Gilgal. Elijah said to Elisha, "Stay here; the Lord has sent me to Bethel."

But Elisha said, "As surely as the Lord lives and as you live, I will not leave you." So they went down to Bethel.

The company of the prophets at Bethel came out to Elisha and asked, "Do you know that the Lord is going to take your master from you today?"

"Yes, I know," Elisha replied, "but do not speak of it."

Then Elijah said to him, "Stay here, Elisha; the Lord has sent me to Jericho."

And he replied, "As surely as the Lord lives and as you live, I will not leave you." So they went to Jericho.

The company of the prophets at Jericho went up to Elisha and asked him, "Do you know that the Lord is going to take your master from you today?"

"Yes, I know," he replied, "but do not speak of it."

Then Elijah said to him, "Stay here; the Lord has sent me to the Jordan."

And he replied, "As surely as the Lord lives and as you live, I will not leave you." So the two of them walked on.

Fifty men of the company of the prophets went and stood at a distance, facing the place where Elijah and Elisha had stopped at the Jordan. Elijah took his cloak, rolled it up and struck the water with it. The water divided to the right and to the left, and the two of them crossed over on dry ground.

When they had crossed, Elijah said to Elisha, "Tell me, what can I do for you before I am taken from you?"

"Let me inherit a double portion of your spirit," Elisha replied. ❧

~ CHAPTER FOUR ~

GOD SPEAKS TO US...
Through Angels

*U*sually when we think of angels, we think in terms of rescue, protection or comfort. They appear, or we become aware of their presence, during moments of crisis or danger. Seldom, on the other hand, do we think of angels as teachers. Guiding someone to a deeper understanding of God's will doesn't exactly seem to fit their job description.

As with so many of our arbitrary limits on the workings of the Spirit, this notion needs to be expanded. Direction can grow out of rescue or comfort. There's nothing like being saved to help us understand that God wants nothing more than to save us. As God's messengers, angels often serve as bearers of that glorious news.

Because God's timing is so different from our own, we may not perceive the stately progression with which grace often unfolds. This is especially true in the midst of crisis. Our focus is on the immediate miracle; only later do we realize that our lives have been changed permanently. The author of our first story in this chapter, Lindsay Thomas (a pseudonym), knows this from firsthand experience.

Only for Me

—By Lindsay Thomas—

Like most high school juniors, I couldn't wait to be a senior. Early in 1994 I was already daydreaming about the big prom and our Class of '95 graduation. But it wasn't long before I had to wake up from my dream. In the spring of junior year I got pregnant.

My boyfriend and I were just too young to make our relationship work. We finally broke up. Problem was, I didn't have anyone else to talk to about this. I was afraid of what my parents might say. Even my friends. So I kept it to myself. Somehow I kept the pregnancy secret. I gained weight, but I was athletic and I carried it well. I wore sweatpants and oversized T-shirts. Nobody noticed my growing belly. And nobody noticed that I was crumbling inside.

In September, before school started, Mom wanted to take me shopping at the mall. "You're going to need some special outfits for senior year," she said.

"Okay, Mom," I muttered. "Whatever." My total lack of excitement gave everything away.

"Lindsay?" she said. "What's wrong?"

My secret tumbled out. It was such a relief. "I'm six months pregnant," I confessed.

"All this time," Mom said, "and you've held it all in."

I was so ashamed, I just wanted to hide. Even from God. "I want to go someplace where no one knows me," I said.

Mom understood and found a home for single mothers in a city a couple of hours away. The facility was next to a hospital. I could stay there, have my baby and arrange for an adoption. I could even continue my education.

The staff at the maternity home was nice enough, but being with so many other pregnant teens just made me feel worse. Each of us lived with another girl, and we shared a bath with our neighbors. The shower stall was so small you couldn't turn without bumping your belly. We could sign out and go into town if we wanted—see a movie, get our nails done, that kind of stuff. But I threw myself into schoolwork. This was far from my dream of senior year. No prom. No dates. No graduation ceremony.

I was cordial to the other girls, but I didn't really want to make friends. I couldn't wait for weekends, when Mom came to get me and we returned to Burlington. "It's so good to be home," I said, hugging her every chance I got. But Sunday night always came, and all too soon I was back in my lonely room.

There were counseling sessions every couple of days, and we talked a lot about self-image. I knew what I thought of myself, and it wasn't good. What must God think of me? I wondered.

One day I saw a notice on the bulletin board. "Bible Study," it read. I'd loved Bible stories and church camp as a kid, but I kind of put my faith on the back burner once I hit high school. I worried what my friends would think if I acted too religious. Here, who cared? I wrote my name at the top of the sheet, the first one to sign up. The meetings would be held on Wednesdays at four o'clock in a conference room.

That first Wednesday, I opened the door, feeling kind of shy. Choir music played in the background. When I saw the teacher, I relaxed a little. She was a beautiful black woman, maybe in her forties, and her face seemed to glow. "I'm Dorothy," she said, "and it looks like you have me all to yourself. Welcome."

Welcome was how I felt each Wednesday when I spent an hour with Dorothy. None of the other girls ever came to the class. It was always just Dorothy and me. She seemed to sense exactly what was on my mind on any given day. One afternoon she took my hand. "You're afraid, aren't you?" she said. I nodded. I was afraid of what I'd done, afraid of giving birth, afraid of what my friends would say if they ever found out. I didn't know how to face life anymore.

Dorothy opened her Bible, and started reading from Philippians 4. "'Do not be anxious,'" she read. "'The God of peace will be with you.'"

"I'd like to believe that," I said. Dorothy traced her finger down the page. "Remember this," she said, pointing to Philippians 4:13. "'I can do everything through him who gives me strength.'"

In our sessions we talked and laughed and cried, and I learned why Dorothy had that glow about her. "I love the Lord," she said. Right before Thanksgiving she gave me a book of Scripture passages called *God's Promises*. "If you have questions and I'm not here," she said, "you can find the answers in this book." Then she put her arms around me. "Your baby will be beautiful." That was the last time I saw her.

My November 27 due date came and went, and by December I wasn't doing well. God of peace, be with me, I prayed. The doctors induced labor when I was a good two weeks overdue. My newborn son was beautiful, just like Dorothy said. Saying good-bye to him seemed impossible, but I was thankful for the loving family who adopted him. Over and over I asked God to give me strength. I had to keep reminding myself that I'd done what was best for my baby.

I returned home a few days before Christmas. Somehow I got through the next several months. I read and reread *God's Promises*. It wasn't easy to think about the past, but I often thought about Dorothy. I told Mom how important she'd been to me.

Eventually I called the maternity home to get Dorothy's telephone number and address. I couldn't believe what I was told. The nurse who answered said that there was no Dorothy at the home. And no one had ever conducted a Bible study there. After I hung up the phone, I could barely speak. "Dorothy must have been there only for me," I said to Mom. We talked about it and decided God had sent an angel to show me that He loved me, no matter what.

My son is now seven, and with the blessings of his adoptive parents, we talk almost every day. I'm married now, and my husband and I have a child of our own. Glancing through a book of baby names, I decided to look up Dorothy. I guess I shouldn't have been surprised. Her name means "Gift of God." ❧

 Do not forget to entertain strangers, for by so doing some people have entertained angels without knowing it.

Hebrews 13:2 (NIV)

We know that angels appear in earthly as well as spirit form. Sometimes they come in bunches, too. Rona Swanson found that out when she and her children moved into a rundown house in the center of town. She also found that sometimes the voice of God keeps whispering the same thing over and over again: Don't lose hope. Don't lose hope.

THE PEOPLE OF MY TOWN
—BY RONA SWANSON—

So this is it, I thought. *This is where we'll spend our worst holidays ever.* My best friend Bodie had driven me up onto the dirt driveway of the ramshackle house I'd rented for my three children and me. Once the general store, it stood in plain view of the café, the hardware store and the post office at the intersection in the center of Glennville, a former silver-mining town in California's Greenhorn Mountains. I took a deep breath and slowly walked up the creaking steps to the porch.

I'd worked hard to make a good home for my family. But over the years my husband had become increasingly abusive, and in November 1985 I'd finally made the decision to take our children and leave. We'd moved in with Smitty, the town sheriff, and his wife, Paulette, while I scraped together enough money to afford a place of our own. This old house was the best I could do for now.

Going inside for the first time was a shock. The last occupants had been kicked out, and it wasn't hard to see why. The stench was overwhelming. "They must've kept a hundred cats and dogs in here," Bodie said, holding her nose. "But I'll help you clean it up."

I've made a big mistake, I thought. *Who could be happy here?*

We were loading Bodie's pickup with trash when Smitty stopped by. "Looks like the place needs a little work," he said with a wry smile as he ducked his head to fit under the door frame.

"Yep," Bodie said, "but we'll have it looking like a palace in no time."

"One nice thing," Smitty remarked as he looked across the front room, "you've got a great view."

He was right. The house had a huge bank of picture windows in front.

Not only could I see everything that was going on in all of Glennville, Glennville could see me! Even though I had been involved with the PTA and attended church every Sunday, I spent most of my time at home with my family. Funny how you can live in a community for years and never know its people very well.

As Bodie and I hauled away truckload after truckload of refuse, the folks in town looked on. I didn't want to become anyone's charity case. I was determined to take care of myself and my children, on my own. I had a lot to prove, especially to myself. *So much for doing it with dignity!* I thought as we drove through town on the way to the dump with yet another odiferous load. When we returned, we found that a few people had walked over after picking up their mail at the post office to peer in at our progress and offer encouragement.

Silver-haired Don and his wife Zo, who owned the hardware store, strolled over that afternoon. "How's it going?" Don asked shyly, shuffling his cowboy boots on the porch.

"It's coming along," I hollered from the front room. I had been pulling up the filthy old linoleum with a crowbar when from under all of the muck and grime appeared the original pine flooring, clean and pure.

"You're going to need some stain for that," Don said and charged out the door.

"See, honey?" Zo said, coming up beside me. "You found something nice here already."

Don came back in with a grin from ear to ear. "Here's some surplus stain that I got as a sample," he said. "Now, no charge for this, okay? You just gotta tell me how it works."

Light bulbs blew and the outlets popped, so it seemed likely the electrical system needed fixing, but our landlady didn't want to spend the money. A fellow named Mark showed up on the back porch one afternoon. "Thought I'd take a look at your wiring," he said. Most folks wouldn't be too happy to see Mark outside their door. He had lots of tattoos and was rumored to have a dark past. But I reluctantly invited him in. He turned out to be a first-class electrician and installed up-to-date wiring for the entire house.

"I liked doing the work," he explained, and his fee was more than reasonable. A home-cooked meal was all he would take for his labors.

That's when things really started happening. Gallons of paint and supplies appeared on the porch. Bodie surprised me with pretty flowered wallpaper for the front room. A rancher delivered a huge gas heater and hooked it up. "It's just been sittin' in the barn," he explained, his face reddening. Molly, the waitress from the café, brought over a freestanding range and oven in the back of her truck. "My new house has a built-in with a microwave," she told me.

Early one morning Jim Richardson knocked on the door. He lived alone in the big house on the hill, and had been a wallpaper hanger by trade. I had only asked for a few pointers, but he insisted on hanging it himself, transforming that front room into a showplace.

After three weeks at Smitty and Paulette's, our house was ready for the kids and me, but we had no hot water. The old heater was rusted through. Jim "just happened" to have an extra one. While installing it he found that our plumbing pipes weren't connected. He hooked up all the pipes and sent me a bill for three million dollars. "A bargain!" I told him, trying to smile through grateful tears.

The kids and I moved into the house in mid-December. Though we finally had a place to call home, I still didn't have much more than a nickel in my purse. Late one night I paced the kitchen, wondering how we'd make it to the next payday with so little in the cupboard. There was a tap at the back door and I looked up to see Paulette's face through the glass. I waved for her to come in, but she just cracked the door a bit and wagged her finger at me.

"Don't say a word," she said, then disappeared. She came back with a box full of canned goods and staples. "Not one word," she warned as she slid the box onto the counter and hurried out of the house.

I stood at the counter, trying to hold back tears as she returned with three more boxes. "This makes me happy," she said, giving me a hug, "so you be happy too. Okay?"

I held her tight. "Okay," I responded, although I wasn't quite sure I remembered how. I was worried about Christmas, only a week away. *Dear Lord, I want it to be special for my kids.*

The next evening, I noticed Don standing outside the front door. "Forgive me for just bustin' in," he said, when I opened it. "Would you like a tree? Zo and I have two, and we thought maybe you hadn't had a chance to get one yet." Before I could say anything, Don went out into the dark and reappeared with a tree, already set up in a stand. Zo followed with a box under her arm. "We had some extra lights too," she said. Don and Zo stayed to help us string the lights, and when we switched them on, the kids clapped as the room danced with color.

The next day Jim came over. "I couldn't help but notice how pretty your tree looked last night," he said. "I don't use these lights. Would it be okay if I hung them around outside?" It was more than okay.

The kids and I went caroling that night with a group of our new friends, riding in the back of a hay wagon, bundled up against the wind and swirling snow. We circled through Glennville, and as we turned up our street I caught my breath.

"Look!" I said, pointing ahead. In front of us, in the middle of everything, was a beautiful house, twinkling inside and out, ready to welcome Christmas. Our house. Not just my kids' and mine, but everyone's. So many folks had looked after us, put their love into that house. I, who had felt so determined to make it on my own, had been cared for at every turn.

As we sang "Silent Night," I said a prayer of gratitude for the people of my town. They had become angels of Christmas for my children and me, reflections of God's everlasting light in the center of our lives. ✢

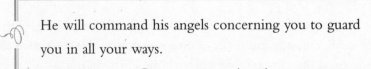

He will command his angels concerning you to guard you in all your ways.

PSALM 91:11 (NIV)

The angels of Christmas who restored Rona Swanson's house participated in an act of holy teamwork. An enormous source of spiritual power is unleashed when an entire community works in concert toward some loving purpose. Anyone who's ever participated in a group ministry project knows the feeling. In the following story,

Rebecca House describes a quieter but no less powerful form of holy teamwork, when both earthly and heavenly angels joined hands to complete another restoration.

THREE MEN IN A CHAPEL
—BY REBECCA HOUSE—

At a retreat I volunteered one afternoon to work in the prayer room. As I was sorting through requests a woman appeared in the doorway. "Is this the chapel?" she asked nervously. "Yes," I said. "Can I help you?" She introduced herself as Mary, and we moved to a small table in the back. As she told me her long, tragic story, two women who knew her well joined us. We pushed our chairs close so we could fit around the table. I feared I had gotten in over my head. I wished there had been a minister to pray with us.

When Mary finished talking, the four of us closed our eyes and prayed, begging for the forces of good to overcome the evil that had brought such sadness into Mary's life. When I lifted my head, I was surprised to see her look so relieved.

A few days later a friend who had been at the retreat called. "By the way," she asked, "who was that man in the chapel with you?"

"What man?" I asked.

"The middle-aged guy with gray hair, slightly overweight. He had on a plaid shirt and sat at the table with you and Mary and the two other women."

But there was no room for anyone else, I thought. Later I spoke to another friend who had been there that weekend. She had come by the chapel while I was praying with Mary and had seen other men besides the one with the plaid shirt. "They looked like ministers to me," she said, "so I figured you were doing all right."

I thought about one description of angels in the Bible: "Are they not all ministering spirits, sent forth to minister for them who shall be heirs of salvation?" (Hebrews 1:14). They had been praying at my side. ❧

Is That You, Lord?

Is it possible to summon an angel?

With prayer, yes. Often, though, angels appear unbidden. People tend to be surprised when an angel arrives, and that is probably as it should be. When our need is great we can pray for an angelic intervention, just as we can pray for other types of miracles to occur. Nothing could be more human than to ask that the cup be passed. But what should we do when the angels *don't* come?

Praying fervently to God in a time of need and not receiving an answer can be one of the most excruciatingly difficult experiences in the life of any believer. It can also be one of our most valuable experiences. When all of our defenses are stripped away, there is no choice but to turn inward, to search deeply within ourselves for a solution. When this happens, we can be stunned to find inner resources we never knew we had. We can also find ourselves closer to God than we ever have been. God loves paradoxes, it seems, and this is one of them. As the writer Constance Fitzgerald has put it, "a situation of no potential is loaded with potential."

The reason for this may be that our defenses or our habits of mind need to be shaken in order for a new truth, a new awareness, to enter in. This is why brokenness is so often a precursor to revelation. The point is not that God *wants* us to suffer, but that God *uses* our suffering to bring us closer to Him. "We know that all things work together for good for those who love God, who are called according to his purpose," wrote the Apostle Paul (Romans 8:28, NRSV). The crucifixion and resurrection of Christ is the ultimate example of this spiritual truth.

What, then, should we do when the angels don't come? Trust that in God's time, an answer will be revealed.

Meanwhile, wait, watch and pray. D.H.

Ideally, God's direction over the course of our lives accomplishes a gradual, thorough cleansing of our souls. As Christians, we don't pretend that such a cleansing isn't necessary. There are dark corners in each of our hearts, places where fear and anger and prejudice reside. If we are faithful, the Holy Spirit will show us these places. Once revealed and recognized, with God's help, healing can occur.

Wendy Smyth's compelling reminiscence, "On the Way to Perpignan," demonstrates that sometimes it is an angel who shines the light that lets us see.

ON THE WAY TO PERPIGNAN
—BY WENDY SMYTH—

With a powerful roar of engines, the plane shuddered as it sped down the runway of London's Heathrow Airport. From my window seat I strained for a last look, a last memory of my summer studying art and theater as part of junior year in college. I was exhausted from lack of sleep and all the painful good-byes. And I was a little scared. Security had been tight at the airport because of the recent bombing of a Pan Am jet over Lockerbie, Scotland, by Arab terrorists. I wished I had opted to go straight home to New York.

Instead, despite the risks, and with almost no money, I was on my way to the south of France for a two-week vacation. I would be staying with a French couple who were like second parents to me—I'd lived with them for a few months out of high school—so once I arrived, things would be fine. All I had to do was fly to Nice and take a train to Perpignan, my destination. "Piece of cake," said a British friend who planned my route.

The plane lifted, and I watched cars and buildings recede till they became like toys. The red seat-belt light went off. I got up and walked toward the rest room. Suddenly, involuntarily, I shrank back in fear. There, in traditional dress, was an Arab. I knew the panic that seized me was irrational, but the fear—and prejudice—was intense.

I recalled the cruel incident where it had begun: a costume party with a bunch of students letting off steam. I, dressed as the Statue of Liberty, was talking with a group of Canadians. A swarthy man in Arab garb strolled over and pushed his way in.

"Are you American?" he demanded in a thick accent.

"Yes," I admitted.

"Then this is for you!" he shrieked, producing a snub-nosed revolver and pointing it at my heart.

Shock rippled across the noisy room, until there was a deathly silence. My knees buckled. Then, suddenly, the man ripped off his headpiece and began laughing.

"It's a joke. Get it?" he said in a Midwestern American twang. No one else, especially me, took it as a joke, and he was immediately ejected from the party. But I couldn't forget being inches from death at the hands of an "Arab."

Back in my seat I deliberately turned my thoughts to more pleasant things. As if an angel were pouring it out, the evening dusk saturated the sky. I have a fascination with angels. Of course, I've never seen a real one (that I know of), but in my travels some special people have come along when I needed help. To me each is a sort of angel because the word means "messenger of God." As I watched this everyday miracle of dusk turning to night, I prayed, "Lord, please let Your angels be on standby for me. Help me get to Perpignan safely."

We landed in Nice at 10:00 PM. I struggled through customs with three heavy suitcases. Even though I spoke French, it was a culture shock to hear it everywhere and see it plastered on the signs. When I asked about a train, I discovered the first chink in my plans. I couldn't get a train from the airport, as my friend had assured me, but had to take a bus across the city to the train station. There went a good part of my food money, not to mention energy.

On the bus I sat up front, not paying attention to the two men across from me till I heard them speaking. In the darkness, I stole a glance at their Arab profiles and felt an instant dislike and fear. I was relieved when they got off at the next stop.

At the station I had more trouble. My French was rusty and my arms felt as if they were about to break from carrying my luggage, but finally I stumbled onto the right train. Then, after an hour and a half, I had to change trains (another unforeseen happening) at a small town. It was 2:00 AM. The station was closed and I had to wait for hours on an out-door platform in eerie darkness broken only by one feeble streetlamp.

I sat on a bench, cold, hungry, tired and scared. A few lecherous Frenchmen came by and offered "help." One said I could spend the night at his place. A drunk stumbled up and sat next to me, telling me his troubles. I remembered my trip-planning friend and vowed never to consult him again.

When the train finally rumbled in at four o'clock, I used my last bit of energy to get myself and my luggage on board. At the first empty compartment, I dragged in my three suitcases, closed the door, pulled the window curtains, and fell instantly and soundly asleep, knowing the long journey was almost over. The conductor had promised to wake me when we got to Perpignan. My French family would meet me.

I woke with a jolt. The first timid rays of light were streaking through a crack in the curtains. The train was still. A Frenchman with a red beret and a potbelly sat across from me.

"Excuse me," I said, "have we gotten to Perpignan yet?"

He began waving his arms excitedly. "You missed it. We're in Spain now!"

It couldn't be. But when I pulled the curtains I knew it was true. There were border guards everywhere. I was totally drained. So I sat there, in a fog, dimly aware that the Frenchman had left the compartment. I sagged deep in the seat, whipped. I couldn't move.

Soon I heard loud voices outside the compartment. Two men were speaking Spanish. The door opened and there was the red-bereted man with someone else. "This man is going to Perpignan. He will help you. He says you must hurry or you will both miss the train. But he speaks only Spanish and Arabic."

I shrank back as I looked up into the dark, distinctive face of an Arab. But the decision was out of my hands; the man picked up my luggage and took off, looking back to make sure I was coming.

In the semidarkness I ran after him. He went across the concrete platform and down a flight of steps. We passed through a tunnel, under some tracks, up yet another flight of steps and toward the sky blushing with dawn. A train was waiting. The Arab found a compartment, piled my luggage on the shelf and on the floor between us. We sat facing each other. He was young, slight of build, with a pencil-line mustache and black, brooding eyes.

I could hear the border guards going up and down the train. Soon
two of them burst into our compartment asking for passports. I offered
mine and it was returned with smiles. But I saw dread in the Arab's eyes.
When he handed over his passport, one guard frowned as he showed it
to the other. Then they both began firing questions at him. Though I
didn't understand Spanish I could hear contempt in their tone of voice.
Finally the passport was tossed back in disdain, and the guards moved on.

I was angry. "Why did they do that?" I asked the Arab uncertainly,
hoping he knew a little French.

"Because I am Arab," he replied, shrugging resignedly.

The train jerked to a start. My new friend left and when he reappeared he was carrying a cardboard tray with two coffees, sweet rolls and
croissants. I hadn't planned on breakfast because I couldn't afford it, but
I reached for my purse. He shook his head no. "Merci," I said, diving in.
I was starved!

Despite our limited communication, I learned the bare bones of his
history. He was Palestinian and had grown up in a camp in Lebanon. For
some reason (I couldn't understand his explanation) he was forced to
leave. He had a wife and child he hadn't seen in more than a year, and
was saving money to bring them to Spain. He was a carpenter by trade.
Because of his nationality, he was often questioned by authorities and
harassed by others. There was a lot of prejudice against Arabs, he said.

An hour and a half later we were in Perpignan. It promised to be hot,
a good beach day. The man carried my bags and stood by while I phoned
my French family. "You don't have to wait," I said, hanging up the
phone. "No, no, I will," he said.

We sat down on a bench, the heavy luggage beside me. I felt refreshed
from not having to haul it, from not having to find my way—and at
having been fed. Was it a coincidence, I wondered, that all this had been
at the hand of my "enemy"?

I stared across the station at the benches scattered with people reading,
dozing, talking. Old people, young people, Spanish, French, Italians,
Americans—and an Arab family, sitting alone. I found myself looking at
them with new eyes, as members of one big family, God's family.

"Wendy! Wendy!" Now my French family was coming toward me. I turned to introduce my friend, but he was already across the room and going through the door to the outside.

I never learned his name. But I will always remember him as one of those unlikely angels God sends. And I will not forget that his kindness has taught me we are all God's children, and that I must never judge any person because of what another has done. ✤

> Do not conform any longer to the pattern of this world, but be transformed by the renewing of your mind. Then you will be able to test and approve what God's will is— his good, pleasing and perfect will.
>
> ROMANS 12:2 (NIV)

Another soul wound most of us carry is guilt. God would have that healed as well.

Even those who are most dedicated to God can take comfort in that fact. The following story by Elizabeth Sherrill tells of a healing experienced by Brother Andrew, a Dutchman who spent much of his life smuggling Bibles behind the Iron Curtain. Despite all the good he had done, Brother Andrew couldn't shake the shame he felt for having been among the Dutch soldiers sent to fight the people of Indonesia. It took an encounter with an angel to free him of that burden.

A HAND OF FORGIVENESS
—BY ELIZABETH SHERRILL—

When the Cold War ended, Brother Andrew decided to return to now-independent Indonesia to assist the people he had once fought. Nothing he did for them, however, served to ease his conscience. The place he most dreaded revisiting was the town of Ungaran, where his army unit had been headquartered.

"At last," he said, "I forced myself to go back there." He made himself walk up the single main road, past the mosque, to the big U-shaped school building the Dutch had used as a barracks. The building had been turned back into a school; on the former drill ground inside the U, some children in ragged clothing were playing.

As Andrew stood watching, a little girl, maybe eight years old, suddenly broke away from her playmates and ran toward him. The other children stopped their game and stared after her, clearly puzzled. The child ran straight up to Andrew, put her small hand in his, looked up into his eyes and smiled. Then she ran back to join her companions.

Andrew stood where he was, tears running down his face. "I knew Who it was Who'd come to me. It was Jesus. Jesus telling me, 'I forgive you, Andrew. Now forgive yourself and serve these beautiful people with joy.'"

> I have swept away your offenses like a cloud,
> your sins like the morning mist.
> Return to me, for I have redeemed you."
>
> ISAIAH 44:22 (NIV)

I have heard God's love described as "gratuitous," meaning that it is given to us freely. It's not something we earn.

The last story in this chapter reminds me of that glorious fact. I chose it mainly because it underscores the unfathomable mystery of God's ways. In trying to discern God's will, we are always limited by our humanness. We see, as Paul said, through a glass darkly.

Reading David Waite's astonishing account of the mysterious visitors who came to his home one Christmas season, we are left with a sense of how utterly strange the workings of God's grace can be.

FOUR MYSTERIOUS VISITORS
—BY DAVID WAITE—

Last Christmas got off to a promising start. Alison and I and the children —two of our four were still at home—had picked out a tree and its lights were twinkling merrily in the living room. I had lit a fire to take the edge off our raw English air. And then-twelve-year-old Matthew hesitantly asked me a question that would have been perfectly natural in any other household: "Dad, would it be all right if I put on some Christmas music?"

"Of course," I said, too quickly.

I braced myself. As strains of "Hark! The Herald Angels Sing" began to fill the house, a familiar gnawing sensation grew in the pit of my stomach. *Not again*, I thought. Christmas carols were one of the triggers that could inexplicably bring on a severe anxiety attack. I slipped out of the living room and met Ali in the hallway.

"Are you all right?" she asked. I shrugged. "Do you want to turn off the music?"

"I can't do that," I said. I went upstairs to my office. Work would keep my mind occupied. I tried to focus on a newspaper feature but succeeded only in staring at the impatiently blinking cursor.

I had hoped the old fears would not plague me this Christmas. All my life I had been beset with vague apprehensions and the awful depressions that followed.

The roots weren't hard to find. Born premature, forty-nine years ago in the village of Styal near Manchester, I spent the first three months of my life fighting to survive. I had been born with a shortened and twisted right leg that, later, made walking difficult. In my first week at school a girl pointed at me. "You're a cripple!" she said. She hobbled off in a perfect imitation of my limp that set the other kids laughing.

Being lame of body was not half as bad, though, as being crippled in spirit. My mental woes may have been inherited. My granddad suffered from free-floating fears and so did my father. Dad was so tense that he and Mum were in constant rows, yelling at each other, slamming doors, hurling crockery, then continuing the battle with silence that could last for weeks.

My first serious depression occurred in my early teens. Dad was the village bobby and on his salary we couldn't afford psychiatric help, even if he had believed in it. Antidepressant drugs were in use by 1960, but I was wary of trying these early experimental medicines.

There were glimmers of hope. I became a Christian at eighteen, and for a while I believed this commitment might help me get better. It didn't— not for more than thirty years. Of course I prayed about my anxieties, always in private because I was far too shy to bring up my need at church.

When I married Alison I hoped I was beginning a new, healthier chapter. But along with the joy of a wife and a growing family came responsibilities that made the problem worse. Six weeks was the longest I could go without suffering an acute anxiety attack. Little things set the explosions off. A bill coming due. A Christmas carol. The family was ready to leave for church one summer day when I realized my cuff links were missing. It didn't matter because I was wearing a short-sleeved shirt, but I held us up until the cuff links were found.

I was spoiling things for everyone. The best I could do was keep out of the way while depressed. Soon I was spending days on end in my room, as my family waited for me to come around again.

Then on the fifteenth of December of 1995, a few days after the renewed battle with Christmas carols, I was putting my good foot, the left one, on a step when I stumbled. Searing pain shot through my leg. Within an hour I could not use the leg at all. It was just the kind of incident that usually sank me into a depressive state. Ali offered to pray not only for the leg pain but also for the funk that would almost certainly follow.

What good would prayer do? We had asked God to help us so often. But this time He was about to answer, and in a fashion I could never have anticipated.

Ali prayed for me and my leg did get better, but not the signs of oncoming depression. That evening, just ten days before Christmas, as we were getting ready for bed, Ali remembered that because of the cold weather she had not opened the windows as she usually did to freshen the room. She picked up what she thought was an air-purifying spray and sent a mist all over the room. But the spray turned out to be a sore-muscle balm with a dreadful menthol smell that I've always hated.

"Whew!" I said. "I'll have to sleep in Daniel's room if I want to get any rest." Our oldest son Daniel was in London and his room was empty.

I kissed Ali good night, walked to Daniel's room and turned down the spread on his narrow bed, which was right up against the wall. I climbed in, turned out the light and lay there staring into the darkness. I was unusually warm and comfortable but still fretting about all sorts of things . . . bills, a close friend in the hospital, an assignment that was due.

At first, the way you can sometimes sense a person looking at you, it seemed to me someone was in the room, focusing attention on me. I thought Alison had stepped in. "Ali?" I whispered.

There was no answer, not a rustling of clothes, not a stirring of air, and yet I knew beyond doubt I was not alone. A friendly presence was near me, at the head of the bed. Had Daniel come home unexpectedly? I whispered his name. Nothing. Maybe it was one of the younger children. "Matthew? Caroline?" No answer.

Slowly I became aware of a second unseen being in the room, this one at the foot of the bed. It seemed to me the two creatures were facing each other. And then I knew there was a third presence too, and a fourth one, these last two facing each other on the left side of the bed . . . impossible since there was no space between the bed and the wall.

I wanted to call Ali, but there was something so benevolent, so full of promise about the four lively presences that I didn't want to do anything that might risk driving them away. I lay perfectly still, strangely warm and expectant.

And then—how did I know this, since I could not see them?—the four creatures began to move toward one another, two on each side of the bed. Their progress was slow and deliberate. They passed one another, turned and repeated the traverse three, four, maybe five times. Every time their paths crossed I felt as if I would burst with joy.

Then abruptly the room was empty. I knew it as surely as I had known a few minutes earlier that angelic creatures were there. The room was back to normal and I was alone again, yet still filled with ineffable joy. *Should I go tell Alison? But tell her what? That I had been visited by four beings I couldn't see?* Still debating, I fell into a deep sleep, the best I had had in years.

By the time I surfaced, the children had already left for school. "You'll never believe what happened last night," I said to Ali. I told her as best I could about the mysterious visitors God had sent me. Alison did believe it and was delighted at my newfound joy and peace, though perhaps wondering, as I was, if this calm would last for more than a few days.

Our doubts were misplaced. I enjoyed every minute of the Christmas season. December was followed by a long gray January and February, two months that in the past had been times of distress but were filled with an exultation new to me. The joy even survived a devastating bout I had with the flu. Winter gave way to a spring, a summer and then an autumn of freedom.

Though I can't be sure how long this freedom will last, I am beginning to believe the victory is permanent. It's not that I've shed pressures like bills and problems at work. But today I confront these issues with a positive attitude unlike my past fearfulness.

Christmas is once again just around the corner. Thanks to my heavenly visitors, I'm anticipating another joy-filled season and I am going to make a statement to that effect. This year I have bought a present for the entire family, a small but very special gift I hope we will use a lot . . . a CD of the world's best-loved Christmas carols. ❧

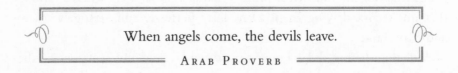

When angels come, the devils leave.

ARAB PROVERB

KING NEBUCHADNEZZAR'S GOLD STATUE
DANIEL 3: 1–28 (CEV)

King Nebuchadnezzar ordered a gold statue to be built ninety feet high and nine feet wide. He had it set up in Dura Valley near the city of Babylon, and he commanded his governors, advisers, treasurers, judges and his other officials to come from everywhere in his kingdom to the dedication of the statue. So all of them came and stood in front of it.

Then an official stood up and announced: People of every nation and race, now listen to the king's command! Trumpets, flutes, harps and all other kinds of musical instruments will soon start playing. When you hear the music, you must bow down and worship the statue that King Nebuchadnezzar has set up. Anyone who refuses will at once be thrown into a flaming furnace.

As soon as the people heard the music, they bowed down and worshiped the gold statue that the king had set up.

Some Babylonians used this as a chance to accuse the Jews to King Nebuchadnezzar. They said, "Your Majesty, we hope you live forever! You commanded everyone to bow down and worship the gold statue when the music played. And you said that anyone who did not bow down and worship it would be thrown into a flaming furnace. Sir, you appointed three men to high positions in Babylon Province, but they have disobeyed you. Those Jews, Shadrach, Meshach and Abednego, refuse to worship your gods and the statue you have set up."

King Nebuchadnezzar was furious. So he sent for the three young men and said, "I hear that you refuse to worship my gods and the gold statue I have set up. Now I am going to give you one more chance. If you bow down and worship the statue when you hear the music, everything will be all right. But if you don't, you will at once be thrown into a flaming furnace. No god can save you from me."

The three men replied, "Your Majesty, we don't need to defend ourselves. The God we worship can save us from you and your flaming furnace. But even if he doesn't, we still won't worship your gods and the gold statue you have set up."

King Nebuchadnezzar's face twisted with anger at the three men. And he ordered the furnace to be heated seven times hotter than usual. Next, he commanded some of his strongest soldiers to tie up the men and throw them into the flaming furnace. The king wanted it done at that very moment. So the soldiers tied up Shadrach, Meshach and Abednego, and threw them into the flaming furnace with all of their clothes still on, including their turbans. The fire was so hot that flames leaped out and killed the soldiers.

Suddenly the king jumped up and shouted, " Weren't only three men tied up and thrown into the fire?"

"Yes, Your Majesty," the people answered.

"But I see four men walking around in the fire," the king replied. "None of them is tied up or harmed, and the fourth one looks like a god."

King Nebuchadnezzar went closer to the flaming furnace and said to the three young men, "You servants of the Most High God, come out at once!"

They came out, and the king's high officials, governors and advisers all crowded around them. The men were not burned, their hair wasn't scorched, and their clothes didn't even smell like smoke. King Nebuchadnezzar said:

"Praise their God for sending an angel to rescue his servants! They trusted their God and refused to obey my commands." ❧

CHAPTER FIVE

GOD SPEAKS TO US...
In Our Hearts

*T*heologians have argued for centuries about the role that emotion ought to play—and not play—in spiritual life.

Should preachers aim to provoke thought with their sermons, or joy?

Should we pray quietly, or raise the rafters with ecstatic song?

Should we read the Bible studiously, or prayerfully?

Most believers would agree, I think, that the answer to all these questions is "both." When you're serious about your faith, you think about it. At the same time, belief can't exist only in our heads. The heart plays an essential, fundamental role. You can study religion till the cows come home, but at some point you've got to feel it, deep in your bones.

Feeling something deep in our bones is one of the principal ways we receive direction from God. Have you ever hesitated before going along with a suggestion because it just didn't feel right? Have you ever instantly trusted, or distrusted, someone you've just met? Feelings *such as these can be cues from the Holy Spirit, and spiritually mature people have learned over time to rely on them.*

The stories in this chapter all center on people who, in one way or another, have responded to the prompting of the Holy Spirit in their hearts. I've chosen Louis Hill's "A House Was Waiting" to begin because it demonstrates so nicely the tension that exists between logic and intuition. Hill shows that head and heart can complement each other, rather than conflict. Ideally, we will learn to maintain a respectful balance between the two. This is reminiscent of the words the Apostle Paul addressed to the Corinthians. "There are different kinds of gifts," he wrote, "but the same Spirit" (1 Corinthians 12:4).

A HOUSE WAS WAITING
—BY LOUIS A. HILL JR.—

We don't have enough money for a place to live! I said to myself after counting our cash. *And to make matters worse, Jeanne won't listen to me. How did I get into this mess?*

I'm an engineer, a very practical fellow who designs buildings and bridges, and teaches engineering students to do the same. I've always had a solid faith, but a practical faith that matches my work. So I'm not a person who hears God's voice telling me things. But my wife is. And that has caused us problems sometimes. Especially during that August of 1965 when I finished my doctorate in Ohio and headed back to teach at Arizona State University. Every time I'd tried to tell Jeanne how dismal our finances were and how hard it would be to find housing that we could afford, she'd get this knowing (maddening!) little smile and say, "God has a house waiting for us. He's told me so. You'll see." Only now she was going to see otherwise.

For two years Jeanne and the kids had made great sacrifices because they knew my future at the university depended on my getting another degree. We had used scholarships for my tuition, lived on our savings until they ran out and finally borrowed up to our limit.

After we pulled into Scottsdale, while Jeanne tucked our three kids into bed, I sat in the motel room calculating our meager money. When she came over to join me, I told her the awful truth. "Remember my big talk when we left here? About how we'd come back with enough money to put a down payment on that dreamy corner lot?" I said. "Instead, we don't even have enough money to rent anything!"

This time she listened. "Could you get an advance on your salary?" she asked quietly.

"Not enough for us to live on in the next few months."

Jeanne slipped a hand into mine. But then she went off on that tangent again. "I remember how scared I got when I was packing and saw our low bank balance," she said. "That's when God whispered in my ear, 'Don't worry. There's a house waiting for you!' Just like He'd *prepared* it!"

"Don't I wish!" I said irritably. "Not that I doubt either you or God. But you know that I've always had trouble with a faith that flies in the face of logic. And when we've got only a hundred and fifty dollars and need three times that to make first and last months' rent in advance, plus breakage deposit, that's tough logic to fly against! Well? Isn't it?"

Jeanne wouldn't argue. "We're worn out," she said. "After a good night's sleep we'll see what's out there."

Nothing! Of all the modest rentals we looked at, we could afford nothing. Yet when we passed the corner lot we'd once hoped to build on, and it was still empty, Jeanne wanted me to call the owner.

"Why?" I was exasperated. "We pestered him enough in the past."

"I'm sorry," Jeanne said. "I just felt a nudge to call the owner, but it doesn't make sense. Let's go back to the room and cook supper."

The next day, Saturday, we lowered our sights. We looked at apartments with broken windows, stopped-up toilets, garbage-strewn kitchens and spaced-out characters loitering in the halls. But we still couldn't make the rent. While Jeanne was cooking, I played Monopoly with our twelve-year-old daughter and ten-year-old son, bouncing the toddler on my knee and silently praying, *What can we do?* We'd feel better tomorrow just seeing some old friends at church, I told myself.

To our disappointment, during our absence most of our friends had moved across town to a new church that was sponsored by our old one. But the new faces at our old church were friendly and the new minister's sermon started with a Bible verse from John (14:2, RSV) that had me bolt upright. "In My Father's house are many rooms; if it were not so, would I have told you that I go to prepare a place for you?" Jeanne had said, "It was as if He'd prepared it for us." Suddenly I felt reprimanded; God hadn't told me, but He had told Jeanne. And I'd downplayed it all, because it seemed illogical. So He'd given me the message this time—a written message straight from the Bible so that even I couldn't miss it. I looked at Jeanne and she reached across our toddler in her lap to squeeze my hand. I squeezed hers back.

When church was over, I told her we were going back to those modest rentals and I was going to talk to some landlords. "Surely one of them will waive the deposits," I said.

But no landlord would. We were on our way back to the motel when I suddenly turned onto the street with the corner lot. "You had a feeling we ought to call the owner, didn't you?" Jeanne nodded. "It's time I turned this whole thing over to God."

When I phoned, the owner/builder remembered me. He even pulled a card on us that was still in his files and said he'd meet us at the lot.

It wasn't until I hung up that I began to feel guilty about getting that man out on a Sunday afternoon all for nothing. *We can't possibly buy that lot!* What will I say to the owner?

But when the owner arrived, he did all the talking. And not about the lot; he kept asking about us. Was I under contract to teach at the university this year? Looked like we still had the same car . . . Wasn't going back to school financially draining? *He's guessed that we can't afford the lot,* I figured.

"You're right," I admitted, "I apologize for wasting your time. We don't have any money to buy this lot." I took Jeanne's arm and we started for our car. "The truth is, we don't even have enough money to rent an apartment."

"I thought so," the builder said. "That's why I met you here. I sold this lot six months ago." Jeanne and I stopped walking. We turned to face him again, puzzled. "But I built a house down this street," he said. "It's almost finished. Walk down with me to take a look."

"It's no use," I said, "I can't possibly buy it."

"This house you might!" he said. "You and I just might solve each other's problems." He started walking and we followed. "A construction workers' strike has really hit me hard. This is the only house I've ever built that I haven't sold before the foundation was poured. It's been vandalized once already, and what's worse, I'm making payments on it to the bank. Mine's a small business, so I can't afford to have my capital tied up that way. I want to dump this house and not lose any more."

Jeanne and I walked beside him, our mouths gaping in surprise. "But I can't sell this house to just anybody," he went on. "I've got to sell it to someone who will keep up those payments. A solid citizen with an excellent credit record. Your card shows that's you, Mr. Hill."

"But I only have a hundred and fifty dollars to my name!" I blurted out.

"It won't cost you that much up front," he said, "as long as you can begin making payments next month." We walked into the house, which smelled of new paint. It had gold carpeting throughout half the house and gold-flecked white tiles through the other half. "Your card listed your needs as four bedrooms and a double carport," he went on. "This house has only three and a single carport. Can you make do?"

Could we ever make do! Two days later we moved in—for seventeen dollars total cost.

That week, working together, the builder and I finished the house. While I installed the light fixtures, I thought about it. All our married life I'd picked on Jeanne about her "illogical feelings, nudgings and voices" from God. She'd never once picked on me about my "logical ('superior' implied) guidance" from Him. Now I knew why. Because she'd always known what I had just discovered: God gives guidance in many different ways, all of them valid. It's really up to us to keep our eyes and ears—and our minds—open. Later, in prayer with Jeanne, I thanked Him for those different ways, and for the house.

Twenty-five years later we're still living in that house the Lord prepared for us. Over the years, when we needed more room for our growing family, we added things—patios, planters and a pool. Last year we redecorated the entire house, and with the children grown and gone, we converted two bedrooms into offices for Jeanne and me. It seemed the logical thing to do. ❧

> "Take heed . . . of the promptings of Love and Truth in
> your hearts, for those are the leadings of God."
>
> GEORGE FOX

Sometimes our hearts serve as divine message centers. God leaves clues there that can guide us along the path he would have us follow, as he did for Louis and Jeanne Hill.

But God has also written upon our hearts more elemental information. If our genes contain the biological data that determine who we are physically, our hearts contain the code of our character, the talents, tastes, needs and sensibilities that make us who we are. Science tells us there is substantial interplay between the physical and the psychological, but faith tells us that God has something to say about it, too.

Also imprinted on our hearts is the capacity to respond to the invitations of the Holy Spirit. Saint Augustine referred to this inborn appetite when he wrote, "You have created us and directed us towards yourself, O Lord, and our hearts are restless until they rest in you."

Often we're unaware of what we have in our hearts until pressed by some challenge. Then our essential qualities blossom forth. Such was the case with Annie Boucher, who was blessed with an indomitable spirit of perseverance. She'd thought her tenacity was mainly of use on the tennis court, but God showed her otherwise.

ONCE MORE OVER THE NET
—BY ANNIE BOUCHER—

I took up tennis when I was nearly forty, an age when a lot of people are giving it up. I'm no pro, but I play seriously. Very seriously. That's because in an odd sort of way tennis became more than just a game to me. It became a way to fight back against my past.

I remember when I first picked up the racket. It was a summer

Sunday afternoon. I was relaxing with my teenage daughter Sandra, when I saw my neighbor Erma dashing for the Rochdale Village courts.

"Hi, Erma!" I called. My, she looks good, I thought. I liked the crisp white tennis outfit she was wearing, and I liked how her legs looked in it—long and sleek—and the way she kind of bounced along the street swinging her racket. Suddenly an idea got hold of me: Why couldn't I learn to play tennis? I had an old five-dollar racket stashed away in a closet; I'd bought it at a garage sale for no other reason than I felt sorry for the people who had to sell off their things. I dashed inside, dug it out, then went to the tennis courts.

I'd been pretty good at sports as a youngster. It was the only part of school I ever liked. I caught on fast that day on the tennis court. I didn't have much style, but I got around the court pretty quickly. This is easy and hard, I remember thinking as I ran back to return a lob. Easy because all you had to do was get the ball over the net one time more than your opponent. Hard because it wasn't as easy as it looked.

When we were through I glanced up at the stands, where a lone woman sat. "Who's she?" I asked one of the players. She laughed. "That's the female champ. But don't get any ideas, Annie. She mostly plays against men."

"I'm gonna beat her someday," I said. "You watch." Six months later I made good on my promise. In straight sets.

So tennis became part of my life, the only real bright spot, except for Sandra, whom I'd raised alone and had made the center of my world. My job was a dead end. I was a keypunch operator. Anyone who has done that job knows what a grind it is. But I never finished high school, and that kept me anchored in the data-entry room of a huge Wall Street brokerage firm, punching in daily transactions.

Every day it was the same numbing commute to lower Manhattan. It could take up to two hours each way. First I rode a bus to the subway. Then I took a subway to Queens Plaza, where I connected with another train. That got me into Manhattan, where I'd change again to another subway line going downtown. At night it was the same heartless thing in reverse. The noisy stations and pushy crowds. Fighting just for a place to stand on the train.

Every day as well it was the same windowless keypunch room, with forty or fifty other operators all doing the identical repetitive job. The strokes I made on the terminal were tabulated so that my supervisors knew if I was making my quota of entries. Half hour for lunch. Two coffee breaks.

The brokers liked to stop and joke with me, and every so often one would say, "Hey, Annie, what are you doing here? Isn't there something better for you?"

They were right, I guessed. But I had my daughter to support. That came first. I had to make sure she got her education so that she wouldn't get stuck in a dead-end job. And I had tennis. I almost always won, for some strange reason. I didn't really have the strokes—not much of a forehand, almost no backhand. I just hustled to the ball and hit it over the net one time more. No one could out-hustle me.

The day came when Sandra got her diploma. It was one of the most emotional moments of my life. I cried. Not just in joy for Sandra but a little bit in pity for myself for never finishing school. I felt like I'd paid for it my whole life with dreary jobs and people looking down at me for being uneducated. But school had been hard for me. My father was very strict when it came to education, so strict that learning terrified me. I dreaded failure. I feared my teachers. I couldn't wait to leave the classroom behind.

Sandra got a job, then a husband, and moved out. For the first time in twenty years I was alone. I figured, *Good, now I'll have time to work on myself.* Slowly it dawned on me, though, *What do I have to work on?* Sandra had been my whole life. I didn't have a career. I had tennis, but that was about it. As the months passed I became more and more depressed about my situation. Until one day I did something I don't normally do.

During rush hour I encountered a man handing out religious pamphlets on the platform at the Queens Plaza station. I had always avoided his type. A long time ago I'd decided that the world wasn't a particularly nice place, and if there even was a God, He wasn't doing His job. For some reason, though, on this morning I took the pamphlet, and before disposing of it in the trash, where I assumed it probably belonged, I actually skimmed some of it. A few days later I saw him again and took another pamphlet, which I stuck in my purse and reread more carefully at home.

I'd run into this fellow on the subway and we'd sit together talking about God. Mostly I said I wasn't so sure about God. But I enjoyed our talks and thought about them afterward. Eventually he stopped riding my line and I began to miss those conversations. Really miss them.

One day I decided, *Maybe I'll try talking directly to God....* That noon I dropped by a church near work. Candles flickered in a warm cross-breeze. All around me people prayed. As a kid I'd been as afraid of God as I had been of my father, school and teachers. I thought of God as some old man in a big chair up in the sky waiting for us to make mistakes so He could punish us. I was afraid of failing Him. Yet these people didn't seem afraid. They seemed at peace.

I started going to church on my lunches to escape the monotony of the keypunch room. Little by little I talked to God about my life. The more I talked to Him, the more certain I was that He heard. More and more I sensed that same peace I saw in those around me, and gradually my idea of God changed from a mean old man to a loving creator.

But still I was unhappy about my work situation. One day I was complaining to a friend. "Annie," she said, "it's simple. Get your high school equivalency degree at night school." Easy for her to say. She'd been to college. But her words stayed with me the next day out on the court. Here I was beating doctors and lawyers, people who'd played tennis their entire lives, people who had a lot more than I. I'd learned to play this game on my own terms. Why couldn't I tackle school again, the way I'd beaten that local champion? If I could learn tennis at thirty-eight, then I could go back to school at forty-five. Besides, I knew something now—that there is an all-loving God in whose name I could do anything.

I went for my GED at night, reading and studying during my commute. The first time I tried the test, I flunked. I took the class again. This time I passed, but by the lowest margin possible. That didn't matter. I received my degree, an accomplishment that had until recently seemed no more possible to me than walking on the moon. Now something inside kept urging me on. Why not higher education?

But registration day at a nearby college was a bad joke. The harried secretary in the admissions office scowled at me. "How old are you?" she demanded to know. "Forty-five," I said as quietly as possible and with the sweetest smile I could muster. The secretary gave a curt glance at my GED. "I'm sorry," she said in a distinctly unapologetic tone. "We don't take scores that low."

Walking toward the door, I began to scold myself. *You deserved that. You never should have come here. You are stupid. . . .* Suddenly a hand touched my arm. It was one of the security guards. "I saw how she treated you," he said. "Why don't you try Queensborough Community College. They hold your hand a little bit there. Just take the Q30 bus."

I thanked him but I wasn't up for any more humiliation. I started walking back to Rochdale Village, hoping that the three miles of meandering city streets would lift my spirits. Did I think that just because I'd learned to play tennis I could change my life? *Annie, God would have made you a lot smarter if He'd wanted you in college.* I stepped off a curb and started to cross the street when a beep-beep startled me out of my fog. I was standing in the way of an impatient city bus. I retreated to the curb. The bus pulled up and opened its door. The driver looked at me as if he expected me to get on. I stared back. Then I heard myself say, "Is this the bus that goes to Queensborough Community College?" There were scores of different bus routes in Queens.

"Bus Q30," he said. "Hop on."

They did hold my hand a bit at Queensborough. I needed it. But I always sat in the front row. I never cut class. If I failed a subject, I took it over. If I flunked an exam, I studied harder. It was like tennis. You hustled. You got the ball over the net one time more than your opponent.

Speaking of which, I got a note one day from the women's tennis coach. "I definitely want you on my team," it said. It was the lady champ I'd beaten years before, the one up in the stands that day I first swung a racket. She was a college coach now.

I ended up captain of the squad, playing girls young enough to be my daughters. When I moved to Alfred University in upstate New York I had an undefeated season and got my picture in *Sports Illustrated*. Sandra had a baby by then, and the story made a big deal about the grandmother who was winning at collegiate tennis and making the dean's list.

But to me it was a lot more than that. More than just winning matches and passing classes. I discovered that I could change my life. It was the most powerful discovery I ever made. And it started with a simple recognition of who God is. He is a loving, forgiving God. Once I understood that, I felt I could win at anything. ❧

> The Lord called me before I was born, while I was in my mother's womb he named me.
>
> ISAIAH 49:1 (NRSV)

Is That You, Lord?

There's no doubt that God speaks in our hearts, leading us with urges and intuition to follow the paths he would have us take. But here's the rub: so does the Devil.

How can we accurately identify the source of the feelings we have in our hearts? This is one of the more important questions of the spiritual life, in part because we humans have a seemingly bottomless capacity for self-deception. (Adam and Eve set the standard.)

One place to look for guidance on this key issue is the Bible. In the fifth chapter of Galatians, the Apostle Paul contrasts the works of the flesh to the fruits of the Spirit. Among the former he lists fornication, impurity, licentiousness, idolatry, sorcery, emnities, strife, jealousy, anger, quarrels, dissensions, factions, envy, drunkenness and carousing. The fruits of the Spirit are identified as love, joy, peace, patience, kindness and self-control.

Paul's point is that the urgings of our hearts will have different consequences, depending upon their source. Before acting on those urgings, therefore, we need to contemplate what those consequences will likely be. Granted, this isn't an automatic litmus test, because some actions aimed at promoting peace in the long run can produce dissension in the short run. The civil rights movement led by Martin Luther King Jr. was a case in point.

For that reason the other disciplines of discernment—prayer, patience and consultation with others among them—must always be brought into play. A good rule of thumb is that feelings are less a call to action than invitations to investigation. Leadings of God don't fade when they're examined; they intensify. D.H.

I have mentioned that God imprints upon our hearts certain charac-
teristics that shape who we are. Among those characteristics are things
like determination, conviction and integrity. These are living gifts
we're all born with, I suspect, but they need to be nurtured, lest they
weaken, become twisted or die.

Like Annie Boucher, Jonathan Byrd had a natural talent—
cooking, in Jonathan's case—and a great resolve to use it construc-
tively. He also had a rock-solid conviction that caused him to stick to
the leadership God had planted in his heart, even when the world
told him that to do so would cost him his dream.

FAILURE WAS NOT ON THE MENU
—BY JONATHAN BYRD—

My whole dream seemed to come crashing down one hot August
evening four years ago as I slumped, dejected, at an old picnic table in
the middle of the construction site. Dark steel structural girders loomed
over me, seeming to overshadow any hopes I had for making a go of the
cafeteria I was building.

I had been in the restaurant business most of my life, and for years I
had dreamed of building the best cafeteria in the world. Yet now many
people were predicting it would fail.

Why? Because I did not plan to put alcohol on the menu.

It wasn't that I had anything against other restaurants doing this; I
simply felt God didn't want me to do it. One evening long ago when I
was eighteen, I made a church call with our minister on the grieving kin
of a whole family who had been killed outright. Their car had been
struck head-on by a drunk driver. In the silence of that sad living room,
I knew that all the money in the world wasn't worth being in any way
responsible for such a tragedy.

But a lot of knowledgeable people had a different view.

"Jonathan," advised a business friend, "here you're planning a restaurant with big function rooms for weddings, banquets and other celebra-
tions. If you won't serve liquor, why, you're writing your own ticket for
bankruptcy."

When I explained that I felt the banquet rooms would be used by church groups, he snickered. "You probably won't make enough off them to pay your light bill."

"Well," I said, "I guess I'll have to leave that in God's hands."

God hadn't failed me in my thirty-six years. But that didn't mean life had been easy. Mom and Dad weren't well off, and to help make ends meet I started working as a youngster selling a skin salve door-to-door. Next I sold tomatoes, then raised sheep, and by the time I was nine I had a thousand dollars in the bank.

Meanwhile Dad and Granddad had started a small ice-cream stand on US 31 in Greenwood, just south of Indianapolis. Eventually it grew into the Kitchen Drive-In, and soon I was flipping burgers, making shakes and greeting customers.

I loved the restaurant business. It touched me to see folks enjoying good food the way I did. Mom said I had a big hole in my stomach that no amount of food could fill. Still, back then I was so skinny I had to wear suspenders to keep my pants up.

I was impressed by how many significant biblical events involved people eating together: Jesus feeding the five thousand; His grilling fish on the beach for the disciples; and that most intimate gathering of all, those awed men sitting down to a meal on the eve of Jesus' crucifixion.

The summer I was fifteen, Dad became ill, and I took over the responsibility of our restaurant and its sixty-some employees. I worked eighty hours a week, convinced this was my calling in life. Dad eventually retired and I went on to Cornell University's School of Hotel Administration. I got a Kentucky Fried Chicken franchise and through the years expanded that into seven KFC restaurants. All the while my dream of opening a cafeteria was growing.

Why a cafeteria? When we were kids my folks often took us to a local cafeteria after church. I loved being able to pick out just what I wanted from the foods displayed before me. Even my little sister Janeen, a finicky eater, always found something she liked.

In the early 1980s, the dream became more persistent as it took shape in my mind. I wanted to serve delicious food with the greatest selection possible at economical prices. For quality assurance I planned on modern kitchens with computer-controlled menus, which had never been tried in a restaurant before, only in hospitals and institutions. Since I wanted to offer at least two hundred items each day, I figured the cafeteria line would be almost a third as long as a football field. I began to see I was thinking about what could well be the world's largest cafeteria.

But would there be enough customers? Jesus told a parable advising that a man who builds a tower should count the cost so he knows he can finish the job (Luke 14:28–30). I had done my homework. Indianapolis was a fast-growing city, and I had picked out a good location near one of America's major crossroads—just off Interstate 65 in Greenwood—where we would serve not only the local community but also many travelers passing through.

After a lot of prayer, I burned my bridges by selling the Kentucky Fried Chicken restaurants. On March 1, 1987, in a dedication service, we turned our first spadeful of dirt on what would be a colonial-style building covering one acre of ground.

But from then on, it seemed every worldly thing set out to stop us. We figured on spending twenty-five thousand dollars for permits; they ended up costing ten times that. Then we had to truck a huge load of dirt off the site to bring it to proper grade. This cost another eighty-six thousand dollars. The contractor advised me to cut back on the quality of materials, such as the raw oak trim throughout the vast dining room.

"No," I said, "I'm putting my name on this place. My wife, two boys and I are going to eat here along with, I hope, a lot of other people. I want it to be right."

The concrete was poured, the structural steel erected, and the walls started going up. But a big storm hit us in July and blew down most of the roof trusses.

Then, in August 1988, came that worst day of all.

My pastor showed up at the work site and passed on a prediction from a fellow church member who was in the restaurant food-distribution business. "He is terribly worried about you, Jonathan, and so am I," he said. "He says you'll go broke in six months, and I thought I'd better come down and warn you." My pastor felt the same way I did about liquor, but he was also sincerely concerned about my well-being.

As he drove away, I sat down at the splintery old table and began calculating my extra costs. By now I was five hundred thousand dollars over budget.

Early dusk had fallen as I sat alone in the tomblike silence of the unfinished restaurant. Then other headlights flashed across in front and a car door thunked. A man in a dark business suit strode up the wooden plank into the building and began peering around. I rose and approached him. "Can I help you?"

The man eyed my old work clothes. "Oh, just looking around," he said. "I own a chain of funeral homes, and I hear the owner of this place isn't going to serve alcohol." He cocked his head. "He'll be bankrupt in six months. With all this space, I figure this could be the biggest funeral home in the Midwest." He shot me a quick smile. "I just wanted to see it now because I figure I'll be buying it from the fool who's building it."

After he left I slumped down at the picnic table and put my head on my arms. An evening breeze blew an old newspaper around my feet. "Oh, Lord," I groaned, "is there any good news?"

At that another car pulled up. *Uh-oh*, I wondered, *now what?*

Two men and two women stepped out of the car. One man began telling the others, "There will be a dining room seating five hundred, an eighty-eight-foot cafeteria line, and some beautiful banquet halls seating six hundred . . ."

He stepped around the corner, and his face lit up. "Jonathan! I'm just showing my friends your place."

It was Dr. Gene Hood, pastor of the Nazarene church in nearby Beech Grove. "What's the matter?" he asked. "You look down. Had a tough day?"

"Well, you kind of picked the worst day of my life." I recited my troubles, ending up with the "funeral" the local undertaker had just conducted.

He laughed at the story. "Well, I'm excited about your plans," he said. "I can just see all the Southern gospel singers in your banquet halls."

Gospel singers? What was he talking about?

Dr. Hood leaned across the table. "If you have enough faith to build this place, I have enough faith to help you keep those banquet halls filled with great gospel-singing groups."

That was the encouragement I needed. Three months later, on November 7, 1988, we opened our doors. Customers began streaming in, and they have been crowding Jonathan Byrd's Cafeteria and Banquet Hall ever since. Dr. Hood was true to his word; every six weeks our function rooms play host to gospel concerts. And even without liquor, our banquet rooms were quickly booked up, and churches began reserving them far in advance.

So the naysayers were wrong. We're thriving. All of which, I guess, proves that if you count the cost, stick to your principles and leave everything in God's hands, you'll have a menu that can't fail. ❧

It is the heart which perceives God and not the reason.

BLAISE PASCAL

We've been talking a lot in this chapter about integrity and resolve, two qualities that characterize the steadfast faithful heart. The following reflection from Karen Barber addresses another type of essential spiritual strength: the ability to acknowledge sin, and to repent.

I   H A V E   A   D R E A M
—B Y   K A R E N   B A R B E R—

My nine-year-old son John ordered a paperback from the school book club entitled *I Have a Dream—Dr. Martin Luther King Jr.* I was quite surprised when the book arrived to find that it was not a book *about* Dr. King, but an illustrated edition of the actual text of his most famous speech. I had been John's age myself when this historic speech was delivered.

As John and I looked through the book together, we came to a picture of a white mob pouring ketchup on the heads of African Americans seated at a lunch counter. John had many questions, and I had to admit the sad truth about our society's history of race relations. *What faith*

Dr. King must have had to believe that such monumental changes were possible, I thought.

Then I read aloud a simple yet moving paragraph from the speech: "I have a dream that one day on the red hills of Georgia, the sons of former slaves and the sons of former slave owners will be able to sit down together at the table of brotherhood."

A shiver went down my spine as the words hit me like a prophecy fulfilled in my own lifetime. We lived in the red clay hills of Georgia, and as difficult as it was to admit it, some of my ancestors had owned slaves. Yet Dr. King's dream had become a reality every time my family had sat down around our turn-of-the-century mahogany dining-room table to share a meal with African-American friends, co-workers and neighbors.

Finally I understood something of Dr. King's faith. Yes, he worked hard for new laws to bring about justice and change, but he also knew that the laws of the heart are the ones that revolutionize the world. Even monumental changes start small—one dining-room table at a time. ❧

"You desire truth in the inward being;

therefore teach me wisdom in my secret heart. . . .

The sacrifice acceptable to God is a broken spirit;

A broken and contrite heart,

O God, you will not despise.

PSALM 51:6, 17 (NRSV)

In the movie Wall Street, *a ruthless tycoon played by Michael Douglas takes a young trader played by Charlie Sheen under his wing. Occasionally the young apprentice is afflicted by pangs of conscience as he witnesses the human cost of the stock manipulations perpetrated by his mentor. The tycoon brushes aside such concerns. "It's all about bucks, kid," he says. "All the rest is conversation."*

This is nonsense, of course. In fact, it's all about getting right with God. That's when you can truthfully say all the rest is conversation.

In the end, getting right with God is an event of the heart. The Spirit touches us deep inside and we are transformed. Often this conversion is perceived as something that happens in an instant, but perhaps just as often it's a process of accumulation. Gradually our resistance lowers and our willingness builds until a tipping point is reached. Finally the moment comes when we allow ourselves to fall back gratefully into the arms of God.

You don't have to recognize the name Paul Harvey (a legend in radio news for decades) to appreciate his lovely account of how being baptized changed his life. Harvey's story underscores that conversion is an ongoing process, not a one-time event. God continually invites us to go deeper.

I FOUND MY QUIET HEART
—BY PAUL HARVEY—

Newsmen are said to have tough hides, cold hearts, "printer's ink in their veins." We see so much of tragedy, disaster, the mud and blood that make news. Understandably, we can become insensitive, cynical, hard. That's why I'm so grateful for something that happened to me one day about thirty years ago up a little mountain road in Cave Creek, Arizona. I think today that all the experiences in my life had been building up to this one.

First, the Christmas Eve when I was three, a gunman's bullet took the life of my policeman father. To provide an income for my sister and me, Mother had apartments built in our house. As soon as I was old enough, I, too, looked around for ways to earn money. Radio was just coming into its own; by age nine I was making cigar-box crystal sets that I sold for a dollar. A few years later I took part in a seventh-grade class play presented over Tulsa's KVOO radio station. After that I spent every spare minute hanging around the studio. Finally they put me on the payroll. I was fourteen and I did everything from sweeping to writing commercials, with a little announcing on the side. I kept remembering what one of my teachers had said: "Paul, in this wonderful land of ours, any man willing to stay on his toes can reach for the stars."

Radio became my star. At seventeen I did some of everything on a local station in Salina, Kansas; then came jobs in Oklahoma City and St. Louis. In St. Louis at KXOK radio I met a lovely girl who was doing educational programs. We were married and she has been the Angel—that's what I call her—in my life ever since. Together we worked hard. By 1945 I had my own network news program. By 1968 I was on television and doing a newspaper column as well.

Seemingly, I had achieved everything for which a man could ask. Everything, that is, except for a quiet heart. Something was missing. There was a vague emptiness in my life—an incompleteness that I could not define.

This emptiness was still with me in March of last year when Angel and I were vacationing near Cave Creek. We noticed a small church on an isolated hilltop. On impulse one bright Sunday morning Angel and I decided to attend a service there. We drove up the mountain road and as we rounded the last turn, the little steeple pierced an azure sky, and white clapboard siding reflected the morning sun.

Inside were a dozen or so worshipers on wooden folding chairs, a scene reminiscent of ones I had seen many times as a youth. During those formative years, there was one Scripture verse I learned that had stayed with me throughout the years: "For God so loved the world, that He gave His only begotten Son, that whosoever believeth in Him should not perish, but have everlasting life" (John 3:16, KJV).

Sometimes I would get to thinking about that—how wonderful it was. I never made it to the altar in any church, but I liked that promise of "everlasting life." So one night, alone in my room, kneeling at my bed, I offered my life to Christ.

Now, as the upright piano sounded a familiar melody in this unfamiliar little Arizona church, I was reminded of my long-ago expression of belief. I did indeed believe.

The minister mounted his pulpit. As his eyes swept the congregation, he said, "I see we have visitors here." He paused for a moment, then added, "I don't often talk about baptism, but today I'm going to talk about baptism." Inside I yawned. But then, for some reason, my attention began to focus on the simple eloquence of this country preacher.

He talked about how alone man is without a heavenly Father, how much we needed to surrender our lives to Him to find any real purpose for living.

But, I thought, *hadn't I done this?*

"Now I'm going to assume," continued the minister, "that most of you here this morning have already made this commitment. But the giving of your life to Jesus is just the first step in your life as a Christian. There is another step: baptism—the way Jesus experienced it—by immersion in water. This becomes the outward expression of your inward commitment.

"This baptism," he continued, "through the symbolic burial of your old self and the resurrection of a new one, is your public testimony to your commitment." He quoted supportive Scripture, paused, let it sink in.

"There is no magic in the water," he added. "One's immersion is simply an act of obedience, a sign of total submission to God."

Submission to God.

I twisted on my chair, new understanding discomfited me. Long years ago I had asked to be saved—but had I offered to serve? I began to realize how much of me I had been holding back. I thought of my prayer time each morning driving to my Chicago studio at 4:30 AM. Often on the dark, deserted expressway I would seem to hear God's plan for the day. But by the time I was halfway downtown, I'd be arguing with Him, making exceptions, bending His directions.

Could this be the source of my uneasiness, the inconsistency within me?

Now the minister was looking over his spectacles at the congregation. "If anyone here agrees with me about the importance of this and wants to be baptized, step up here and join me beside this pulpit."

I found myself on my feet, down the aisle, by his side.

The preacher had said there was nothing magic in the water. Yet as I descended into its depths and rose again, I knew something life-changing had happened. A cleansing inside out. No longer did there seem to be two uncertain contradictory, Paul Harveys—just one immensely happy one. I felt a fulfilling surge of the Holy Spirit.

Afterward I cried like a baby, a kind of release I suppose. I remember looking at Angel and her eyes were shining. She knew well what this meant to me, for she had been blessed with the same experience as a girl.

The evolving joy has been escalating. Yesterday I was praying for guidance and not really meaning it; today the difference is in a genuine desire to know what He wants and an eagerness to do as He says. Though I had learned John 3:16 early in life, it took me till last year to learn John 14:15 as well: "If you love me, keep my commandments." The Christian life is one of obedience, not partnership.

The change this simple act has made in my life is so immense as to be indescribable. Since totally yielding to Him through the symbolism of water baptism, my heart can't stop singing. I've shaken off a lifelong habit of fretting over small things. A thousand little worries and apprehensions have simply evaporated.

Also, perhaps because baptism is such a public act—and because one's dignity gets as drenched as one's body—I've discovered a new unself-consciousness in talking about my beliefs.

The other evening, on a speaking trip, I was flying over west Texas into a beautiful sunset. My heart swelled with joy in my new surrender and I thought, *how wonderful*: If this is no more than what the unbelievers believe, a sort of self-hypnosis, it nevertheless affords an inner peace that passes all understanding. And, if it is what we believers believe, then we have all this—and heaven too! ❧

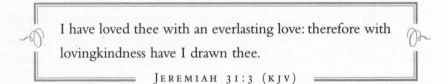

I have loved thee with an everlasting love: therefore with lovingkindness have I drawn thee.

JEREMIAH 31:3 (KJV)

The Parable of the Sower
Matthew 13:1–15 (NIV)

That same day Jesus went out of the house and sat by the lake. Such large crowds gathered around him that he got into a boat and sat in it, while all the people stood on the shore. Then he told them many things in parables, saying: "A farmer went out to sow his seed. As he was scattering the seed, some fell along the path, and the birds came and ate it up. Some fell on rocky places, where it did not have much soil. It sprang up quickly, because the soil was shallow. But when the sun came up, the plants were scorched, and they withered because they had no root. Other seed fell among thorns, which grew up and choked the plants. Still other seed fell on good soil, where it produced a crop—a hundred, sixty or thirty times what was sown. He who has ears, let him hear."

The disciples came to him and asked, "Why do you speak to the people in parables?"

He replied, "The knowledge of the secrets of the kingdom of heaven has been given to you, but not to them. Whoever has will be given more, and he will have an abundance. Whoever does not have, even what he has will be taken from him. This is why I speak to them in parables:

"Though seeing, they do not see; though hearing, they do not hear or understand. In them is fulfilled the prophecy of Isaiah:

"'You will be ever hearing but never understanding;
you will be ever seeing but never perceiving.
For this people's heart has become calloused;
they hardly hear with their ears,
and they have closed their eyes.
Otherwise they might see with their eyes,
hear with their ears,
understand with their hearts
and turn, and I would heal them.'"

CHAPTER SIX

GOD SPEAKS TO US...
In Our Thoughts

*T*hinking is good, as long we don't get carried away.

A balance needs to be maintained. On the one hand, thoughts are one of the principal vehicles through which we receive divine direction. God puts ideas in our heads.

On the other hand, promptings of the Spirit can be drowned out by the din of other thoughts racing through our minds. The problem of mental noise has become acute in this day of TV, cell phones, e-mail and a billion other distractions. That's why so many people are learning contemplative prayer: They are trying to stop their own minds from talking so God can get a word in!

The stories in this chapter depict God speaking through thought in a variety of ways. Sometimes loudly, sometimes softly. Sometimes in the midst of private battles, other times in the middle of a crowd. Sometimes in response to prayers, sometimes out of the blue.

"Where can I go from your Spirit?" the psalmist asked. "Where can I flee from your presence?" (Psalm 139:7, NIV).

The answer is, "Nowhere." The Lord is with us always, in all ways. Including in our thoughts.

Why I Quit the Gas Company
—By Bill Bair—

I sat in a pew near the rear of the church on that October night in 1967, thinking back over my life and feeling—well, satisfied. I looked at my family sitting alongside me, my wife Marilyn and the five kids. The three oldest were foster children whom we'd had since they were tykes: Ted, Marlene, Judy, all teenagers now. I thought of our cottage at the seashore and the fun we had there every summer. Not bad for a guy who flunked two grades before he ever finished grammar school.

I was the kid everyone said would never make it. I never did get past the ninth grade at school and then bummed from job to job. At twenty-five I was digging ditches.

And now, at forty-two, I had a good job in sales at the People's Natural Gas Company, already thinking about the day when Marilyn and I would retire, buy a home in Florida, fish, travel. . . .

Bill, I want you to work for Me.

That thought cut across my self-congratulations as sharp as though a voice had spoken. I was so startled I actually glanced behind me. I'd heard of God "speaking" to people, but—to me?

"Gee, Lord," I stammered, "I—I do work for You, don't I? Look at the Bible class I teach Sundays. And the youth work so many nights."

I want you full-time.

The preacher, Leonard Evans, climbed into the pulpit and started speaking, but all I heard was the uproar in my own mind. "I've got a full-time job, Lord—with the gas company! About as much job as a guy like me can handle."

Quit the gas company.

Quit the—with five kids to support! Now I knew I was hearing things. "Lord Jesus, this can't be You talking. Look at the kids!"

Look at the kids. . . . Suddenly, without any conscious will in the matter, I was seeing them. Not only ours but faces of kids I'd never seen. Dozens of them—frightened or rebellious or withdrawn—kids who were never going to make it.

Look at them, Bill. My children have no homes.

Interesting idea. To offer a home to such kids—not just the appealing, moldable little fellows, but to the older ones—the ones who'd been in trouble. The ones nobody wanted. It would make a full-time job for someone. Maybe when I retired, Marilyn and I could—

Now.

"Lord, a man can't just pick up and leave that way! Look, in two more years I'll be eligible for a pension. With that money we could—"

Don't you think I can care for My workers as well as the gas company can? I want you to quit your job today and I want you to go up to the front of this church and tell this congregation what you've done.

I looked around desperately, wishing the door were a few feet closer. "Lord, if this is You talking, okay. But what if it's just some crazy idea of my own? You're going to have to give me a sign."

This was no way to talk to God Almighty, but I was too scared to care. "Lord, if this is You, have that preacher up there say my name right in the middle of his sermon."

I settled back in the pew, enormously relieved.

"Isn't that right, Bill Bair?"

Far down in front, Mr. Evans was looking straight at me. The church was tomb quiet.

"Don't you agree, Bill Bair?" he repeated.

This time as my name rang out from the pulpit I managed to reply, "Yes, Mr. Evans, that sure is right!" I had no idea what he'd been talking about. He went back to his sermon while I sat in the rear of the church knowing I was trapped.

The sermon ended with the most stirring altar call I'd ever felt. I stood and made that long walk.

At the front I turned around and, talking as rapidly as I could, said I was quitting my job and starting a home for delinquent kids and would they please pray. Then I turned back to the altar because I couldn't look my family in the eye.

I felt a hand on my shoulder. "Bill." It was Marilyn's voice. "I don't know what you're doing, but I'm with you all the way."

I turned cautiously around. Not only Marilyn but all five kids as well were standing there. And with them maybe forty other people, all of them reaching out to clap my shoulder or grip my hand.

Monday morning I told my boss I was quitting. Well, he treated me real nice, the way you do when someone is sick. He talked about all the legal red tape involved in chartering a nonprofit organization. It would take eight months at least. By then, you could see, he thought I'd be recovered.

But I began to have some tooth trouble about then, and of course the dentist turned out to be a member of the Pennsylvania legislature, who saw the application through personally. We had our charter within six weeks.

A Home for Kids to me meant having a great big place, maybe an old school building; or a farm. But as it turned out, God didn't have that in mind at all. We first began to realize this when the Lawrence County Child Welfare Department heard about our willingness to take troubled older children. Placement for this kind of child, they said, was almost impossible to find. Since Marilyn and I had already been approved as foster parents for our own three, they wondered if we. . . .

Before we knew it, Kitrick was with us; two days later, Johnny.

In a matter of weeks there were thirteen people in our family, and still the phone kept ringing. Our own five children were wonderful, sharing rooms, moving onto sofas and bedrolls while we borrowed cots and moved furniture around. Far from being mad at the new turn of events, our kids were the ones who could really get to these lonely, angry youngsters.

But all the love and furniture arranging in the world couldn't push out the walls of the house. I was still thinking of one big house, when one day a couple came to visit us.

"Bill, we know this is a wild idea. But do you think we could get county approval to take in a boy like Kitrick?"

And suddenly I glimpsed His idea. God's plan, I believe, for kids in trouble all over this nation is not another institution, but individual Christian families opening their doors. I talked about the new dream with the board of our nonprofit organization, and they caught the excitement. What a troubled kid needed, we all agreed, was Jesus. He needs to be part of a family who live their faith, who pray together when problems come up, who lean on the Holy Spirit's wisdom instead of their own.

And one by one, we found such homes. Here in New Wilmington we started with those forty folks who were standing behind me that October night when I turned around from the altar.

The kids come to our house first—usually straight from the court with a probation officer to see they make it through the door. They stay several days or several weeks while we get to know each one's strengths and needs. Then we begin to pray for wisdom in placing each child with the right family. One kid will need a big bunch of brothers and sisters; another should be an only child for a while.

Then we place the youngster in what we call a "love home." But in doing so we also place the child in a Christian community. For beyond the smaller community of the family there are the Christians next door in the church and throughout the entire town. Each takes a part in the child's renewal.

And as we help and pray for one another, we find that we ourselves are being helped. Families are knit together, churches reinvigorated, streets become neighborhoods. Today, sixty-seven families in this area are open to these youngsters; more than one hundred fifty "unwanted" kids have found homes. And the idea is spreading. Already, similar community projects are starting in Bridgeport, Connecticut, and Toronto, Canada, and in several Ohio cities.

Sometimes when I walk through our silent house late at night, checking a dozen sleeping kids, I'll remember how I kicked and struggled that night four years ago. I was like Johnny, the second little fellow who came to us. He gave us a terrible scowl as the social worker left.

"I'm only staying ten days."

"Well, that's okay, Johnny," I said. "We'll have a real good time those ten days."

Ten days later he sidled up to me at supper. "Papa Bair?" he said. (Wouldn't you know it, Marilyn and I are Mama Bair and Papa Bair.) "Papa Bair, which comes next, fall or spring?"

"Spring," I said.

"Well," he announced, "I'm staying till fall."

You and me both, Johnny. We don't like to commit ourselves. We hang on; we make conditions. But, Johnny, once we let go, what a God He is! ❧

O the depth of the riches and wisdom and knowledge of God! How unsearchable are his judgments and how inscrutable his ways!

R O M A N S   1 1 : 3 3   (N R S V)

Bill Bair's story is a dramatic example of God speaking through thought. Most of the stories in this chapter are equally dramatic—drama makes for good reading. Still, we should remember that such moments of overpowering grace are rare. Far more common are the subtle signals God plants in our minds, those that gently turn us in His direction, away from doubt, fear, anger or impatience. Such moments of quiet grace can occur any time, anywhere, as Edward Grinnan reminds us in the following meditation.

R E N E W E D   B Y   G R A C E
— B Y   E D W A R D   G R I N N A N —

The morning before my birthday, I stand in line under the big RENEWAL sign at the Department of Motor Vehicles. I've been whisked through the eye test, had a photo snapped so quickly it felt like an ambush, and now find myself in a bit of a bottleneck waiting for a clerk to certify the paperwork and take my check.

I keep thinking about that word *renewal*. It seems an unlikely description of the process a dozen of us are going through, moving sleepily from station to station (we're the ones who are convinced that the earlier we get here, the faster we'll be out), studying the newspaper and sipping coffee from Styrofoam cups ("Hold the cup down so it doesn't show up in the photo, please"). *Ordeal* would be more apt.

The older I get, the more I think of my birthday as an unwanted reminder of the inexorable aging process. *Another one down*, and all at once I realize I have more birthdays behind me than I am likely to have left. It's a strange thought.

I glance at my four-year-old license picture. *Not a bad shot*, I muse. As a rule I am very critical of myself in photos, a kind of reverse vanity. I was wearing my hair slightly longer four years ago—or maybe I had just needed a haircut; I can't recall. I don't look that different, otherwise. I remember feeling old on that day, too, yet looking at the picture now I seem young, younger than my age, even. Four years from now, will I look at the ambush photo taken today and think, *Not bad?*

The thought strikes me: When I look at my life *today*, when it counts most, can I help but think, *Not bad?* Things have changed in the past four years, certainly, and most of what has come to pass couldn't have been foreseen when I last stood here in the DMV renewal line. And life will change more in the four years to come. But today, standing in this line on a gray, sleepy morning, waiting for a free clerk, I can't help but feel grateful for God's careful guidance and for what I believe is my increasing awareness of it. In that respect, I know I am different. I am four years closer to God.

I look up again at the sign that says renewal, and smile. *Not bad.* ❧

> Happy is the man who listens to me, watching daily at my gates.
>
> —— PROVERBS 8:34 (RSV)

It's been said many times that the glass is either half empty or half full, depending on how we look at it. One of the ways God works through our thoughts is by encouraging us to view life from the more bountiful perspective, seeing a world of possibility and grace rather than one of scarcity and resentment.

This next story is a remarkable demonstration of just how much power we have to define our circumstances. It reveals as well another of those paradoxes God seems so fond of: Surrendering to His will never means giving up.

120

Use the Health You Have
—By Linda Williams—

It happened at the dentist's office two weeks before I was to be married. I had gone in to have a wisdom tooth pulled. "You don't want a toothache on our honeymoon!" David had urged me.

"All done!" the dentist said, bringing the chair upright. "All done," he repeated when I didn't get up.

I couldn't move. I was hurried to a hospital, where doctors attributed the strange paralysis to the anesthetic used by the dentist.

Very slowly, movement returned. I remained in the hospital for a month, and it was six months before I could return to nursing school. David still wanted to get married right away, but I insisted on waiting. What if it hadn't been the anesthetic? How could I ask David to take on a sick wife?

We were young; I was twenty, he was twenty-three. We could afford to wait. I completed nurse's training and got a hospital job. The paralysis did not recur. There were a few unrelated things—or so I thought. Days when my vision blurred. Sometimes at the end of my shift my left foot would start to drag. "You're just working too hard," David would say. In 1974, three years after our original wedding date, we were married.

The following year Jenifer was born; two years later, Trisha. Was the string of complications—dizziness, kidney infections, ulcers— pregnancy-related, as the obstetrician assured me?

Wanting to raise our family in the country, we bought a secondhand mobile home on fifteen acres in Washington state. I worked the 3:00 PM to 11:00 PM shift at Bess Kaiser Hospital in Portland, Oregon, thirty miles away, leaving when David got home from his work repairing welding equipment. Making my rounds, I began to notice that my whole left side often lagged behind the right.

David and I always got up at 5:00 AM to pray together before he left for work; daily now we asked for healing. I started losing weight so rapidly that the hospital shifted me to part-time work and put me through a battery of tests without arriving at a diagnosis.

By 1980 I was down from 130 to only seventy-five pounds, and doctors insisted on putting me in the hospital. Two days after being admitted I woke in the hospital room to discover I could not lift my head, legs, arms or hands. As in the dentist's chair ten years earlier, there was no response.

By week's end catheters and feeding tubes were keeping me alive. Around me the room darkened. Finally I knew when it was daytime only by asking the nurse. Then, as the paralysis spread to my throat, I could not even do this.

Finally, a specialist confirmed that I had multiple sclerosis.

As a nurse I was all too familiar with this disease, which progressively destroys nerves. I was thirty years old and I realized that I might be dying.

After two months in the hospital, I was to be released to a nursing home. Blind, mute, paralyzed, I would require total care. David held my unresponding hand as the doctor named several institutions. "You can look at them, Mr. Williams, and let me know."

"I don't need to look at them." That was David's voice. "Linda is coming home."

And over the doctor's protests, home I went. I was sure that at six and four, Jenifer and Trisha would be terrified by the forest of tubes. But I heard only excitement in their voices: "Mommy's home!"

Mommy? What kind of mother could I be as I waited for death in that little mobile home? Attended by nurses the insurance paid for, I lay week after week, unable to move or see or speak, wanting the end to come quickly. Worse, God, who had always been so close, now seemed a million miles away. I knew God could heal because I had watched Him do it for patients I had prayed for. But when I prayed about my own health, there was no answer.

You have health. Use it.

I had . . . what? Where had such a ludicrous thought come from? Certainly not from me. I was sick. Helpless. Why, the only part of my body I could move at all was a single finger on my right hand!

Then move that finger.

There in the dark, I moved that one finger. A mere quiver, but I moved it. Next day, and the next, and the one after that, I took my mind off all I could not do and focused it on that responsive muscle. Physically it was a movement of centimeters, but in my understanding, a journey of light-years. Instead of bombarding heaven for healing, I was to concentrate on the health I had.

Hearing, for example! I could hear the wind in the firs, the chatter of the girls as they dressed their dolls.

Thought! I could reason. I could pray—thanking God for husbands, for children, for Himself.

What could a single finger do? Gesture a greeting when I heard footsteps in the room!

One day as I "waved" at David this way, a second finger trembled into motion. A week later I coaxed a few croaking sounds from my throat. Soon afterward I saw one blur of brown and another of yellow beside the bed. The darker was Jenny's brunette curls, the yellow one, blonde Trisha.

As my sight improved and more muscles responded in my right hand and arm, I discovered an amazing range of activity within inches of me. Jenny and Trish developed an uncanny ability to make sense of my garbled speech. With the girls translating, I communicated an idea to David. Would he wedge pillows behind me till I was sitting up? Would he put my sewing machine on the bed table? And now, would he tuck the foot treadle beneath my right arm?

So it was that the girls and I began making their spring wardrobes. They cut the fabric and guided it through the machine, but I was the one who used the bit of motion I had to start and stop the needle.

Doctors cautioned that such temporary reversals were not unusual with MS. A patient could improve, but sooner or later the disease might reassert itself.

I had stopped focusing on the disease, however, simply enjoying each gift of health. Like the time when, strapped in a wheelchair, I was first wheeled out of the bedroom. Like teaching the girls to cook. (They pushed me into the kitchen, and together we baked bread, and made soups and pies.) David built a ramp beside the front steps so that I could be wheeled outside. When growing season came, he mounted a foam-rubber pad on a board with wheels, narrow enough to be pulled between the rows of beans and carrots. Lying face down I dug my fingers into the damp soil.

Use the health you have, God kept telling me, and how many uses there were for each regained ability! Much as I had improved, it was obvious that I couldn't go back to nursing, not in a wheelchair. But there were so many things I *could* do. Parenting, for example—teaching, encouraging, loving. When we learned that our church supported an orphanage in Guatemala, we asked to be considered as an adoptive family, and in 1984 four-year-old Sarah became ours.

Caring for a small child used every ounce of the health I had. And the more health I used, the more seemed to come. To continue the stretching, as Sarah grew older, I enrolled in foster-care classes offered by the state social agency, and proudly heard our home declared "ideally suited for nurturing children."

But MS was advancing again. Breathing was often a struggle, even with oxygen. Time after time I was admitted to the hospital, pronounced terminal, but survived to return home once more. To use the health I had was hard, as the pain in my abdomen became constant. A postsurgical patient is given ten milligrams of morphine; by 1990 I was receiving four hundred milligrams a day.

When even this was not enough, surgeons in August 1992 proposed severing my spinal cord. That would mean I'd never walk again—but of course I couldn't anyway. Another option was partial removal of my digestive tract. As it was eleven years since I'd taken food by mouth, this too would make no difference.

My reason for refusing both procedures must have seemed ridiculous: the conviction that God was still saying, You have health. Use it.

A few months after the surgeons' radical proposals, our first foster child was placed with us. With my mounting handicaps I would never have attempted it alone, but our three girls were so eager that we went ahead. Already a veteran of twelve foster homes at age three, Brandon was a silent child who never smiled. It was a joy to see him soon turning into a lively, laughing little boy who could never get enough hugs.

One day I was wheeling about the kitchen getting Brandon's lunch when I heard an unfamiliar sound: the growling of my own stomach. I stopped, peanut butter jar in hand. Was it time to attempt some food by mouth?

That day I sipped a teaspoon of watermelon juice, and the next day a swallow of carrot juice. Slowly I progressed to solid food, reveling in the forgotten sensation of taste. And strength began returning to my legs. One day David walked in from work to find me sitting on the couch. He looked from me to the empty wheelchair where he'd placed me that morning. "How . . . ? Who . . . ?"

Eating. Walking. Driving a car. Coming off morphine. Addition after addition to my inventory of health. As my healing has progressed, more "problem" children have been entrusted to us: Autistic. Retarded. Deaf. The evaluations that accompany each child are accurate, just not important. Unique, lovable, brave—there is so much more to say about these children.

I have discovered, you see, that it's not what's wrong with us that counts, but what's right. That's what I told the neurologist recently when he showed me the results of my latest tests. "I don't understand it," he said. "I see nothing but health here."

"I know," I told him. "I've seen nothing but health too, for a long, long time." ❧

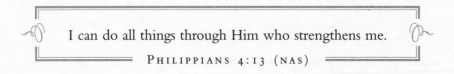

I can do all things through Him who strengthens me.

PHILIPPIANS 4:13 (NAS)

Most of the time when we're talking about the Lord's business we tend to be pretty serious, and I guess that's as it should be. It's easy to forget, though, that perhaps more than anything, God is about joy!

The following story by Gina Bridgeman is an excellent reminder that happiness is evidence of the Holy Spirit at work.

OUR OWN PARADE

—BY GINA BRIDGEMAN—

We were visiting my husband Paul's parents in Ohio, and Grandma thought we'd enjoy watching the Fourth of July parade in a neighboring town. But when we arrived, the main street was empty. She had misread the time of the parade in the newspaper, and we had missed it. All we could do was turn around and head home. My daughter Maria, who'd been jabbering to her brother like a typical six-year-old, didn't realize what had happened until Grandpa turned the car onto their street.

"We're going home?" Maria asked. "But what about the parade?"

"I goofed," Grandma answered, sounding sad and a little embarrassed. Nobody said anything. I knew that whatever happened next to fill the silence would set the mood for the entire day. *Help me say the right thing*, I prayed. Then an idea that didn't even take the time to pop into my head first popped out of my mouth: "Let's have our own parade."

Everyone jumped on the idea. "I'll drive the lawn mower, with Maria in the cart in back," said my twelve-year-old son Ross, running off. "I'll push Dan," Paul said, helping his big brother out of the car and into his wheelchair. "We need music," Paul's brother Tom said, heading to the garage and returning with an old plastic horn, a metal bucket and some sticks. "I'll get the camera," Grandpa said, while Grandma ran into the house and returned with a toy piano and a huge smile. Tom's wife Ann brought their dog Randy out on a leash, and I grabbed the big American flag from the front porch to carry myself. We marched our horn-blowing, bucket-banging parade around the neighborhood, laughing and waving, bringing neighbors out to cheer and laugh with us.

Later, I wondered how many of those decisive moments I have faced unawares, especially when someone's feelings were involved. I can't always control what happens, but I can control how I react when things don't turn out right. By bringing love instead of scorn, and with the help of God's joyful Spirit, I can do more than make the best of it—I can have a parade. ❧

The glory of God is a human being fully alive.

IRENAEUS, BISHOP OF LYONS

In the last chapter I mentioned that ultimately a conversion experience is a matter of the heart. I believe that's true, but for many people, thought prepares the ground for their transformation. They wrestle with God, much as Jacob did at Peniel (Genesis 32:24–30). This is especially true of skeptics who are confident of their ability to reason their way through life.

Once I was one of those skeptics. So was Jeremy Levin.

A Hostage Finds Freedom
—By Jeremy Levin—

That morning I got ready to go to work as usual. I was Cable News Network bureau chief and correspondent in Beirut, Lebanon, a city long ravaged by fighting among Muslim, Druze and Christian factions. The last thing my wife Sis said to me as I kissed her good-bye was, "Will you go with me to the service tonight?"

It was Ash Wednesday, March 7, 1984. She knew that I wasn't interested in going. I'd lived for fifty-one years without religion and never felt the lack. "Sure," I said, just to please her.

I walked out of the apartment house and headed down Rue Bliss. Just as I approached the Saudi Arabian Embassy compound, I felt a tap on my shoulder. I turned to face a bearded young man who jammed a green pistol into my stomach.

"You come," he muttered, motioning me to a small gray sedan at the curb. He shoved me into its backseat and, as the car accelerated, growled, "Close eyes! You see, I kill!"

Soon the car stopped. A rag was tied around my eyes and I was hustled into what seemed to be a back room.

"Why have you kidnapped me?" I demanded.

"You are spy."

"No, I'm a television journalist."

"You are CIA."

"No!" I protested. And then: "Is my wife safe? What have you done to her?"

"We do not harm women."

After more questioning, I was gagged and, still blindfolded, tightly wrapped from head to feet with packing tape, carried out and dumped on what felt like a truck bed. An engine roared, and after two and a half hours of jouncing, the truck stopped. I was dragged out, the tape unwound and, with feet and legs tingling, was led stumbling up stairs to what seemed to be a tiny room. A steel chain was tightened on my left wrist and fastened to a wall. The chain was only two and a half feet long. I wasn't able to stand. I could only sit or lie on my left side or back.

A pistol barrel was shoved under my blindfold.

"Blindfold okay, you okay," a voice intoned. "Blindfold not okay, you not okay." The trigger was pulled, clicking loudly in my ear.

Footsteps left the room, a door slammed and I slumped onto a thin foam-rubber pallet. I knew from their conversation that my captors were Muslim Shiites. They were fanatics. They could hold me here indefinitely.

Two guards came in. They led me blindfolded to an adjoining toilet, letting me know that I was to relieve myself only once a day. As I walked with them, they seemed to enjoy poking and pinching me. After knocking on the toilet door to be let out, I was taken back to my room and chained. Alone again, I peeked under my blindfold to see dingy walls and a painted-over window. Some food had been left for me: dry pita bread and two little foil-wrapped triangles of cheese.

The room had an icy chill to it, and even in my sport coat and sweater, with ragged blankets pulled around me, I shivered. I tried to sleep, but was waked constantly by the clanking chain. Finally the day ended.

The next day came. Then the next one like the other, and soon they blurred together. The only way I could tell when night had come was by the changes of light in the room.

By scratching tallies on the wall, I watched a week grind by, then two. My left shoulder ached from lying on it. My leg muscles cramped and spasms shook my body. My stomach ached from hunger. But worst of all was the worry about my family. I knew I had to do something to keep my mind occupied. I tried thinking pleasant thoughts. There was my tenderhearted, loving, perpetually-in-motion wife of seven years, whom everyone called "Sis." There was the wonderful ready-made family she had given me, five incredible young people aged eighteen to twenty-nine.

I created lists in my head, all the operas I had seen, the original major-league baseball teams, the parks they played in when I was a youngster. I formed a list of the starters on the 1945 World Series Champion Detroit Tigers, the team from the city where I grew up.

But always the cold and pain dragged me back to reality. Shifting my thinning arms and legs on the soiled pallet, I tried again to "escape," this time by reliving my favorite pastime—grand opera. I pictured the curtain rising on Beethoven's *Fidelio*. It was easy to see myself as the political prisoner, Florestan, chained to a dungeon wall, singing, "God! This is miserably dark. How horrible the silence here in my lonely cell." I envisioned Florestan's wife Leonore coming to save him. "I see her, an angel," he sings. "She leads me to freedom. . . !" And I envisioned Sis coming to rescue me.

The words of Beethoven resounded in my memory—Beethoven, who defeated deafness and adversity. "I will not submit," he once wrote. "I will take fate by the throat. It shall not overcome me. . . . I shall shout! I shall sing! Man. Help yourself! For you are able!"

But positive thinking could not ease my terrible loneliness. Aching for someone to talk to, I began talking to myself, then stopped. Would I become like those demented people I'd seen babbling to themselves on the street?

But I had to talk to someone. The guards? That was hopeless, for outside of a few grunted commands they left me alone, not even taunting me anymore at the toilet. Then who? As my mind searched, I began to think about God.

As an atheist I shrank from the idea. Yet I kept thinking about Him. I wrestled with the thought. Everything I had heard or read about God began coming back to me.

Who can grow up in America without hearing about God, from reciting the Pledge of Allegiance to overhearing a street preacher, or catching a few words of an evangelist before switching television channels?

Words surfaced in memory: "God loves you" . . . "Love thy neighbor as thyself." Even snatches of what little I had read in the Bible came back to me. Yet trying to remember what I heard was like a thirsty man holding his mouth open to raindrops.

I kept thinking about Sis. She had never pushed her beliefs on me. But

I couldn't help note that she lived her Christian convictions—sometimes, I felt, to the point of impracticality. I always felt she forgave others too easily, especially when they had hurt her badly. I was not a forgiving person.

As I thought more and more about the help other people seemed to receive through their faith, it began to make more sense. *Could it be*, I wondered, *that this "God" they believed in was real? Could I talk to Him?*

Then I caught myself. I realized that before I spoke one word to God, I would have to believe in Him too. If I started talking to God with even one millionth of one percent of doubting His existence, I wouldn't really be talking to Him, I would be deluding myself, and I felt I surely would go crazy, like those poor demented people on the street.

It was a cosmic Catch-22.

That I had not bathed for four weeks, that my rank, filthy clothes stuck to me, was not important now. I was consumed with pondering everything I had heard about God and the One called His Son, Jesus. Closer and closer I approached a spiritual Rubicon; if I crossed the boundary of believing in God, I would be committed irrevocably to Him and His Son.

Then came April 10, 1984—and then, one moment in that day. Before it, I was not sure. After it, I knew: He was real.

My first words to Him were simple: *Oh Father, please take care of my wife and family. Please reunite us.*

Then I did what I would never have done before. I forgave my captors —and asked God to forgive them too.

For the first time in my life I felt whole. Strange, I thought, to be cold and starving, and yet feel so well.

With Someone to talk to, I found life in my cell taking on a new dimension. I felt more sure of myself. When left alone in the bathroom I pressed my eye to a tiny scratch in the painted window. Looming across the valley was the easily recognizable white ridge of Mount Lebanon. We were in the Bekaa Valley, near the city of Baalbek.

Could I escape? Just as the idea rooted and began to grow, my guards took away my eyeglasses and shoes. Could they possibly sense what was going on in my mind?

Now I was taken to another house. It was May and the Mediterranean heat pressed down. Sweating in my underwear, stung by mosquitoes, this time I was chained to a radiator.

But what was that? Knocks sounded on the bathroom door adjoining me. There were other people nearby. Prisoners like me?

On July 5, 1984, four months after my capture, I was taken to a room where I was made to read a statement for videotaping. The statement urged our government to intercede with the government of Kuwait to free seventeen Shiite Muslims convicted of bombing the American and French embassies there in 1983. At last, for the first time I knew why I was being held captive. I also knew that our government had declared that it would not deal with terrorists. No matter what happened, I now felt there was a strong possibility that I would end up dead. I was moved to another house, and then to another, but all in the same area.

The guards were becoming careless. They didn't always keep the chain as tight as they once had. But what difference did it make? A severe intestinal infection now left me helpless. For weeks I writhed with stomach spasms and diarrhea. Finally the guards brought a doctor who gave me pills. They helped.

December brought freezing temperatures. I huddled, teeth chattering, under blankets. *How ironic*, I thought, *that this would be the first real Christmas of my life. How would I celebrate it? Would the guards bring a hot meal as they had done occasionally?* Then I realized that just by knowing the One Whose birthday it was would be celebration enough.

The shocker came on Christmas Eve. One of the guards actually wished me a "joyous Noel" and handed me a chocolate cake, oranges, grapes, some Lebanese Christmas cards and, of all things, a ballpoint pen!

I got a second shock when he said, "Your wife is in the Middle East talking about peace and asking about you." I had been certain that she wouldn't take my kidnapping sitting down, but the extent of her efforts was still surprising.

Then I got a third shock. The guard asked, "What do you want for Christmas?"

I looked up at him in astonishment.

"A Bible!" I blurted.

Two days later he handed me a small red-bound New Testament, a Berkeley translation from the Gideons.

I thanked him, and the instant he left I lifted my blindfold and began devouring it. I used my new pen to underline passages that had special meaning to me. Day after day I drank deeply from it. In searching for direction to help me pray more effectively, I read in Matthew, "And everything you ask in prayer you will obtain, if you believe." Then I came to a similar passage in Mark where, in telling His disciples how to pray, Jesus said, ". . . whatever you ask in prayer, believe that you have received it and it will be yours."

This hit me like a thunderbolt. Jesus didn't simply say, "Believe you will receive," He said that when you pray, believe you already have it.

I stared at this revelation, my mind reeling with its limitless implications. For the first time I realized that, despite my chain, my cell, my guards, I was free, really free.

I was moved again to another house. From knocks on the door of an adjoining bathroom I deduced that new hostages had been added. Now I felt certain that our government was sticking to its no-negotiation, no-deal policy, and in angry frustration my captors were taking more hostages. I thought that if they did not get what they wanted, eventually they would kill me.

I prayed for a chance to escape, believing that I could. On the night of February 13, 1985, more than eleven months after my capture, a guard was again careless with the chain. I could get away. Late that night I listened. It was quiet.

I tied three blankets together, then carefully pushed open the window to a second-story balcony overlooking a mountainside. I tied one blanket to the railing and then lowered myself to the ground. The frozen earth chilled my shoeless feet.

The city seemed to be asleep. Heart pounding, I began to run, zigzagging down the mountainside. As I reached a road, a dog barked, I froze. Another joined in and soon a whole pack was howling. Then came the concerned mutter of voices.

My captors?

In panic I flattened myself under a truck on the cold gravel. Flashlights raked the dark, footsteps crunched closer. A light swept across the gravel; I squirmed from it but it slanted across my feet.

Guns went off and men started shouting Arabic, which I did not know. It seemed as if they were telling me to get out from under the truck.

Trembling, I crawled out and stumbled toward the blinding light. Then I saw red berets. They were Syrian soldiers, friendly Syrians bemused by the wild-looking shoeless man in a dirty warm-up suit babbling at them in English and fractured French. I was safe. I was free.

Two days later I held Sis tightly in my arms at the Frankfurt Airport in Germany. Our ordeal was over.

Now I carry the gift my captors gave me at Christmas, the little New Testament. I look at it daily and often think about the reasons for my captivity. When I do, I am reminded of Joseph's words to his brothers, who had sold him into slavery: "You meant evil against me; but God meant it for good" (Genesis 50:20, RSV). And I believe that, like Joseph, my captivity wasn't meant just for my good—by leading me to my faith—but also for the good of the hostages I left behind when I fled my lonely cell. Now I at least had the chance to help them. ❧

> There can be no personal freedom where there is not an initial personal surrender.
>
> HOWARD THURMAN

Is That You, Lord?

Hearing yourself think in a world full of distractions is a problem. Hearing what God would have us think is even harder. How can we create some quiet around and within ourselves in case the Holy Spirit is trying to tell us something?

One expert on that subject is a humble monk who worked in the kitchen of a Parisian monastery in seventeenth-century Paris. His name was Brother Lawrence, and the account of his method (told to another monk, for Brother Lawrence was illiterate) are collected in a book called *The Practice of the Presence of God*.

As befits a simple man, Brother Lawrence's technique was simple: He worked to keep his mind focused on God regardless of what he was doing. He talked to God while he did the dishes and praised God when he cleaned the floor. He worshiped God while he was setting the table for dinner and asked God's blessing while he cleared it. Over time he got to the point where he was constantly aware of God and constantly in communion with Him. "In the noise and clatter of my kitchen," he said, "while several persons are at the same time calling for different things, I possess God in as great tranquility as if I were upon my knees at the blessed sacrament."

Most of us aren't as dedicated as Brother Lawrence, but there are easy steps that can move us in his direction. Try taking "minute retreats" whenever a few moments of downtime present themselves during the day. Think of God when you're stopped at a traffic light, standing in line at the supermarket, or waiting on hold on the telephone. It may be helpful during such moments to say a simple, repetitive prayer. Believers have recited the Jesus Prayer ("Lord Jesus, son of God, have mercy on me, a sinner") for centuries. A shorter alternative is to repeat "Abba," the word Jesus used for "Father."

The key to practicing the presence of God is directed attention. The more we focus our thoughts on God, the better we will hear Him. D.H.

Guideposts *magazine was founded by Dr. Norman Vincent Peale and his wife, Ruth Stafford Peale, in 1945. Already well-known as a motivational speaker and pastor, Dr. Peale became an international celebrity upon the publication of* The Power of Positive Thinking *in 1954. Positive thinking is the foundation upon which* Guideposts *is built, as the organization's mission statement affirms:*

"Guideposts *helps people from all walks of life achieve their maximum personal and spiritual potential.* Guideposts *is committed to communicating positive faith-filled principles for people everywhere to use in successful daily living.*"

Our last selection in this chapter is a vintage essay by Dr. Peale, reprinted from the Guideposts *issue of August 1958.*

How to Defeat Defeatism
—By Norman Vincent Peale—

I overheard two men talking the other day. "Well," said one, "I suppose it's about time we had a depression. We've had good times for many years now." The other man nodded, and his face took on a gloomy look, too.

What a contagious virus this pessimism is! Those who can't conceal their moods of defeatism, or rise above them, will soon infect everyone they meet.

"Attitudes," said a great American psychiatrist, "are more important than facts."

The late Dr. Albert Cliffe once told a story that illustrates perfectly this statement. A young couple he knew in Canada set themselves up in business, but soon ran into financial difficulty. One day when Dr. Cliffe dropped in to see them, their faces were glum.

"We've got six hundred dollars in bills to pay by the end of the month," the worried husband told him. "We'd be all right if only the people who owe us would pay up." And he pointed to a pile of past-due statements he was about to send out.

Dr. Cliffe looked from the tense face of the husband to that of his tired wife. Then he gazed about the store.

"As your spiritual counselor," he began, "I'm going to speak frankly.

This place reeks with gloom; it's a sunny day outside, but in here it's overcast. And not because your merchandise isn't attractive. You people have to sell yourselves to your customers and you're not doing it."

He pointed to the pile of statements. "Would you be willing to try an experiment with those?" he asked.

The man and his wife were willing. Dr. Cliffe then sat down at a table with them.

"Let's start by changing our thinking," he said. "Not just the three of us, but as four." Then Dr. Cliffe put his hand on the stack of statements and closed his eyes. His prayer went something like this:

"Father, we know that bad situations do not change unless people change. This couple has worked hard; they know that they need Your help. Please show them how to brighten up their lives—as well as this store.

"We also want to pray for the people who are to receive these statements. Perhaps they have had serious troubles and can't pay. If so, be with them in their need, and if it is Thy will for them to settle their accounts, we know they will do so promptly."

Within a week over nine hundred dollars from the delinquent accounts had come in, three hundred dollars above what was needed. More important, however, was the spiritual transfusion this young couple received. For Dr. Cliffe's counseling not only gave them a new approach to business, but helped to save a marriage.

This experience, and others like it, confirm what the Bible said more than two thousand years ago:

"As a man thinketh, so is he."

I wonder if these truths aren't being evidenced today in America's industrial system. If people are confident, buoyant, optimistic, if they have faith in the future and in themselves, they will go out and spend their money with the calm assurance that they will earn still more money—and then spend that.

Here, it seems to me, the leaders of industry (and by leaders I mean not only executives, but also the foremen, the salesmen, and outstanding workers on the factory floor) have a great challenge. If they refuse to be discouraged, if they react to declining sales figures with increased energy and determination, if they oppose defeatism with strong, positive, affirmative attitudes and actions, they will be doing much to restore people's confidence and their country's prosperity.

For those worried about their jobs, their business or any personal problem, I would like to recommend these words of Emerson:

"This time, like every time, is a very good time, if we but know what to do with it."

What Emerson is telling us is that the person with imagination and faith can take any problem, any crisis, any obstacle and from it draw not defeatism but stimulus; he can regard it as a challenge. Once he does this, invariably, he begins to think harder, pray harder, work harder. As a result, instead of gloom and pessimism, creative insights and ideas and intuitions begin to flow.

Here is where Christianity can help all of us so much. If anyone ever had cause to be depressed and disillusioned it was Jesus Christ. A study of the Bible shows us that during His ministry Jesus suffered every kind of indignity and rejection. Yet, at all times He carried high the banner of hope and the promise of an abundant life. Even His death was a great victory. ❧

 Free will, though it makes evil possible, is also the only thing that makes possible any love or goodness or joy worth having.

C. S. Lewis

AT THE HOME OF MARTHA AND MARY
LUKE 10:38–42 (NIV)

As Jesus and his disciples were on their way, he came to a village where a woman named Martha opened her home to him. She had a sister called Mary, who sat at the Lord's feet listening to what he said. But Martha was distracted by all the preparations that had to be made. She came to him and asked, "Lord, don't you care that my sister has left me to do the work by myself? Tell her to help me!"

"Martha, Martha," the Lord answered, "you are worried and upset about many things, but only one thing is needed. Mary has chosen what is better, and it will not be taken away from her." ❧

CHAPTER SEVEN

GOD SPEAKS TO US...
In Dreams and Visions

*T*he Bible was way ahead of modern psychology in appreciat-
ing that the subconscious is an important source of insight
and direction. From the story of Jacob's ladder in Genesis to
the apocalyptic landscapes of Revelation, Scripture shows us God's
using dreams and visions as vehicles of blessing, guidance, prophecy
and correction.

Part of the beauty of dreams and visions is their freedom from
rational logic. They don't have to make sense, in the usual fashion,
and neither does God. Their strangeness prompts awe and humility.
There are secret worlds and languages hidden to us. We listen, try to
understand, and wonder.

Because they are unfiltered by the conscious mind, dreams and
visions can also be especially potent sources of spiritual power. They
give us access to an interior reservoir where the Holy Spirit flows, wild
and unrestrained. When that power spills out into our daily lives, it
transforms and heals, as the stories in this chapter attest.

A DREAM OF LOVE
—BY RHONDA LINN MCCLOUD—

One winter night in 1994 the confrontation that had been brewing for months finally erupted. When I heard my fourteen-year-old daughter stumble into our apartment past curfew again, I summoned her to my bedroom. "I love you, Kellee," I said, "but I've had it. This behavior can't go on."

She lifted her chin defiantly. How had my innocent daughter turned into a wayward teenager? I could see the sweet, vulnerable little girl inside her, but I just didn't know how to reach her anymore.

Kellee and I had moved to Huntington Beach in the middle of the previous semester, and adjusting to a new school was hard for her. So I had looked the other way at first when I found her hanging out with a bunch of older kids whose top priority seemed to be having a good time. Kellee had never taken her studies as seriously as I, a former teacher, would have liked. At least she's making friends, I tried to reassure myself.

Then she started coming home at all hours, her eyes glazed, her breath foggy with alcohol. "I'm disappointed in you," I'd harangue her. "I have high expectations for you, and I know you can live up to them." Kellee didn't listen. If anything, her behavior got worse.

That February night I'd had all I could stand. "I won't have you drinking and taking drugs," I said firmly. "Not while you live under my roof. If you stay here, you live by my rules."

"Fine," Kellee snapped. "I'll leave, then. You won't have to worry about me anymore."

"I'll never stop worrying about you," I protested. "I'm your mother." Not saying a word, Kellee snatched her purse and walked out. "The door's always open . . ." I called after her feebly. I was pretty sure she was just going to stay with a girlfriend for a couple nights. Still, a terrible fear crept into my thoughts. *What if Kellee had walked not just out of our apartment, but out of my life altogether?*

I sank down on my bed, more discouraged than I had ever been. My fiancé had called it quits recently, a blow that hurt almost as much as my divorce from Kellee's dad. Now my daughter was gone too. For as long as

I could remember I had pictured myself as a wife and mother. I'd failed miserably on both counts. *What do I have left to offer?* I wondered. Despair swept over me and I gave in to it, sobbing so hard it ached to breathe.

Finally, drained, I got up to try to pull myself together. But when I saw my reflection in the bathroom mirror the hopelessness of my situation struck me anew. Not only had I been unable to handle the all-important responsibilities of wife and mom, I couldn't even find a job to give me the smallest sense of accomplishment. No employer would hire me looking the way I did, and I couldn't blame them.

My face was covered with ugly blisters, the result of osteomyelitis, a type of bone infection. It had started after a minor accident during a root canal nine years earlier. The tip of a metal file had broken off and lodged in the root of my tooth, causing an infection in my jawbone that had failed to respond to treatment, and had spread to other parts of my body. Now my appearance frightened even me.

I turned away from the mirror. Back in my bedroom I paused at the window. Gazing out into the starry night, I started praying. *God,* I pleaded, picturing him wrapping a deep-purple blanket around Kellee to keep her safe, *please protect my daughter.* I knew it was up to Him now. *And please help me find peace in my life.*

I lay down again. The last thing I saw before I closed my eyes was the electric, treetop angel I'd saved from Christmas and hung above my bed. The soft glow of its lights always brought me comfort, comfort I desperately needed that night. *God, release me from my pain. What's the point of going on? Everyone I love leaves me.*

I hadn't been asleep long when I found myself getting out of bed. I walked out the front door and stood on the balcony, looking at the sky, a canopy of midnight blue. Then, amazingly, I was floating over the balcony railing, up into the velvet expanse. I realized I must be dreaming but I felt fully awake.

The stars were so near that I couldn't resist touching them. Their texture felt like snow melting in my hands. I peered more closely at them. All around me, as far as my eyes could see, were tiny angels! Garbed in a glistening crystalline substance so they looked like snowflakes, they whispered past me, drifting somewhere on the breeze.

The next thing I knew I had glided to a stop in a cloud. Someone was standing beside me, and I glanced over to see who it was. Love, pure and boundless, streamed from him, suffusing me immediately with a cosmic sense of well-being. I knew I was in the presence of Christ. And I knew He was directing the angels—to earth, to do His work.

Gently he wrapped his left arm around my shoulders and held me close to him. Neither of us spoke, yet communication flowed between us. *I am your brother,* he told me. *And I will always be with you.*

I nodded. I know that now, but I need to know one thing more. What is my purpose on earth?

His answer was unhesitating: *To give and receive love; to give and receive forgiveness.*

"Love and forgiveness." Those words were on my lips when I woke, rested and renewed. But whom did I love? Whom did I need to forgive?

In the days following I began to make a list. I prayed over every name during the next months. My ex-husband, Kellee's father, for our failed marriage. I'd had my part in it too. My dentist, for causing the infection in my jawbone during that root canal. It was an unfortunate accident and I knew he felt bad. My former fiancé, for ending our relationship. It wouldn't have been right for either of us. Slowly I let go of my anger and hurt.

But what about Kellee? Six months later she still hadn't come home. Technically she wasn't a runaway. She sporadically checked in with my mother to say she was okay. But Kellee didn't want to speak to me. Though I longed to talk with her, I had to accept that she wasn't ready to re-establish our relationship. The longer she stayed away the more I came to accept that she was her own person. *I forgive you for not being the serious student I wanted you to be,* I told her in my thoughts. *I love you the way you are: bright, creative, free-spirited. I hope you'll forgive me. I only wanted to protect you.*

I could feel my emotional wounds beginning to heal. With the help of prayer, the problems that used to drive me into despair gradually became bearable.

Yet somehow I didn't feel completely free of the pain of my past. *Do I still harbor negative feelings toward someone I need to get over?* I wondered.

One morning, as I gave myself the usual cursory once-over in the mirror, I noticed the blisters on my face weren't as inflamed. My skin actually looked as if it was getting better! Marveling at how my illness seemed to be abating, I gave thanks to God.

Almost like an answer, the words Christ had communicated to me in my dream came back. *Love and forgiveness.* Gazing at my reflection, I knew what I had to do before I could be whole again. It was going to be a long, complicated process, but I needed to learn to love and forgive myself.

It helped when Kellee finally came home nine months after she left. "I love you, Mom," she said. "I want to try again. Will you give me another chance?"

"If you'll do the same for me," I replied. I hugged my daughter tight, and I didn't think anything could feel better.

When Kellee told me she had started going to a twelve-step recovery program to help deal with her drinking and drug abuse, I was proud of her. I was grateful. I knew God had sent His angels to watch over Kellee when I couldn't.

Now it was time to find something to give me a sense of purpose. I thought of counseling over the telephone, where people wouldn't be put off by my appearance, and where my education in behavioral science and my experiences in life might be of use.

I contacted mental-health programs in the area, and New Hope, a suicide and crisis hot line, had an opening for a counselor. When I saw the title of the manual I received on the first day of training I knew I had found the right place: "Giving Life by Giving Love."

Not long after that I was led to a doctor who was able to treat my osteomyelitis successfully, and eventually the infection in my jawbone cleared up completely. My appearance returned to normal.

Love and forgiveness. They have brought me a release from my pain far beyond what I could ever have imagined. As my faith in myself has grown so have my job and my relationship with my daughter. At New Hope, I train new counselors. I also teach parenting classes in Huntington Beach. Under my guidance Kellee studied at home and earned her high-school-equivalency certificate. She is now a student at a local college. Today, four years after that desperate winter night when I nearly gave up all hope, God's blessings continue—carried into my life, I like to think, on the snowy wings of His angels. ❧

> In the year that King Uzziah died, I saw the Lord seated on a throne, high and exalted, and the train of his robe filled the temple. Above him were seraphs, each with six wings: With two wings they covered their faces, with two they covered their feet, and with two they were flying. And they were calling to one another: "Holy, holy, holy is the Lord Almighty; the whole earth is full of his glory."
>
> ISAIAH 6:1–3 (NIV)

Artists have been called to function as full-time visionaries. They see things many of us do not, and bring them to life in their art.

This is not always a pleasant assignment. Perhaps you are familiar with the paintings of Hieronymus Bosch. He was the fifteenth-century Dutch artist who painted dramatic visions of Hell. His canvases are filled with leering demons, tortured humans and nightmarish landscapes. These are not happy images to carry around in your head.

Thankfully, other artists were as skilled at evoking God's glory as Bosch was at evoking the agonies of damnation. One of these was George Frederick Handel, the composer of Messiah. *The birth of that glorious choral masterpiece is the subject of the following account by Rick Hamlin.*

VOICES OF THE HEAVENS
—By Rick Hamlin—

The servant trudges up the rickety flight of stairs once more. He puts down his tray full of food, and knocks on the closed door. No answer. He raps again. Silence. Very quietly, so as not to disturb the man at work inside, he lets himself in.

Pages of manuscript paper are scattered about the floor. The tray from yesterday's dinner lies where the servant had placed it the night before, the food untouched. And the master sits at his desk in a trance, his quill pen scratching almost continuously on the page.

It is the end of summer in London, 1741, and the servant is the lone employee of George Frederick Handel, the great composer and musician who has now fallen upon hard times. In earlier days his orchestral music had been commissioned by the royal family. The king was so appreciative of one Handel concert "that he caused it to be repeated three times in all." His operas and oratorios had played to full houses in the finest London theaters. So successful were the performances of his works that Handel became one of the first composers in history to live off the profits of his writing, not the lowly wages of a court musician.

A portly man, he had a loud voice and a boisterous manner. With his wry sense of humor, he could be modest about his work. When a friend once commented on the unpleasant music they were hearing in a public park, Handel replied, "You are right, sir, it is very poor stuff; I thought so myself when I wrote it."

Born in Germany in 1685, the same year as Johann Sebastian Bach, he was soon singled out for his natural musical gifts. His surgeon-barber father wanted him to become a lawyer. Then a duke heard the boy playing an organ postlude and persuaded the father to provide formal musical training. By the time he was twelve, Handel was already substituting for his teacher at the keyboard.

Quickly mastering a variety of instruments, he gave up his legal studies and set out for other lands to practice his trade. In Rome he impressed the musicians of the day with his composing skills, but it was in England where he was to have his career.

And what a career it was! He triumphed with one opera after another—*Radamisto, Giulio Cesare, Orlando*. These were, in the famous words of Samuel Johnson, an "exotic and irrational entertainment," the texts in Italian and the plots complicated and convoluted. But because of the world-famous singers, lavish costumes, sophisticated scenery and special effects, people flocked to these operas.

In the meantime Handel also continued his work as an orchestral composer and organist. Once, after attending services at a country church, he asked the organist's permission to play a postlude. His playing so captivated the congregation that they reclaimed their seats and refused to leave until he finished.

Then came the first of many setbacks. An opera in English, *The Beggar's Opera* by John Gay, premiered in London, satirizing the convention of songs sung in a foreign tongue. Fashion changed. Italian operas became the subject of ridicule. People scorned them. One of Handel's friends urged him "to deliver us from our Italian bondage."

Handel was not dissuaded by the turn of his fortune. When one of his pieces was about to be played to a nearly empty auditorium, he joked, "Never mind. The music will sound better in an empty hall."

Adapting himself to the tastes of the era, the composer began writing oratorios, long compositions based on biblical texts, such as *Esther* and *Deborah*. But these too met with mixed success. Some clergy felt they were a sacrilege: "What are we coming to when the will of Satan is imposed on us in this fashion?" The London audiences were fickle. And the foreign singers, as one contemporary observed, "made such rare work with the English Tongue you would have sworn it was Welch!" Underwriting performance after performance, Handel soon found himself in financial difficulty.

Exhausted from overwork and disappointment, he suffered a paralyzing stroke, leaving his right arm useless. How would he ever be able to conduct or play again? Doctors sent him abroad to bathe in natural thermal waters. Handel was fifty-two years old, in debt, and it looked as though he would never compose another piece.

And yet, one day in France where he was recovering, he sat down at a convent's harpsichord and started improvising. Astonishingly, he could play with both hands, even the one that had been paralyzed. The nuns listened, amazed. It was as though an angel were fingering the keyboard, one of them claimed.

He went back to London and to his furious pace of work. He took out huge loans to put on performances of two new oratorios. He rented theaters, hired singers, and formed an orchestra. But both works were financial disasters.

Now he found himself in danger of ending up in debtors' prison. He gave what he termed his farewell concert and then retired from public life. It looked like the end.

Except there was one last commission Handel had to fulfill.

Commission is a grand word for it, because he would be paid next to nothing. A charity in Dublin wanted him to write an oratorio to be performed to raise funds for debtors who had landed in prison.

He set to work feverishly on August 22, 1741. In the grip of inspiration, he didn't leave his room for three weeks. He hardly ate. One friend who visited him found him sobbing with emotion. His text was the life of Jesus, the words taken from the Bible, and the music inspired. When later describing the mystical experience of the oratorio's composition, Handel referred to the apostle Paul's words, "Whether I was in the body or out of my body when I wrote it I know not."

And then came that day when his servant walked in on him in the midst of his writing. Tears streaming down his face, Handel cried out, "I did think I did see all heaven before me!" The servant looked down at the manuscript paper and saw the text: "Hallelujah! Hallelujah! Hallelujah!"

The oratorio premiered on April 13, 1742, raising four hundred pounds and freeing 142 men from debtors' prison. (The following year the composer conducted it himself in London. Afterward someone congratulated him on an excellent "entertainment" for the people, and he responded, "I should be sorry if I only entertain them. I wish to make them better.")

Since then millions have been inspired, moved and made better by this music. Handel himself raised thousands of pounds in his lifetime by conducting his masterpiece for benefit concerts. His fortunes improved and his faith grew. A contemporary once noted him in church, "on his knees, expressing by his looks and gesticulations the utmost fervor of devotion."

Mortally ill, he conducted one last performance of *Messiah* during Lent of 1759. On his deathbed he declared his hope of "meeting his good God, his sweet Lord and Savior, on the day of his Resurrection." The day before Easter, he died.

Today the words of the angels' song that Handel set to music can be heard wherever Christians sing. For if indeed he did see heaven, many people would be surprised to discover the immortal "Hallelujah Chorus" wasn't a direct transcription. As many a *Messiah* listener has exclaimed, "I have heard the music of heaven!" ✍

> In my vision at night I looked, and there before me
> were the four winds of heaven churning up the great
> sea. Four great beasts, each different from the others,
> came up out of the sea.
>
> DANIEL 7:2–3 (NIV)

Visions don't have to be spectacular in order to be gifts from God.
Sometimes they can be very specific, aimed at a very specific purpose.
That doesn't make them less mysterious, or less miraculous.
The vision that changed the life of Betina Beard is a case in point.

JOURNEY TO NUBBLE POINT
—BY BETINA BEARD—

The vision came to me one blustery winter day, as if blown in on the icy
wind rattling the eaves of my house in State Line, Pennsylvania. With
unmistakable clarity I saw it: a huge, gray, flat rock jutting out over the
ocean, a churning surf charging the beach below. I was seized by an urge
to travel to Maine. I had never entertained any thoughts of visiting Maine.
I certainly had no intention of going there now. Yet the urge, and the
rock so clear in my mind's eye, became a part of me. I asked God to reveal
what it meant; but instead of an answer, I continued to receive the powerful mental impression of that great gray rock leaning out over the sea.

On June 21, 1989, I sat in my Ford Thunderbird, parked in the lot of
a local restaurant, blotting up the soda I had just spilled. I had been crying
when I climbed into the car because I had just finished lunching with my
ex-husband Jim. Our meeting had left me in agony and confusion.

Our marriage of twenty-six years had ended a year earlier. Once, I
had been so in love with my tall, handsome, athletic, brown-haired husband. He had been my Prince Charming. We shared a tremendous pride
in our children—a married son, and a daughter in college. But in the
latter years of our marriage he had hurt me so badly that I felt an almost

bottomless sense of betrayal. We had drifted far apart emotionally and spiritually. Finally it had all fallen to pieces.

I had battled loneliness and put my life back together slowly and painfully, and at times I wondered how I would go on. Yet I sensed that God had something in store for me; He wouldn't forsake me, and I begged Him to reveal what lay ahead. The only answer I got was the strange vision of the rock.

Jim and I had occasional get-togethers like today, usually over lunch. We would discuss the children and other safe topics, working hard to find a common ground; we didn't want to be estranged totally. On one occasion Jim surprised me by saying he had given his heart to the Lord and returned to church.

I didn't know how to respond. "That's wonderful," I finally managed. I was glad Jim's life was changing, but I didn't know what it meant. During one visit, we were in a restaurant when Jim suddenly reached over and put his hand on mine. "Bets," he said earnestly, "do you think we could ever get together again?" His blue eyes searched mine for an answer.

I could never trust him again, I knew. Never forgive him. But I didn't want to say that, not after we had come so far. "Jim, we're friends now. Why don't we just leave it at that?"

Pain rippled through his gaze. He withdrew his hand and we sat quietly for a minute before Jim signaled for the check. My heart went out to him, but I didn't love him that way anymore.

Then came that June 21, Jim's birthday. My daughter was home from college and wanted to take the three of us to lunch. Jim and Julie laughed and reminisced about her childhood days. I felt such warmth watching them talk, almost like the old days. The intensity of the feeling surprised me. As we left the restaurant and Julie said good-bye and walked on ahead to her car, Jim suddenly took me by the arm. "Please, Bets," he pleaded gently, "why don't you give us another chance?"

I pulled away. "I . . . I don't know what to say, Jim. I need time." I started to cry quietly as Jim stared at the ground.

I knew he didn't want to push me. Seeing the to-go cup of soda in my shaking hand, he smiled and said, "Don't spill your Coke, Bets." He turned, walked to his car and drove off.

But I did spill it, bumping my elbow on the T-bird's door. Now as I sat behind the wheel blotting up soda with a wad of tissue, so many emotions were doing battle inside me. I begged God to give me a clear mind. Once more, the image of the rock loomed before me.

That's when I knew what to do. Yes, it seemed insane, but I also knew I must trust the answer would be there waiting for me.

Stopping at home, I threw some clothes into a bag and almost as an afterthought I tossed in a novel that Julie had been strangely insistent I read—*Colleen*, by Eva Gibson. She kept asking me if I had gotten to the end yet.

Interstate 81 was just outside town. I got in a northbound lane, telling myself, *This is crazy.* Yet as I rolled through the lush Pennsylvania hills, my crying stopped; my confusion lessened. If God had shown me a vision, he would guide me.

North of Harrisburg, I paused at a rest area to check my atlas for the route into Maine. I continued, heading northeast on I-84. As the miles ticked off, my thoughts kept drifting back to Jim. Feelings for him were emerging within me, feelings I couldn't quite identify. They were powerful, unformed between bitterness and forgiveness, resentment and love. *How could I trust these feelings?*

Somewhere ahead was my rock. I would find my answer there. I turned onto I-95, heading north. In Massachusetts I stopped at a cozy diner for a fried clam sandwich, the kind of place where Jim and I might have met for one of our lunches. It was dusk when I crossed into New Hampshire. I found a motel near Kittery. In the morning I would cross the Piscataqua River and start my search up the Maine coastline. I fell asleep almost as soon as I climbed into bed, clutching the novel I had brought.

When I awoke, brilliant sun flooded me with anticipation. After breakfast, I hurried to my car, savoring the sharp, salty ocean breeze. I crossed over the bridge and I was in Maine! I followed the coastal road north. Time after time I stopped to observe the rocky shore, beautiful granite crags around which surf crashed and foamed. But none was the rock from my vision.

I drove on. At a picturesque village called York Beach I spotted a distant lighthouse standing bright against the intense blue of the ocean sky. As I drove to see it I passed an imposing gate beyond which several large houses sat on a grassy point of land. A sudden urge overtook me. I drove through the gates and followed the road to the end. I parked and walked across a lawn at the water's edge.

And there it was—the rock. My rock. A huge gray monolith overhanging the water. The sight of it filled me with awe. I returned to my car and got my camera, a blanket and my book. I clambered onto the rock and spread the blanket on its smooth, sun-warmed surface. Calmed by the healing vista of the endless horizon and soothed by the surf sighing and gurgling below, I felt a joy I hadn't experienced in years. It was more than a feeling. It was a transformation. It was as if angels had set the scene just for me, even to the detail of the small fishing boat that ventured close. Leaning back, I opened my book. I rested and read for a few hours.

Then, as I finished the last pages of the novel, an overwhelming realization struck me. The book told the story of a woman who felt bitter and betrayed. In the conclusion, God leads her to mercy, forgiveness and a new life. Healed by God, she returns to her family to help heal their hurts.

I set the book down on my lap, my tears moistening its pages. So that's why God had brought me here—to show me how His love can heal. *Could I forgive Jim? He said he had turned his life over to the Lord. I sensed something different about him. But could I ever trust him again?* Was God saying, Trust Me first and I will show you how to trust Jim? God had brought me, the rock and the book together. By leading me to Maine, He showed how I must trust Him.

Eight days later Jim and I became engaged on what would have been our twenty-seventh wedding anniversary. On July 22, 1989, we were remarried in a beautiful old-fashioned ceremony, with more than 115 friends and family members looking on.

Where did we go for our honeymoon? To Maine, of course; to our rock at Nubble Point, where I had learned to trust a new foundation in faith. ❧

Because Joseph her husband was a righteous man and did not want to expose her to public disgrace, he had in mind to divorce her quietly. But after he had considered this, an angel of the Lord appeared to him in a dream and said, "Joseph son of David, do not be afraid to take Mary home as your wife, because what is conceived in her is from the Holy Spirit.

MATTHEW 1:19–20 (NIV)

Most of the visions we've read about so far in this chapter have come to those who had them involuntarily. They were bestowed as gifts. The exception was Handel's inspired creation of Messiah: *Like all artists, Handel was in the habit of actively seeking visions—his work depended on it.*

Artists are not the only ones who can consciously go about trying to create visions that will grant them access to the deep wells of Spirit that lie hidden in the subconscious. Visualization is a form of prayer that can be cultivated. Harry DeCamp knows this from experience: The visions he created saved his life.

BELIEVE, BELIEVE, BELIEVE!
—BY HARRY DECAMP—

I am a man who lives today in a state of amazement. For most of my many years I had only a nodding relationship with God; how extraordinary, then, that when I was dying He would bother to reach down and heal me. And yet He did just that.

Even when I was told I had cancer of the bladder, my first thought was not that I should pray to God. In fact, I wasn't all that desperate; it didn't seem like the end of the world to me. Actually, it was harder on my wife Bess. Her mother had been a nurse, and Bess had been brought up hearing all the cancer horror stories. But I felt that somehow medicine was going to save me. I had confidence in my doctor, and I followed his instructions.

I eased up. I sold my insurance business to my son-in-law. Although I was in and out of the hospital several times, the cancer moved slowly. Life seemed fairly normal until that day when I went to the hospital for exploratory surgery. When I returned from the recovery room, my doctor was there. "Harry," he said, "I consider myself a competent surgeon, but you need somebody much better than I am."

For the first time I was afraid.

The doctor went on to say, "We're sending you to the Sloan-Kettering Cancer Center in New York. It's the best in the world." The idea that one of the finest surgeons in the world was going to operate on me gave me hope.

I knew when I went to New York that my bladder would have to be removed. As terrible as it was, I was prepared to live with the inconvenience of all kinds of medical contraptions. I was ready for anything if only I could be rid of the cancer.

But back from the recovery room on the day of the operation, through a haze of pain, I learned the truth. The great surgeon had sewn me up without removing my bladder. I cried in great racking sobs: My cancer was inoperable!

That afternoon, one of the surgeon's assistants came to talk to me.

"No lies," I said.

"Well. . ." he said, his brow furrowed with concentration, "the cancer has spread so extensively to the surrounding tissue that to remove it all would mean . . ." he trailed off lamely.

"How much time do I have?" I whispered.

"We can't promise you anything: a year, a month . . . or even a day . . ."

I swallowed and licked my parched lips. "Where . . . do I go from here?"

"I don't know," he replied.

Now I was facing the reality I hadn't faced before. I was going to die. They gave me some pain killers as big as thumbnails, and a supply of sleeping pills.

Bess, bless her, put on a brave show. "Now, Harry, we'll beat it yet," she said, as she propped me up in my easy chair in our living room. "We'll try the chemotherapy. And there are all sorts of other theories . . ." Somebody sent us literature from California about cancer patients being injected with massive doses of vitamin C. Bess pounced on it as if someone had thrown us a life preserver.

But I knew I was dying. Whenever I lay down, I felt as though I were smothering, so most of the time I sat in my easy chair and stared at meaningless images on the TV screen. I wondered if I could commit suicide and, if I did, what would be the best way?

The smell of food made me ill. "Harry!" Bess fumed. "I don't care if you're not hungry! EAT!"

I waved her away. What was the use? I'm a big man, but my weight plummeted steadily.

Occasionally I thought about praying to God, but I really didn't know how. I knew God was there, but He was some mystical Being, far away. It didn't seem right that after I'd ignored Him all these years I should start begging now. The words I said seemed to bounce off the ceiling.

Then two things happened, one right after the other.

The first was the card. It didn't seem to be that much different from all the other get-well cards. Yet for some reason, I kept returning to it. A friend had scribbled a message beneath her name: "With God all things are possible" (Matthew 19:26, KJV).

How I wanted that to be true! Again and again I'd take out the card and look at it. Suppose it were true . . . How do you go about making contact with God? . . . Isn't it too late in the game to think about going to church? . . . Should I pray harder? . . . Read the Bible? I floundered; I was so confused I didn't know what to do. Yet the phrase kept coming back to me ". . . all things are possible."

Then the magazine came—an issue of *Guideposts*, with a cover story about a cancer victim. She, too, was sent home to die—just like me. But she refused to die. Instead she began to read and reread about the healings of Jesus in the New Testament. She prayed constantly. She went to God determined that He was going to heal her. "Most of the time," she said, "we knock on the door so timidly, and open it just a little crack. We really don't expect God to reply."

Wasn't that what I was doing? Wasn't I knocking timidly? Should I knock more boldly, like the woman in that story?

In the same issue of that magazine, there was the story about a seriously wounded soldier who recovered by creating mental pictures of himself as a healthy, whole individual. The soldier also went to Jesus with utter confidence. He trusted the words of Jesus Christ that "whatever you ask in prayer, believe that you have received it, and it will be yours" (Mark 11:24, RSV).

For the next three days I spent all my waking hours reading and rereading those two articles. I read them a dozen times—three dozen times. I saturated my consciousness until the details of what these two people had done became part of me. The thing that both of them had in common was a simple, childlike trust that God loved them and would heal them. I decided that I was going to believe the same way they did. Right there in our living room, while Bess was clattering about in the kitchen and the TV was blaring with the noise of a game show, I bowed my head.

"God," I said with conviction. "I am knocking on the door. I am here before You to say that I know without any doubt in the world that You are going to heal me."

Don't ask me to explain, but in that one incredible moment, the door swung open. For the first time in my life, God was close to me. He was at my elbow, literally. He was there. And for the first time in prayer I felt as if I was talking to Somebody, not just to myself. A deep joy stirred within me.

"Bess! Bess!" I called out. Bess came running. I wanted to tell her what had happened, but I didn't have the words yet.

"Yes, Harry? What's the matter?"

"I'm hungry," I said.

She looked at me peculiarly. "Would you like a cup of tea?"

"No." I said, "I want food." At first she thought I was kidding. I hadn't asked for anything in over four weeks. So she kidded back. "Well, why don't I run out and get you a nice big submarine sandwich?"

"Fine," I said with a grin.

And Bess did just that. She ran out and bought a sandwich of ham and cheese and tomato and lettuce and watched in astonishment as I ate every crumb of it—with gusto. She was only a bit less surprised when I ate a complete breakfast the next morning, after my first full night's sleep in bed in weeks, and then took a walk—just a short one.

For the first two days after I found God, I prayed, not in the old, stilted, self-conscious, unbelieving way, but in my new informal faith way. I prayed as I walked, I prayed while I sat in my easy chair, and I prayed when I went to bed. I was having a non-stop conversation with God, in Whom I now believed and trusted with all my heart.

On the third day, like the soldier in the story, I began to picture my healing with images just as clear as if they were coming in on our TV screen. I could see an army of white blood cells, led by Jesus Christ, sweeping down from my shoulders into my stomach, swirling around in my bladder, battling their way into my liver, my heart. Regiment after regiment they came, endlessly, the white corpuscles moving relentlessly on the cancer cells, moving in and devouring them! On and on the victorious white army swept, down into my legs and feet and toes, then to the top of my body, mopping up stray cancer cells as they went, until, at last, the battle was over and Jesus Christ stood in triumph.

Day after day I replayed that battle scene in my mind. It made me feel terrific. I felt full of health. My energy returned dramatically. I walked, drove my car, played eighteen holes of golf and walked all the way. I dutifully went through with my chemotherapy treatments, but more to please Bess and my doctor than myself.

Six months later, I went back to my original doctor for an examination. He seemed surprised to see me looking so healthy and well.

I tried to prepare him. "Look. Doc," I said, "you're not going to find a thing. Believe me. I'm all better!"

Smiling indulgently he replied, "Well, Harry . . . let's take a look anyway, shall we?"

He performed several tests and found that the malignant mass behind the bladder had disappeared. Everything seemed to be normal. The doctor was astounded but, nevertheless, cautious.

"Harry," he said, "'the only way we can prove conclusively that you're free of cancer is to do another exploratory. But you look so healthy we're not about to do that. We'll keep an eye on you, but it looks very good."

That was over a year ago, and today I feel fit as a fiddle. So I continue to live in a state of amazement. I'm amazed at His love. I'm amazed at His closeness. I'm amazed that it's all so simple, while I've spent my life making it so complicated. Jesus told us the way to be healed—simply, powerfully, in two words, " . . . only believe."

When I saw him, I fell at his feet as though dead. Then he placed his right hand on me and said: "Do not be afraid. I am the First and the Last. I am the Living One; I was dead, and behold I am alive for ever and ever! And I hold the keys of death and Hades."

REVELATION 1:17 (NIV)

Is That You, Lord?

The power of visualization in prayer has been appreciated at least since Saint Ignatius of Loyola imagined himself as an active participant in scenes of Scripture more than 450 years ago. More recently visualization has become a common tool in psychotherapy; one psychologist called it "directed daydream."

There are two basic ways to pray with images. One is to consciously direct your attention toward a specific goal, as Harry DeCamp did by imagining white blood cells attacking his cancer. Directed imagery can also be used to pray for others. Say you have a friend who is ill. Picture that person bathed in God's healing light. Do the same for someone with whom you're having an argument.

The goal of the Ignatian method of visual prayer is to sink yourself more deeply into Scripture. In his meditation on the birth of Christ, Ignatius imagined himself a slave serving Mary, Joseph, and the baby Jesus soon after Jesus was born. You can use this technique to imagine yourself sitting with the disciples as Jesus delivers the Sermon on the Mount, or praying at the foot of the cross on the day of His crucifixion.

The second basic approach to visualization is more like meditation. The idea is to use images to help you let go of your daily concerns so that you can find the peace of God within you. This approach can also give you insight and healing by allowing hidden images and emotions to surface. One way to do this is to picture a peaceful spot you know of in nature—a favorite beach, perhaps, or a familiar meadow. Imagine yourself walking or sitting there, breathing in the clean air and basking in the sunshine. Simply let yourself be, and let yourself be embraced by the presence of the Holy Spirit. Add other visual elements to the scene, if you wish. Envision Jesus sitting beside you. Imagine talking to loved ones who have passed on. The only limit is your imagination. D.H.

I had mentioned in my introduction to this chapter what I think are the essential points about dreams and visions: They are sources of great spiritual power, and they are deeply mysterious. Sharon Crisafulli's "The Dream" underscores both those points emphatically. Her story also shows that other sources of great spiritual power—namely, prayer and angels—can often work hand in hand with dreams and visions to accomplish miracles.

THE DREAM

—BY SHARON CRISAFULLI—

"Good night, Jason." I leaned down and gently kissed my eight-year-old son's forehead as he snuggled under his comforter. He was wearing his favorite baseball pajamas. His hair, always a little too long, fanned out over the pillow. His eyes were already closed when I turned to leave. But as I was pulling the door shut, he called to me.

"Mom? I just had a dream."

I returned to Jason's bedside. "Honey, you haven't even been to sleep yet. How could you have had a dream?"

"I don't know, Mom. It just came to me right after I said my prayers." His brown eyes held a serious expression. "I was in school, at my desk," he said in a strange, matter-of-fact tone. "All of a sudden, I fell over onto the floor. People were staring at me. I was dead."

I sat with Jason until he fell asleep. His "dream" was disturbing; it seemed more than just a child's imagination.

Several times in my life I'd had similar experiences. I remember suddenly knowing my grandmother would die. Though she appeared to be perfectly healthy, she left us three days later. And I remember being certain a seemingly happy couple were having deep marital difficulties. I don't know how I knew; I just knew. Outwardly, they were the picture of marital bliss. A year later they admitted they had been near divorce at the time.

I went to bed wondering what Jason's dream was all about. *Was it some kind of warning?*

By the following week, however, the incident had been pushed to the back of my mind. Our home in Merritt Island, Florida, was a busy place, and I had plenty of other things to think about. Jason's school activities and caring for Nicole, his lively three-year-old sister, for example.

Then one night a week later, I sat up abruptly in bed, wide awake. It was after midnight, and Jack, my husband, was sleeping soundly. For a moment I thought it was he who had woken me. But before I could give it another thought, I was overwhelmed with the need to pray—to pray for Jason.

As I eased out of bed, I felt tears streaming down my face. I crept into his room and gathered him into my arms. I cradled his warm body against mine as I prayed. I rocked him as I had when he was a baby. Jason slept soundly through it all.

Then it was over. The need to pray ended as suddenly as it had begun.

The next night it happened again—the sudden need to pray for Jason. And again the night after that.

There was a time in my life when I would have felt silly praying the way I did. There was a time when I would have told no one. There was a time when I would have been afraid.

But now I knew it was time to pray, and so I prayed.

By the third morning, my midnight prayers were becoming as predictable as the other routines of my life. As usual, I spent the few minutes before the children woke sipping coffee and savoring the quiet.

Nicole was usually the first to rise. But this morning she was still snoozing even after Jason was up and dressed for school.

It was gloomy and overcast. As I looked out the window, I was seized by a sense of sadness. Even as I made Jason's breakfast, my heart grew heavier by the moment.

I walked Jason to the end of our driveway. Right on time and with a whoosh of air brakes, the school bus pulled to a stop across the street, its red lights flashing.

Jason and I both looked up and down the busy highway. I gave him a quick kiss and he was on his way.

He never made it to the bus. His left foot had barely touched the pavement when a speeding station wagon came from nowhere and slammed into Jason, hurling his body fifteen feet into the air. He came down hard, headfirst.

It all happened so fast. Now, there he was, lying in the middle of the highway.

I fell to my knees beside him. His eyes were rolled back. His tongue was swollen and protruding. In a matter of seconds his right leg had swelled, straining the fabric of his jeans. His left arm was bent at a grotesque angle. I leaned close to his face and realized he wasn't breathing.

"No," I whispered. Then I lifted my head and screamed, "No, no, Lord, You can't let him die!"

A crowd gathered. They were all staring, horror-struck.

"Somebody call an ambulance!" I was amazed at the sudden control in my voice. "And get my husband. He's working in the orange grove down the road."

I bent over Jason and prayed aloud, "Dear God, I know You've raised people from the dead. Please raise up my son!"

I don't know how many people were in the crowd of onlookers, yet in their midst I suddenly felt a distinct presence. I glanced up and found myself looking straight into the eyes of a bearded man standing a few feet away. He had reddish-brown hair and stood relaxed with both hands in his pockets. Though it was only a second or two, it seemed like an eternity before he spoke in a surprisingly soft voice: "I have oxygen in my car."

Moments later the man knelt beside me and gently placed the mask over Jason's face. Almost instantly, Jason gasped and drew a long breath. Weeping with relief, I leaned over and whispered into his ear, "It's okay, Son, just think about Jesus. You're going to be okay."

But when I turned to thank the mysterious stranger, he was gone. And although the road was jammed in both directions, no one saw him leave.

Jason was in the hospital for months. His thigh and arm were broken. He had a severe concussion. But amazingly, there was no permanent damage.

Now, ten years later, I still shudder when I think about what might have happened if I had not heeded those urges to pray, and pray hard. You see, I know that the bearded man who saved Jason's life wasn't just some passing motorist. He was part of something bigger. Something that involved Jason's dream. Something that required my waking three nights in a row to pray for Jason.

That mysterious man was part of a heaven-directed rescue, and he was there in answer to my prayers. ❧

JACOB'S DREAM AT BETHEL
GENESIS 28:10–17 (NIV)

Jacob left Beersheba and set out for Haran. When he reached a certain place, he stopped for the night because the sun had set. Taking one of the stones there, he put it under his head and lay down to sleep. He had a dream in which he saw a stairway resting on the earth, with its top reaching to heaven, and the angels of God were ascending and descending on it. There above it stood the Lord, and he said: "I am the Lord, the God of your father Abraham and the God of Isaac. I will give you and your descendants the land on which you are lying. Your descendants will be like the dust of the earth, and you will spread out to the west and to the east, to the north and to the south. All peoples on earth will be blessed through you and your offspring. I am with you and will watch over you wherever you go, and I will bring you back to this land. I will not leave you until I have done what I have promised you."

When Jacob awoke from his sleep, he thought, "Surely the Lord is in this place, and I was not aware of it." He was afraid and said, "How awesome is this place! This is none other than the house of God; this is the gate of heaven." ❧

·~ CHAPTER EIGHT ~·

GOD SPEAKS TO US...
Through Signs and Coincidences

*W*hat is a sign? I looked it up.

The HarperCollins Bible Dictionary *defines sign as "a significant event, act, or other manifestation that betokens God's presence or intention."*

That's helpful—but what exactly does "betoken" mean?

The American Heritage Dictionary *lists a number of synonyms, including "indicate," "attest," "testify" and "witness." All these verbs, the dictionary said, are meant to imply the existence or presence of something else. A fever betokens illness, for example.*

In short, a sign points us somewhere. It isn't the real thing, exactly, although it may be of the real thing. In any case, it points in the real thing's direction. A parable does that. So does a guidepost.

I also looked up "coincidence."

The American Heritage Dictionary *defines coincidence as "a sequence of events that although accidental seems to have been planned or arranged."*

That definition displays an obvious secular bias. From the point of view of faith, coincidences—at least some coincidences—are not at all accidental. Author Elizabeth Sherrill has described coincidence as "a drum roll from the great conductor." God uses coincidence to get our attention, Sherrill says. Coincidence cries out, Stop! Look! Listen! You, too, have a part in the universal hymn.

Coincidence, then, is a type of sign.

Jesus warned that we shouldn't get too hung up on signs. (See, for example, Matthew 16:4, Mark 8:11–12 and John 4:48.) Faith, after all, is about believing in things unseen. But at the same time the Bible is filled with signs, many of them performed by Jesus Himself.

The reason for this seeming contradiction, I think, is clear. We humans spend a lot of time and energy worrying about the future, which in itself displays a lack of faith. Consequently we tend to become obsessed with trying to read signs that will tell us which way the wind is about to blow. That's a trap that can lead us in the wrong direction, into superstition and away from God. The signs to take note of are those that point toward God. Such signs point toward confidence in the ultimate security of God's loving grace, and toward acceptance of His will.

As we will see in this chapter, signs that are truly of the Spirit tend to encourage as well as guide. The arrow points up.

At a Crossroad
—By Irma Burrill—

I couldn't bear the thought of leaving California. After twenty-two years of being moved all around the country, I felt we'd found a home in Merced. Now my husband Chuck had retired from the Air Force and was planning to settle us back in Illinois, where we'd both grown up. He felt we should be near our families. I felt we'd put down new roots right where we were; our home, our church and our friends were in California.

For weeks I had been struggling with the decision as I ferried children about in my job as an elementary school bus driver. That was another thing: I loved my job, I loved the kids and I even loved the big yellow school bus. So, as the final day of school drew near, I began to wish I hadn't agreed to move, and I pleaded with God: Please change Chuck's mind.

But Chuck's mind was made up. And before I knew it, the last day of school arrived—my last day as a bus driver.

"Well, this is it, Lord," I whispered that afternoon as I prepared for the routine safety check, I slipped the rubber mallet out of its boot and gave the old bus an affectionate pat on the side as I circled around, thumping each of the tires to check for proper inflation. Then I climbed onto the driver's seat, ready to pick up the kids for the last time.

And all the while I prayed, "Lord, I still don't want to leave all this, but You haven't told me what You want."

So far He hadn't answered.

As I sat waiting for school to let out, I kept mulling over all the reasons for staying. Our three boys had so taken to life in California. They had paper routes, girlfriends, a pet desert tortoise. I thought of the good times we'd had overhauling motorcycles on the living room carpet and sleeping on the roof of our station wagon to study the stars.

The people at church were like family. The church nursery had been my second home for several years, and the Bible study I was in seemed tailor-made for me. And Chuck, why, he was a trustee, a deacon, an usher—he'd even helped put a roof on the church.

"Bus driver," came a child's timid voice, "would you like some candy?" I looked down to see a grubby hand shoving a dripping glob of melted chocolate toward me. I gulped. I'd learned a long time ago that to refuse would be to break a little one's heart.

"Thank you, Maria." I said, smiling as I scooped up the brown mass from the grimy palm. Her face beamed as I poured it into my mouth.

How I loved these little guys and gals, with their jars of caterpillars and ladybugs, the limp roses and half-eaten apples, the hugs, the tears, the nosebleeds, the "Tie my shoe" and "Gee, bus driver, you're older'n my dad!"

As I drove down Bear Creek Drive, I thought of the many times I'd asked God to lift my spirits and He'd sent a covey of baby quail scurrying across the highway, or some kit foxes romping on the hills.

I dropped off the last little guy and watched him wave good-bye to me, appearing as downcast as I was. I swallowed hard and shifted into gear. "I know how you feel, little guy," I sighed.

Back at my reserved space in the bus barn, I switched off the engine and sat for a long moment in the driver's seat, fighting back tears. I had to get it over with. I made my last entry in the log book, then picked up the broom and cleaning cloth from the storage chest under the rear seat.

One by one I turned up the seat cushions, picked up debris and wiped the seats clean as I worked my way toward the front of the bus. But all the while, I kept wondering why God had seemed so silent to me. I thought He always answered prayer.

I stooped to pick up a scrap of cardboard, a piece of a jigsaw puzzle that had fallen face down on the floor. *What good is a puzzle with a piece missing?* I mused.

Then I turned it over and caught my breath. Even in the ninety-degree heat I felt goose bumps springing up all over my body. My downcast spirit began to revive. How could I have doubted? God had answered my prayer after all.

For there in the palm of my hand lay a tiny map of the state of Illinois. ❧

Wait on the Lord: be of good courage, and he shall strengthen thine heart.

— Psalm 27:14 (KJV)

A friend who's a recovering alcoholic tells me that acronyms are very popular in Alcoholics Anonymous. HALT reminds newcomers not to get too "hungry, angry, lonely, or tired." FEAR is what you're really feeling when you want to "forget everything and run." KISS stands for "Keep it simple, stupid."

Although He is a little more gentle in His delivery, sometimes I think God follows the KISS formula because He so often makes use of signs that are literally signs, and obvious ones at that. Not that being obvious makes them any less glorious.

Here is a quartet of short stories on that theme.

A SIGN OF PEACE
—BY BETH SWAIN—

Driving down Highway 22, I grumbled to God. Why had He handed me so much to do and too little time to do it? Then I noticed a dusty old camper in front of me with a cardboard sign taped to the back door: "Only By His Grace." I thought of the many good things in my life, and my stress level dropped. The next day, however, I was back to complaining as I darted through traffic. Then, right in front of me, was the very same camper! The driver was probably thinking, "How long, Lord, must I travel this route before that lady gets Your message?" ✎

A SIGN OF ASSURANCE
—BY BARBARA HAMLIN—

Some years ago my mother was hospitalized because of a severe allergic reaction to a commonly prescribed antibiotic. While she was recovering I stayed with her at night so my father could get some sleep.

Restless, uncomfortable, Mom kept waking up. "Can I go home now?" she would ask anxiously. "No, Mom," I replied, struggling to find some words of comfort.

At two o'clock one morning, I walked to the window and gazed down at the nearly deserted parking lot. It had been snowing all evening. Orange streetlights cast an amber glow on a thick blanket of white. A man emerged from the employee exit and walked to one of the two cars that remained. Bundled up in a long overcoat and a hat with earflaps, he began brushing snow from his windshield. Then he started walking around in the snow.

"Mom," I said, "there's a man down in the parking lot. He's making letters in the snow with his feet."

"What's he writing?" she asked groggily.

Slowly I read each letter aloud: first a *G*, then *O* and *D*. And as I deciphered the words I realized I was seeing the message I most needed to receive, and the one I most wanted to give. All night I repeated those words to Mom whenever she woke up, and every time she smiled softly and went to sleep again.

The words in the snow? GOD LOVES YOU. ✎

A S I G N O F P R O T E C T I O N
— B y D o r o t h y S. P r e s l e y —

"I saw your sign and must talk to your pastor," the distraught young woman said as she entered our church office. She had noticed the message on our letter-board outside, which read, "Give God Time."

Our pastor sat down with the woman and prayed with her. She was worried about her eighteen-month-old son who was in the intensive care unit. Only later did I discover why the sign meant so much to her. The *e* at the end of *Time* was missing. The message received by that young mother was "Give God Tim."

Her son's name? Tim, of course. ❧

A S I G N O F S E C U R I T Y
— B y D o r o t h y N i c h o l a s —

We were sitting at the table in our Florida home and talking to our next-door neighbors. This young couple had helped us a lot in the past year and a half, after my stroke and my husband's leg injury.

Unexpectedly, the husband began telling us the story of his troubled past. At age sixteen he'd fallen in with the wrong crowd in his hometown of Greenwood, South Carolina, and had spent a year in a reformatory. When he was released he'd had good intentions, but because of his record, he couldn't find a job.

He became desperate and decided to rob a local service station so he could have enough money to leave the state. He stole his father's car and gun and just before closing time, drove up to the service window of a gasoline station. He was about to demand all the money from the woman manager.

"But just then," he explained, "I looked up and saw the sign overhead. It read, 'God Is Our Security Guard—Always on the Job.' And I knew I couldn't rob that place. I then rushed home and prayed all night. I was determined to get my life straightened out. And with God's help, I did."

As he finished, I looked at my husband. Both of us remembered a night thirteen years ago when I sat at our kitchen table in the same town of Greenwood, South Carolina, trying to make a sign for our business. I had scribbled down several words. Then finally it came, the slogan that my husband put on the sign that stood on the roof of the small service station that we managed:

God Is Our Security Guard—Always on the Job. ❦

> Signs are given to us because God meets us on the level where we operate. . . . In guidance when God shows us a sign, it doesn't mean we have received the final answer. A sign means we're on the way.
>
> BOB MUMFORD

One of the glories of God's guidance is the infinite number of ways He reaches us. It is a measure of the depths of our human frailty, I suppose, that we need His guidance in so many ways!

This thought struck me as I was comparing our next story, "Love in Another Land" by Terry Kennedy, to the first story in this chapter, "At a Crossroad" by Irma Burrill.

Irma Burrill was looking for reassurance that a planned move was in accordance with God's will. She was insecure about a decision that had been made. Terry Kennedy, by contrast, was insecure about a decision that hadn't been made. She knew something was wrong in her life, but she wasn't sure exactly what it was, which meant she also didn't know how to fix it.

In both cases, signs appeared, pointing the way.

LOVE IN ANOTHER LAND
—BY TERRY KENNEDY—

On a muggy March afternoon in Bangalore, India, I settled into the back of a cab. It had been a hectic day of meetings, wrapping up production on my company's latest book. In my mind I ran over the options for passing the time till my last appointment—from getting a massage to going window-shopping.

I had come to India in early 1995, looking for a fresh start after a painful divorce. I settled in a small village in the south and built a successful book-production and video-production business called Tiger Moon. Still, my life felt busy but not full. Somewhere in the midst of running the fast track, careerwise, and struggling through my marital problems I had lost a sense of God's presence in my life. I felt numb and disconnected. During the two years since I made my journey halfway around the world I had visited religious sites and read spiritual books, but I had yet to undergo the transformation I had hoped for.

"Where to, *memsab*?" the cab driver asked.

I looked out the window, my eye caught by a little girl in a faded green dress limping among the passersby asking for change. Suddenly I was very conscious of my designer suit, my gold necklace, the expensive perfume on my wrists. Tomorrow I would be headed to more meetings, and she would be begging for more coins in order to eat. And there were so many other children like her here, so many hands held out to me every day that I saw them even in my dreams.

"Ma'am, where to?" the driver repeated, drawing me out of my reverie.

I asked him for suggestions and he made several—a park, an outdoor bazaar, a first-rate beauty salon. But somehow none of those, which ordinarily would have been tempting, appealed to me.

"No, no." I shook my head. "Something different."

"There's an orphanage not far from here. I visit sometimes to play with the kids."

Not more sad faces and empty hands, I thought. Yet I felt strangely drawn to the idea. Somehow it seemed the right choice. I nodded to the driver.

We drove up to a small stucco building surrounded by colorful bougainvilleas, marigolds and geraniums. I could hear the laughter of children. The driver waved to two nuns in tan habits, who were pruning the flowers. I paid him and emerged into the sharp sunlight, squinting to make out the words on the wooden sign in front. Jyothi Seva, it read. As

I came closer I could pick out some words of the nuns' conversation. *Was it Polish they were speaking? But how . . . ?*

After we made introductions, Sisters Adella and Agata explained the name Jyothi Seva means "service of light." "We are called the Servants of the Cross," Sister Agata said, wiping her spectacles on the generous folds of her robe. "Our founder was from Poland. After she lost her sight she dedicated her life to helping blind orphans."

My mother was Polish and, though I was born in the United States, Polish was my first language. It seemed more than mere coincidence. *Maybe God has led me here,* I thought suddenly.

The sisters took me inside the building and up to a group of children, most of them blind, some with other disabilities. *Poor little dears,* I thought, feeling awkward. *What am I doing here?* A girl with one leg shorter than the other hobbled up to me and gave me a salute. Her chapped lips cracked into a faint smile. I smiled back and patted her head softly.

"That's Manjulka. She's a little mother to the younger children," said Sister Adella. The girl couldn't speak or hear and could hardly see, but the warmth she exuded was almost palpable.

"And this is Martushka, our songbird," said Sister Agata, bringing before me a small girl who was dressed all in yellow. "Will you sing for the nice lady, sweetheart?"

Martushka looked up toward my face with her opaque eyes. "If you're happy and you know it, clap your hands," she began in a clear, high voice, clapping her hands lightly. Immediately, the other children joined in.

As they sang, Sister Adella leaned over to whisper in my ear. "Isn't she a treasure? She was abandoned in a rubbish heap as an infant. When we found her she was so malnourished her eyesight couldn't be saved. But what a voice God gave her!"

I nodded. I thought of the beggar girl on the street. At least these children had one another and the nuns to care for them.

"How do you look after them all?" I asked Sister Adella.

"It's not easy. There are almost thirty now and only eight of us to run the home and teach them."

"Would a donation help?" I asked, digging for my checkbook.

"You are very kind," Sister Adella replied, "but the truth is we have plenty of wheelchairs and not enough people to push them. Every day we pray for new postulants to commit their lives to these children, to take our place when we're gone."

The children finished the song and Sister Adella led them into the front courtyard to play with a few old dolls and toy cars she carried. Meanwhile, Manjulka stayed inside and entertained Nila, a severely retarded toddler, with a hand-puppet show.

"See what we meant about being a little mother," Sister Agata said, smiling. "She also loves to hold Tomak here," she continued, picking up a boy the size of an infant. "Maybe you would too," she said, holding out the child to me.

Wrapped in a white blanket, Tomak looked as delicate as a snowflake. I hesitated. "Go on," she urged. *You have a meeting to go to*, I reminded myself. But then the boy was in my arms. I cradled his head in my palm, and found myself staring deeply into his huge eyes. He made soft mewling noises as I rocked him gently back and forth. A peaceful feeling came over me.

Sister Agata went outside to join the children, and I lost track of time. Holding Tomak seemed like the most natural thing in the world. Then I felt a tug at my sleeve. Manjulka stood beside me, beckoning me outside. I gently put Tomak back in his crib, and Manjulka and I walked out together into the fading light. Again the children broke into song. They swept toward me, reaching out to touch my skirt, my hair, my face. Manjulka did a little dance. And at that moment I saw there was nothing pitiful or sad about these children after all—they were filled with the joy they were singing about.

I bent down to hug Agni and Faru. Prithwi tugged at my earrings and giggled. I looked into each of their faces and saw a love I had never known before—boundless, transforming love.

"If you're happy and you know it, laugh out loud." And I laughed, even as Prithwi wiped away the tears streaming down my cheeks, because I too, perhaps for the first time, was truly happy.

I never did make my meeting that day. God had scheduled a more important one, to show me I needed only to reach out to feel connected to others—and to Him. "Auntie, will you come again?" Shakuntala asked. Yes, I would. And I did, again and again, eagerly clasping the hands that used to haunt me in dreams.

A year after I first walked through the gates of Jyothi Seva orphanage, my priorities have changed. I'm always on the lookout for medical equipment that can help the children. And I donate a portion of the profits from my business to that effort. Thanks to surgery, some of the children now have their sight. They occasionally stay with me before hospital visits, and when I travel with them to the ophthalmologist, the fields of rice, the rows of eucalyptus, the open-faced sunflowers all seem more exquisite, reflected in their eyes. At last, I've truly begun a new life, far from home, but always close to God. ❧

"This will be a sign to you: You will find a baby wrapped in cloths and lying in a manger."

LUKE 2:12 (NIV)

Is That You, Lord?

As I mentioned in the introduction to this chapter, watching for signs from God is fine as long as it doesn't become a preoccupation. The recent outbreak of End Times Fever is a case in point. There are people who seem to spend more time looking for signs that the Rapture is upon us than they do going to church, or serving others, or praying. That's a distortion.

Probably the most common error when it comes to spiritual discernment is overspecificity. By that I mean that too often people look to God for very specific answers to very specific questions. It's true that amazingly specific signs do sometimes appear—most of the stories in this chapter are accounts of just such incidences. But to postpone a decision waiting for such a miracle would be a mistake, and a setup for wishful thinking.

People often see signs because they want to see them: A man thinks he can read the word "go" written in the clouds and changes careers; a woman reads a Scripture passage that tells her she should say "yes" to a proposal of marriage. These are examples of what the well-known pastor Charles Swindoll has called "voodoo theology." God leads through *general principles*, Swindoll says. It is up to us to prayerfully apply these general principles to our lives in order to find the answers to our specific questions. D.H.

The apostle Paul was an extremely eloquent man, but nowhere was he more eloquent than in his comments to the Corinthians on the qualities of love. You know the passage, I'm sure, but it bears repeating:

"Love is patient, love is kind. It does not envy, it does not boast, it is not proud. It is not rude, it is not self-seeking, it is not easily angered, it keeps no record of wrongs. Love does not delight in evil but rejoices with the truth. It always protects, always trusts, always hopes, always perseveres" (1 Corinthians 13:4–8, NIV).

It's that quality of perseverance I find especially striking in relation to our subject here. Love often makes use of both signs and coincidence in order to transcend the usual constraints of time and space. There are countless examples; two of them follow.

A BABY NAMED BRIAN
—BY LYNDA JAMISON—

I couldn't wait to have a baby of my own. My husband Bob and I had been trying since we got married a year earlier. Meanwhile, I was volunteering at an adoption home where I helped look after hundreds of babies who were waiting for permanent families.

I cared about all of them, but one blond boy named Brian stole my heart. Brian was underweight and cried all the time. Most of the staff members could do nothing to comfort him, but in my arms, he was calm and quiet. Only there could he fall asleep.

It was obvious Brian would need a very special home. A big part of me wanted that home to be with Bob and me, but the timing was wrong. I heard a family was ready to adopt Brian at about the same time I found out I was pregnant. *Let him be going to good people who'll love him as much as I do*, I prayed, when I said good-bye to Brian.

I gave birth to a son and another soon after. With each of their milestones—first step, first word, first day of school—my thoughts turned to Brian. I could only pray he was doing as well. After seven years, I could still see his sweet face clearly in my mind.

One evening my husband and I were invited to have dinner at the home of a couple we had met through a prayer network, and whom we hoped to get to know better. Paul and Maggie invited us in, and I looked around their beautiful home. My eye fell on a baby picture hanging on the wall. I gasped. "That's Brian!"

Maggie came over to my side. "That's our son, Christopher," she said, nodding at the picture. "But he was called Brian when we adopted him. How could you have known that?"

I poured out my story. Then a blond boy in pajamas padded into the room. The baby who couldn't stop crying had grown into a boy with an irresistible smile. In an instant he was in my arms again.

Paul and Maggie became our dearest friends and Christopher like another son to me. I sang at his wedding, and one year later, I held his new baby in my arms. ❧

Faith is the assurance of things hoped for, the conviction of things not seen.

HEBREWS 11:1 (RSV)

MY FATHER'S LOCKET
—BY DONNA BOSMAN—

My husband Harvey and I were visiting Ashland, Wisconsin, when I spotted a secondhand store. I coaxed Harvey into going inside with me. He didn't have much patience for antique shopping, but I loved poking around old shops, looking for that unexpected treasure. My eyes took in the clutter—a monogrammed silver baby cup, a guitar with no strings, a wedding dress that was advertised as "never used"—while Harvey stood near the door, waiting.

I was drawn to a glass case filled with beautiful old jewelry—rings, bracelets, brooches and a small gold locket. It took me back to when I was young and my father was frequently away on business. He always brought home a few little gifts. Once he returned from a long sales trip with a gold locket for Mom and, as always, a big hug for me.

That was long ago. Mom was gone and Dad had died twenty years back. Toward the end of his life Dad and I had a terrible disagreement. We never patched things up. If only I'd had one last chance to say I loved him, to feel his arms around me. I often told myself that there was no reason to cling to this sadness. Just as often, I'd find myself asking God for assurance that somehow my father had not died thinking I didn't love him.

"Could I see that locket?" I said to the sales clerk. He took it from the case and I ran my thumb over its surface, worn smooth by the years. I started to open it when I heard Harvey clear his throat. "How much?" I asked the clerk quickly. "Ten dollars," he said.

"I'll take it," I replied, tugging a ten-dollar bill from my purse. "Just a second, dear," I said to Harvey. The clerk smiled as he put the locket back in its box and handed it to me. "Enjoy."

In the car I finally got a chance to examine the locket. I clicked it open with a fingernail and gasped at what I saw: a tiny black-and-white photo of my father that he'd given to my mother years ago. It was the very same locket I remembered. A gift that expressed his love all the more the second time around.

> Every happening, great and small, is a parable whereby God speaks to us, and the art of life is to get the message.
>
> Malcolm Muggeridge

So far in this chapter we've been talking of signs on a relatively small scale: road signs, an old locket, a lost piece from a child's puzzle. The meaning of these objects was magnified tremendously when they became vehicles of the Holy Spirit. There are no small miracles.

Still, on the scale of signs God has been known to unleash, they remain fairly modest. Jesus Christ, for example, is a sign from God, a signification of His infinite love for His creatures. According to

Luke, Christ's birth was announced by a multitude of the heavenly host, an event that declared that the birth of a baby in a manger was worthy of special attention. An empty tomb represented that Christ had risen. These are major-league signs. They signify the most profound tenets of our faith.

Among Christian signs, probably none is more meaningful than the Cross. Indeed, the Cross is at the very center of the greatest of all dramas, the role that Jesus played in reconciling God to humankind. The Cross has also come to represent our faith that, through Christ, life and love will triumph over death and despair. The Cross stands for hope. It stands for resurrection.

Our last two stories in this chapter speak movingly to that theme.

TRANSFORMED
—BY REBECCA ASHBURN—

Easter morning I woke to the shrill ring of my alarm clock. I hit the off switch and sank back on my pillow. Outside my window, the whole world seemed to sing of spring. Except me, I thought. Even though it had been a while since my divorce, I couldn't seem to get past it. Would I ever feel joyous again?

"Mama, get up!" my seven-year-old daughter Elise cried, jumping on my bed. "We have to get to church!"

That was exactly what I was dreading. There had been too many reminders of my marriage at our old church, so Elise and I joined a new one. She'd adjusted fine but I felt out of place there, as I did pretty much everywhere since the divorce. I knew seeing the rest of the congregation at Easter service with their families would only remind me how I'd failed with my own. At least put on a happy face for Elise, I told myself as I climbed out of bed.

"All right, sweetie, let's get dressed."

Twenty minutes later, Elise was standing by the door, holding three drooping daffodils, the stems wrapped carefully in a damp paper towel. Her Sunday school teacher had asked the class to bring flowers to church for the Easter Cross, and yesterday Elise had found three lonely daffodils poking out of the soil in our yard. She'd picked them right then and there. "I was afraid we'd forget later," she'd said. Now Elise smiled at me from the doorway. "Don't my flowers look great, Mama?" she asked.

At church, Elise presented her three bedraggled blooms to the women in charge of decorating the Easter cross. They were busy arranging the children's flowers, most as sorry-looking as Elise's, in the holes of the chicken wire covering the rough wooden cross. To me, the whole thing looked as if it didn't belong in church any more than I did.

I took my seat just as organ music signaled the beginning of the procession. I turned to watch Elise walk down the aisle with the other kids when I caught sight of the cross. One large, red poppy rested at the center and daffodils and narcissus radiated out in gorgeous waves of gold and white, sprinkled with lilac, japonica and forsythia. The effect was stunning. All those wilted flowers together created a transformation. Each had its place in the cross. I looked at Elise. She was beaming. And for the first time in many months, I felt a joyous smile blossoming on my own face too.

For the message of the cross is foolishness to those who are perishing, but to us who are being saved it is the power of God.

1 C O R I N T H I A N S   1 : 18   (N I V)

T H E   C R O S S   A T   G R O U N D   Z E R O
— B Y   F R A N K   S I L E C C H I A —

I'm an excavation laborer, and a member of union local 731. Pick-and-shovel work is my trade. I live in New Jersey, but I'm a New York City native, Brooklyn born and bred. After the Towers collapsed, my city was hurting. When I heard they needed guys like me for search-and-rescue work at Ground Zero, I couldn't get there fast enough.

I'd seen the news coverage, but that didn't prepare me for the reality. Down there it was like hell on earth. Fires burned out of control. Destroyed vehicles littered the streets. Everything was blanketed with dust; the air was filled with a choking stench. I soaked a bandanna with water before wrapping it around my head to cover my nose and mouth. I went to work wondering if I'd be able to get through this.

Six firefighters and I entered Six World Trade Center, which had been flattened by Tower One. We took a smoke-filled stairway down into the garage levels, searching for survivors. There were no cries for help, no signs of life. We spray-painted orange Xs to indicate where we'd searched and to help us find our way back.

After twelve hours of searching, we'd recovered three bodies. By then I was exhausted, but I couldn't quit. "Think I'll take a look over there," I told the firemen, motioning toward the remains of the lobby atrium.

Picking my way through the massive piles of debris, I peered into what had become a sort of grotto. Illuminated by the pale light of dawn were shapes . . . crosses. What? How did these get here? The largest was about twenty feet high. It must have weighed a couple of tons.

In that little grotto I felt a strange sense of peace and stillness. I could almost hear God saying: The terrible thing done at this site was meant for evil. But I will turn it to good. Have faith. I am here. I fell to my knees in front of the largest cross. Tears came, and I couldn't stop them. I cried like a baby. Finally I was able to pull myself together. I grabbed my gear and left the strange grotto to go back to search-and-rescue work. But first I spray-painted "God's House" on the atrium ruins.

Digging day after day at Ground Zero was the hardest work I'd ever done. Often I was so drained I felt I couldn't go on. That's when I'd go to God's House. Standing there in front of that twenty-foot-high steel-beam cross, I always felt my strength and spirit renewed.

Word spread. The cross had the same healing effect on others too. Firemen, police, volunteers, grieving survivors, visiting dignitaries and clergy. They would walk into God's House, see the cross and fall to their knees crying, like I had. Some people sang, some prayed. Everyone left changed.

There are some who say that the cross I found is nothing more than steel. That it was just plain physics that broke the steel beam into the shape of a cross when it plunged through the roof of the building. But I believe differently.

So does my friend Father Brian Jordan. He was a chaplain at Ground Zero, and is a priest at St. Francis of Assisi in midtown. When the time came for what was left of the building to be removed, God's House faced demolition. Father Jordan talked to officials and persuaded them to save the cross. After it was removed from the site, ironworkers fixed the cross to a concrete base, then hoisted it up and mounted it atop a forty-foot foundation that had been a pedestrian walkway outside the World Trade Center. It stood high enough that the rescue workers who were down in the pit could see it whenever they lifted their heads.

Ground Zero was not obviously a place of hope. But it was there that I learned we can always have faith. In fact, we must have faith if we are to go on. New life will rise from the ashes. I know that because the cross was a sign, a promise from God that He is with us even in the face of terrible evil and untold suffering.

Especially then. ❧

If you carry the cross willingly, it will carry you.

THOMAS À KEMPIS

GIDEON ASKS FOR A SIGN
JUDGES 6:36–40 (CEV)

Gideon prayed to God, " I know that you promised to help me rescue Israel, but I need proof. Tonight I'll put some wool on the stone floor of that threshing-place over there. If you really will help me rescue Israel, then tomorrow morning let there be dew on the wool, but let the stone floor be dry."

And that's just what happened. Early the next morning, Gideon got up and checked the wool. He squeezed out enough water to fill a bowl. But Gideon prayed to God again. "Don't be angry at me," Gideon said. "Let me try this just one more time, so I'll really be sure you'll help me. Only this time, let the wool be dry and the stone floor be wet with dew."

That night, God made the stone floor wet with dew, but he kept the wool dry. ❧

CHAPTER NINE

GOD SPEAKS TO US...
By Opening and Closing Doors

I admit I have control issues, which is another way of saying I
have faith issues.

I like everything to go smoothly, according to plan. That's why
I'm a nervous traveler: There are just too many opportunities for
things to go wrong. I find flying, in particular, an ordeal. During takeoffs, I tend to grip the arm rests, as if I could steer the plane with
them, should it turn out the pilot needs assistance.

Henri Nouwen wrote a beautiful little book on prayer called With
Open Hands. The title refers to the posture of surrender with which,
on our better days, we turn ourselves over to our Creator. "To pray
means to open your hands before God," Nouwen said. "It means
slowly relaxing the tension which squeezes your hands together and
accepting your existence with an increasing readiness."

This, you will note, is the opposite of the posture I assume on
takeoffs.

We can open our hands in faith as we embark on all sorts of jour-
neys. As we go through our lives, God directs us along the paths—
inner as well as outer—He would have us follow. Sometimes He does

this by creating opportunities. Other times He does this by closing opportunities off.

It is often easier to see in retrospect than it is at the moment just how thoroughly our lives have been shaped by the opportunities God has presented or withheld. It also becomes obvious with distance how seldom we've followed the itineraries we ourselves had planned. I'm sure there are people whose lives have progressed pretty much along the lines they expected. Mine has not.

The personal stories in this chapter are accounts of what might be called the grace of the opening and closing door, told by people who walked—sometimes boldly, sometimes reluctantly—toward the destinations God offered. We begin with Carol Osman Brown's "A New Point of View," a wonderful tale of discovery in the unexpected, written by a woman who seems to be about as comfortable traveling as I am.

A NEW POINT OF VIEW
—BY CAROL OSMAN BROWN—

No problema.

That's what the Alitalia airline official kept saying as he scurried between the busy ticket agents and the impatient passengers waiting in line at John F. Kennedy International Airport in New York City. But as far as I could see, there was a big *problema*. On the departure board a yellow light flashed insistently: My flight to Rome was leaving—without me!

Months ago, with great excitement, I'd signed up to be part of a church-sponsored medical mission to Kenya. I'd always dreamed of going to Africa, and now was my chance. My husband, though, was more cautious. "It's a long trip," he said. "A lot could go wrong. It might even be dangerous." Nonetheless, he agreed to take over my university teaching duties for the three weeks I'd be gone, and I set about planning my travel itinerary to the last detail.

I'd fly, along with two women from Phoenix, to Kennedy Airport, where we'd catch the night flight to Rome and link up with some other members of our group. Then from Rome, we'd all travel together on the last leg of our trip to Nairobi. Even my husband breathed a sigh of relief—things were set to go like clockwork.

But the clock malfunctioned right from the beginning. The flight we took out of Phoenix was late arriving in New York. My travel companions and I made a mad dash to the international terminal, but by the time we converged on the Alitalia check-in desk, the flight for Rome was in its final stages of departure and we weren't allowed to board.

"You go to Milano instead," the agent announced jovially, punching at some computer keys to change our tickets. "In Milano, there you get a plane for Rome."

We staggered warily aboard the flight for Milan and dropped into our seats. As the engines roared for takeoff, I looked across the aisle. Row after row of passengers were murmuring in Italian and crossing themselves. What did they know that we didn't? What else was going to go wrong? I tried my best to think positively, but my anxiety about this trip was mounting by the minute. I sighed and dropped off into a night of fitful sleep.

It was around eight o'clock on a Sunday morning when the three of us disembarked in Milan. Weary and wrinkled, my companions and I stood blinking in the quiet corridors of the airport, at this time nearly deserted. How soon would our flight to Rome be leaving? "Not long," the Alitalia agent told us. "*Quattro ore.*" When I looked at him blankly, he translated: "Four hours."

I groaned out loud. By now my enthusiasm had totally disintegrated. My best-laid plans had been disrupted, and it seemed to me our whole expedition was in jeopardy. Would the others in Rome know to wait for us? Why had I even wanted to go on this trip? My dream was turning into a nightmare. It probably served me right for thinking I could have this kind of adventure in the first place.

Seething with frustration, I paced up and down, then whirled to face my companions. "I can't stand sitting around," I burst out. "Let's pool our money for a taxi and go into Milan."

We found the main entrance and piled into a taxi. "*Dove?*" the driver asked. "Where to?"

I didn't know a thing about Milan, and we didn't have a guidebook. But I spied a map sticking out of the back pocket of the driver's seat.

Unfolding it, I scanned a maze of streets and minuscule names in Italian until my eye fell on a name I recognized—Leonardo da Vinci. As we hurtled along the expressway, through the countryside of northern Italy, I leaned up to the driver and pointed at that patch on the map.

"Take us there," I said.

For some forty-five minutes we drove through the outlying suburbs into the city, the three of us in the backseat trying to figure out how to say something sensible in Italian. Then the driver turned off the main road, slowed down and maneuvered the cab through a winding passageway.

In an instant I felt as if I'd stepped back in time. We threaded our way through a web of narrow cobblestone streets lined with ancient buildings. The early morning sun cast wavering patches of light on red tile roofs and aging walls; we passed under encrusted grillwork and through worn portals that had clearly been there for centuries.

And then the taxi stopped. Apparently we'd arrived at our destination. "*Ecco!*" the driver said, pointing across a courtyard. "There!"

We gazed out at a small but majestic church made of weathered brick and terra cotta, with a beautiful curved dome. As we stepped out of the taxi, we saw that a plaque in the courtyard wall read Piazza Santa Maria delle Grazie.

After exchanging gestures that we hoped meant our driver would wait for us, we crossed to the church, our footsteps echoing on the worn piazza tiles. Nowhere did we see a sign indicating anything about Leonardo da Vinci. In the isolation and quiet of the early morning, feeling ill at ease in an unfamiliar situation, I wondered once again: *What have I got myself into?*

And then I turned and saw some people walking toward the stone building next to the north side of the church. "It must be the refectory," one of my companions said, "the dining hall where the monks ate." Hesitantly, we walked over and tried the door. To our surprise, it opened.

We walked down a chilly corridor, to where a woman sat in the gray light selling tickets. Six thousand lira, she requested—about four dollars and fifty cents. Since we'd come all this way, why not? We paid and stepped inside a dim and somewhat dingy stone room.

And then I caught my breath, unable to believe what I saw. Covering the entire length of the far wall was a fresco I had seen countless times as a reproduction. But I never imagined I would be standing in front of the original, and that it would have such a powerful impact on me.

I was staring up in astonishment at *The Last Supper,* the fifteenth-century masterpiece painted by Leonardo da Vinci.

Although the room itself was dark, the painting was glowingly illuminated by a few lights and the small windows above it. Somehow it seemed that Jesus and His disciples were actually present in the room, seated at a table perhaps thirty feet long, sharing a meal together. In the background of Da Vinci's painting, the windows of the upper room were flung open to show vistas of blue sky, green hills, and sun-warmed houses. In the foreground, because of the artist's amazing use of perspective, the table and the men seated behind it appeared to stand out from the wall, drawing viewers into the drama of the event.

Even though the painting was mottled by patches of deterioration, the body language and facial expressions of the men who sat on both sides of Jesus were full of passion, agitation, sadness, frustration.

The minutes passed as I stood mesmerized. The room was quiet, like a place of worship, and people spoke only in whispers. Slowly, bits of information I'd read came back to me. I remembered that Da Vinci had chosen to visualize the moment just after Christ had announced, "One of you will betray Me." In this work of art, the apostles had pulled back from Jesus in shock and confusion and were huddled together in questioning groups—and Judas, rather than sitting apart, was among them.

And at the very center of the consternation and uncertainty, sitting quietly with His arms outstretched and the palms of His hands resting open on the table, was the figure of Christ. His countenance was calm and His expression gentle but full of strength. And most compelling of all were His eyes; there was no doubt in my mind that they followed me, looking down at me, lovingly, as I moved slowly around the refectory.

The past hours of my own frenzy and stress melted away. What had Jesus said to the disciples at the Last Supper? "I will not leave you comfortless." Those words applied to my own anxieties as well. Somehow it seemed that these words of reassurance uttered centuries ago were meant for me personally. Whatever disruptions—or surprises—the rest of my trip might bring, I knew I could handle them. Because I wasn't the one in charge. If I was willing to travel with faith and a willingness to embrace the unexpected, I would gain far more than could ever be offered by a guidebook and a strict schedule.

It was time to go. We headed back to find our taxi driver, who was indeed still waiting across the square. As we headed through the countryside back to the airport, into my mind came the image of Christ as the peaceful center of Da Vinci's painting. As the peaceful center of any tumult that might disrupt my own life.

Could I handle the ups and downs that were bound to occur with even the best-laid plans?

No problema.

You have enclosed me behind and before,
And laid Your hand upon me.
Such knowledge is too wonderful for me;
It is too high, I cannot attain to it.

PSALM 139:5–6 (NAS)

As Americans we live in a can-do society that celebrates success. Some people say that success is a sign of God's blessing. What's often overlooked is that failure can be a blessing, too. Defeat provides opportunity for reflection on God's purpose for our lives, and for bringing ourselves more closely into line with His will. A closed door can be God's way of leading us to where our true joy lies. As the Apostle Paul wrote, in all things God works for the good of those who love Him (Romans 8:28).

In several passages the Bible likens the purification of the soul to the refinement of precious metals. The dross must be burned away so that, in the end, only gold remains. (See, for example, Zechariah 13:8–9, or Malachi 3:3.) Failure, in this sense, can be a furnace, a cleansing fire. A composer named George Fischoff discovered the truth of this metaphor when his dreams of Broadway success crashed and burned at a theater in New Jersey.

J O U R N E Y T O P R O M I S E D L A N D
— B Y G E O R G E F I S C H O F F —

I knew things had been going wrong, but the phone call told me just how bad they were. It was my lawyer.

"George, I just don't think the Theatre Guild is going to continue with the play. I'm sorry, but *Sayonara* won't make it to Broadway."

Sitting in my bedroom, I couldn't believe what I was hearing. A bin not three feet from the phone contained about thirty rave reviews for the musical production, including one in *The New York Times* that called it a "sumptuous spectacle with soul." But now my lawyer was telling me that the whole thing had fallen apart.

I felt numb as I hung up the phone. How could this have happened? *Sayonara* had been my prize project for more than twenty years. It was based on a James Michener story. Hy Gilbert wrote the lyrics to my music. The show made its debut in 1987 at the famous Paper Mill Playhouse in Millburn, New Jersey, just across the river from Broadway. It looked as if it was headed straight for the Great White Way.

But then trouble began. The cast and crew started to argue with the director. We tried to find a new production team, but Paper Mill wouldn't release the costumes and sets. Finally I had to face reality. *Sayonara* wasn't going to Broadway. It wasn't going anywhere.

Before this, my musical career had been going steadily uphill. Ever since I was a little boy in South Bend, Indiana, I had been interested in making music. From studying classical piano, I switched to Broadway-type tunes and pop singles.

During the sixties I wrote such hits as "98.6" and "Lazy Day." Later I developed a one-man show on the piano and went on tour.

But *Sayonara* had always been my great dream. And now it had collapsed. Why? Why had God allowed this to happen? In my apartment in Rego Park, New York, I mentally wrestled with Him. I had to know if I could ever write music again or if my career was finished.

I was raised a Reform Jew but had never given a great deal of time to prayer or worship. I had always had a love for the Bible, though. Now, in my moment of despair, I turned to it for comfort.

As I read, Proverbs 3:5–6 (KJV) arrested my attention: "Trust in the Lord with all thine heart; and lean not unto thine own understanding. In all thy ways acknowledge Him, and He shall direct thy paths."

It was a familiar passage, but suddenly it seemed to take on new meaning. "In all thy ways acknowledge Him," I read again. I had used my talents to make a lot of money for myself, but how much of this had acknowledged God? Could I put my abilities to work for Him?

As I considered that prospect, an idea came to mind: Maybe a biblical musical would be the answer. I thought of the story of Moses. Such a musical would have an appeal to both Jews and Christians.

Now I had a concept, but I had no idea where to begin. As I studied the books of Moses in the Bible, I found pages and pages of laws and rules of life—not the sort of material that lends itself to catchy tunes!

While I was tussling with this dilemma, I took my wife Gladys to see a student musical revue at Forest Hills High School. Our daughter Lisa was involved with the production, and it promised to be fun.

In the auditorium, relatives and friends of the kids on stage shouted their enthusiasm for virtually every line. Lisa was energetically prompting the young performers from a space in the wings.

Sitting in the audience, I felt totally alone. I was probably the only person there who wasn't having a good time. In fact, I felt miserable. "I've got to get some air," I told Gladys during the intermission.

I walked out of the building into the freezing February night. I had finally hit bottom. All my musical ability seemed to have fizzled out. I wanted to do something for God, but I couldn't even get an idea for one song.

Suddenly, in my mind's eye I saw a Hebrew slave in Egypt crying out for freedom. It was as if I could hear him actually crying, "Oh, my Lord, deliver us from darkness."

That was what I needed. The next morning I sat down at my desk and wrote and scored the first song. The words reflected the despair I had been feeling:

> Oh, my Lord, deliver us
> from darkness.
> Oh, my Lord, deliver us
> from pain
> Will this night of bondage last
> forever?
> Will we ever see the light of
> Your love again?

Now the ideas were flowing. For the next three months I wrote and composed—until I had created a whole production. It was the first time I had written both words and music.

With a dozen musical numbers, *Promised Land* tells the story of how God and Moses brought the Hebrews out of slavery into freedom. As I wrote it, I felt I was being liberated from my own bondage of despair and self-doubt.

For the first performance, I decided to go back to my roots. With the help of a theater critic in South Bend, I got in touch with the theater staff at Indiana University.

The world premiere of *Promised Land* was staged there in my hometown in April 1989. It was a huge production, with a thirty-five-member cast and giant pyramids. It drew four thousand people for six performances, and the production staff was ecstatic. But was staging the musical on college campuses the way to go?

Back in New York I called Joseph Beinhorn, a producer with whom I had worked in the sixties. After reading the libretto, he said, "Let's try something different. Let's do the show in churches and synagogues, with a small cast, no big stage effects, and you playing the piano at each performance."

I decided to try his idea. *Promised Land* made its New York debut in March 1990—at Central Presbyterian Church in Manhattan.

This time there were only nine people in the cast, there were no giant pyramids, and the overture was done solo by me at the piano. But the production was special in several ways. Central Presbyterian, an affluent congregation based on Park Avenue, had never before hosted a theatrical presentation in its sanctuary. The musical played to a full house of about four hundred people.

The overture faded, and all the lights went out. Then I played the first note of the first song, and I heard the line sung with great emotion, "Oh, my Lord, deliver us from darkness."

As the show progressed, the audience seemed to be waiting for a chance to show its reaction. It came about halfway into the production, at the end of a number called "Sound the Trumpet."

This particular song comes just after Pharaoh finally gives Moses permission to lead the Hebrews out of Egypt. In a halting, almost unsure way, Moses tells Joshua:

> Sound the trumpet loud
> and clear.
> Freedom is at hand.
> Soon we journey far
> from here
> To the Promised Land.

Joshua repeats the lines with a little more enthusiasm to the assembled Hebrews. Then the whole group takes up the message, which gradually rises to a joyful climax of singing and dancing as the people celebrate their liberation.

The audience had been quiet until this point, but at the end of the number, people rose from their seats to cheer and applaud. A chill ran down my spine. It was an outpouring of emotion that I had never experienced at a production of *Promised Land* before, nor have I since. And the small, intimate atmosphere of doing the show in a church sanctuary rather than a huge theater seemed to have helped make it happen.

This is the way it should be done, I thought. A production on this scale helps each person identify with the story of how God leads from bondage into freedom. I knew without a doubt that God had been leading me, and this was the result.

And that's the way it's been ever since with *Promised Land,* through more than one hundred fifty productions, from schools and libraries to the Spoleto Festival in Charleston, South Carolina. People from black churches and Orthodox synagogues alike have told me how the show has inspired them and even rekindled faith.

I realized now that if *Sayonara* had made it to Broadway back in 1987, I might never have used my talents to glorify God. And all the people who have had their faith strengthened through *Promised Land* would never have seen the play or heard the songs.

Over the years, I have learned not to quit just because a situation is very hard. God sometimes gives us tests to see how much we want something. He gave me a big one, and He brought a success out of what had been a failure. But then, isn't that just like God?

> In your unfailing love you will lead
>
> the people you have redeemed.
>
> In your strength you will guide them
>
> to your holy dwelling.
>
> Exodus 15:13 (niv)

We've all run into closed doors before, and we've tried to walk through doors that somebody seemed to be leaning against from the other side. But what about the doors we've closed and locked ourselves? Sometimes we need to be reminded that we still have the keys, in our hearts.

Leaning into the Curves
—By Anne Dueck, as told to Helen Grace Lescheid—

I heard my husband's motorcycle roar out of the driveway of our home. Another holiday alone, I thought bitterly. It was July 1. Tony, my fifty-nine-year-old husband, would be spending this gloriously sunny Dominion Day (Canada's Independence Day) motor biking with friends from church.

"At the age of fifty-three," I had warned him, "I'm not about to start riding a motorbike! People would wonder, *What's that gray-haired woman doing on the back of a bike?* Besides, it is a cold, dangerous and stupid thing to do." Freezing while staring at the back of my husband's neck and pivoting helmet was not my idea of seeing the scenery, even the lush farmlands and the magnificent views of our British Columbia.

I stormed into the garage that I'd made into a sewing room for my drapery business, and I began to cut fabric. All day my machine whirred furiously as I simmered out loud: *Last weekend he took off to the west for Victoria and the coast. . . and this weekend he's gone southeast to Mount Baker. Where will he be next weekend?*

Mount Baker with its snowcapped peak was perfect for a summer outing. It was only an hour's drive away. I checked my watch. By now they were probably having lunch on the mountain.

He could at least have asked me to go along! Angrily I yanked a piece of material from the machine. "It would have given me the pleasure of turning him down."

We used to spend our weekends and holidays together. The thought filled my eyes with tears. Tony and I were both from German Mennonite homes in the plains of Saskatchewan. I was eighteen and he was twenty-three when we married, and in the thirty-six years since then we had shared not only four wonderful children but also many intimate times—long nature drives, Sunday visits with close friends, gardening sessions among the rows of organically grown vegetables and herbs in our yard.

In 1965 we moved to a four-acre strawberry farm in Abbotsford, where Tony worked as a mechanic and I worked as a drapery maker. Then, after moving to town, we each started our own business: Tony had his driving school and I fashioned draperies.

Over the years, we'd grown so compatible that words oftentimes weren't necessary, just the touch of a hand, or a smile, or simply a look meant we were having a lovely time. We enjoyed being together, at least until recently.

I'd tried to discourage Tony from buying a motorbike, but he'd gone ahead and bought it anyway. Initially our teenage sons had been the ones to influence their dad into motor biking. But they were grown now, and their dad had just gone out and bought a powerful bike for himself. Ridiculous!

It's forcing a wedge between us, I thought resentfully.

I was banging away in the kitchen, throwing together supper, when

Tony rumbled up and parked in front of the house. Sunburned and bright-eyed from his ride, he tried to tell me about the day. "What a super time . . ." he began. But my look warned him to keep silent. I was too hurt to trust myself to speak.

Day by day I nursed my self-pity. Tony tried to reason with me: "Give it at least one try, Anne." Tony, the big strong silent one, eyed me anxiously, but I gave him the cold shoulder. His gentle pleading annoyed me and made me feel guilty.

He'd leave for his driver-training school and I'd bury my angry self in the business of shaping yards of material into decorative window hangings. I used to love sewing, but now it seemed like sheer drudgery. It became just a job, and I went through the motions mechanically while anguishing over the trouble between Tony and me. I wanted that bike off the yard, and the sooner he got the message, the better.

Evenings became strained. Meals were eaten in forced silence. Afterward Tony would busy himself in the garden or work alone in the darkroom on a photography project. And without a look or a word in his direction, I would return to my sewing room.

I'm usually a happy person, but now resentment and jealousy consumed me. After three weeks of this ugly pattern I was miserable. A heavy spirit of sadness left me feeling drained, lifeless.

Seven years earlier Jesus had become very real to me. I'd felt alive and full of joy. Like two close friends, the Lord and I had kept in touch as the sewing machine hummed away at my work. At that time I had rejoiced in these words of King David: "You have made known to me the path of life; you will fill me with joy in your presence, with eternal pleasures at your right hand" (Psalm 16:11, NIV). And I had always longed for some way of passing on that message to others.

Now, though, reading those words failed to bring me joy or comfort. God too was silent, distant.

At the sewing machine that day I wondered aloud, *What's happening to me?* The work in front of me blurred as tears streamed down my cheeks. *There's no fun in life. There's no fun in me. I'm a bitter old woman, the kind I vowed I'd never become.* The thought terrified me. Alarmed, I sat down on a chair and sobbed to the Lord.

"I can't stand it anymore. Either make Tony hate riding that bike or make me love it, but let us be together in this for Your glory."

Sitting there, feeling desolate, I wondered whether God was listening anymore. Would He answer? All my senses were alert, waiting, but the only thing I was aware of was the radio playing softly on my cutting table.

The next weekend dawned sunny and clear. "Anne," Tony asked kindly, "would you like to go to the Minter Gardens with me?"

These were magnificent formal gardens with sculpted hedges and flowers laid out in elaborate designs. They had recently been opened to the public, and yes, I wanted very much to visit them. But they were an hour's drive from home.

"By car?"

"No," Tony said sheepishly, "I thought we'd take the bike."

Then, after a slight hesitation, I heard these incredible words coming out of my mouth: "Okay, I'll go. But what should I wear?"

A sparkle came into Tony's eyes. "Something warm," he replied. "Be sure to wear two pairs of slacks."

Two pairs of slacks weren't enough. Neither were the extra sweaters and jacket. As the scenery sped past, I clung to Tony and shivered in the cold. The bike roared beneath us.

"Relax," Tony encouraged. "Lean into the curves with me."

Awkwardly at first, I tried to synchronize my body movements with his. Then, as we harmonized more and more, my heart swelled with joy to feel the togetherness, to feel the freedom. It was like riding the wind. And it didn't seem to matter that my curls were gray, nor that I was fifty-three, nor that my husband with his receding hairline was nearly sixty.

As the cold caught at me, I smiled at God. "Are You cold too?" I asked. How natural it felt to be talking with Him on friendly terms again.

That bike I hated actually brought me back together with Jesus. Today I have a Honda CB 650cc. Tony and I have joined the International Christian Bikers Association, which gives us a chance to study and pray with other bikers and to pass along His message at rallies, even to those bikers who call themselves Hell's Angels.

And if anyone asks me, "What's a gray-haired woman like you doing on a motorbike?" I simply reply, "I'm having the time of my life!" ❧

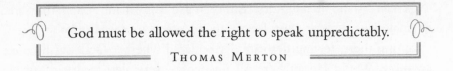

God must be allowed the right to speak unpredictably.

THOMAS MERTON

Some people have the impression that the religious life is a passive life. Not so.

Getting ourselves to move through the doorways God opens requires action. Getting to a point of acceptance when a doorway closes often requires hard spiritual work. Either of these tasks can require determination, persistence and raw courage.

In "Seizing the Moment," Shirley Farmer demonstrates it's possible to have all of those qualities in spades and still remember that God is ultimately in control.

SEIZING THE MOMENT
—BY SHIRLEY FARMER—

On New Year's Eve 1979, and in the wee hours of the first day of 1980, I stepped out of the way, and a Power far greater than my own took over and in a few short hours accomplished what I had been trying for six years to do with all my might. On that night my husband Jim took his last alcoholic drink.

I sat up late. My two little girls lay asleep upstairs, snug on top of their covers in the slumber bags they'd received from Grandma for Christmas. Jim was out again, drinking his usual case of beer.

I was married to an alcoholic. For three months there had been no more room for doubt. It seemed incredible now that I could have lived with him for six years in the advanced stages of the disease without knowing what was wrong. Before we were married, though, I saw his drinking as normal bachelor immaturity—objectionable, but nothing that the responsibilities of marriage and a family couldn't cure. The fact that he didn't stop drinking after our wedding night was a decided disappointment, but, I reasoned, "Give him time. A loving wife will mend his ways."

Wrong again. At that time, though, it was impossible for me to think that I could be wrong in something that basic. How much easier to condemn myself for having somehow failed in the "loving wife" role! Never mind, though. Give me time and I would figure out what I was doing wrong. Then I would fix it, and everything would turn out okay.

I fixed it, all right, in six short years I completed the transition from loving wife to screaming shrew. Throw in "hysterical mother" and "self-righteous scold" and you have a pretty good picture of the Shirley Farmer of the late 1970s. Everyone near me of course knew what I was; but my own parents and siblings, insulated by the miles that separated us, still thought of me as steady, sunny Shirley. This family support was my anchor, my ray of hope, for all the years I suffered in ignorance. I treasured my family's favorable opinion of me. It pains me to think how I ultimately revealed to them what a wreck I had become.

Late in the summer of 1979, my mom and dad took me and my two baby girls on a trip to Kansas City to visit my older sister Sylvia. One night there, over something so trivial I can't even remember what it was, I lashed out at my little girls in a tirade that sent a shock wave through everyone there. Dear God, it brings tears to my eyes to think of the damage it—and previous attacks—did to my innocent children. I'm a tough nut to crack, but that did it. In the eyes of my nearest and dearest supporters I saw the horrible reflection of myself. I was ready for the help that Sylvia offered.

My sister handed me a book titled *The Booze Battle* by Ruth Maxwell. I read it and found in it a mirror image of my own situation. In the ensuing three months I grew enough to struggle through denial, anger and self-pity to some semblance of acceptance that alcoholism is a disease, and I was as irrevocably infected by it in my own way as my husband was in his. It was a complete change of attitude for me. I could look at Jim with love, compassion and understanding instead of with guilt, anger and disgust. I was ready to "Let go and let God."

For some unexplainable reason, on that fateful New Year's Eve I broke my usual habit of making sure I was asleep in bed to avoid an ugly confrontation on Jim's drunken arrival. Instead, I found myself addressing belated Christmas cards. In my stack of unanswered greetings, I came across a letter from Aunt Nora. In it she had written that she hoped Jim would stop trying to control his drinking by himself. "Ask him," she suggested, "if he has ever tried to use his willpower in trying to control a bad case of diarrhea!" Crude, perhaps, but graphic and, I thought, very apt.

Aunt Nora also gave me the address and number of an alcoholic treatment center, and now I penciled it in on a file card, along with several other treatment-center numbers that I'd cross-referenced. I had just finished when Jim arrived home. That greater Power kept my tongue still and my eyes calm. This time Jim was the first to speak.

"Well, I guess I did it," he mumbled through the haze of his intoxication.

"What did you do?" I managed to say, imagining all sorts of horrors.

"I guess I proved I can't do it by myself. I promised myself I'd quit drinking—like I quit smoking cigarettes. But I couldn't do it. I guess I need help."

"Do you want to talk to somebody about it?" I asked. It was two o'clock in the morning, but Jim was in the habit of calling old friends long distance in the middle of the night.

"Sure," he said. "I'll talk to somebody."

I knew this was an opportunity I could not pass up. Now, right this minute, in the middle of the night, I had to get Jim professional help. And this time I had the right numbers at my fingertips.

There was no answer at the hospital I called in Scottsbluff, the nearest choice. But the number that Nora had given me of the Harmony Foundation in Estes Park, Colorado, finally answered. True to the nature of alcoholism, Jim was already getting out of the mood to seek help. He said some awfully besotted things to the lady on the other end of the line. I was sure she was going to tell him to call back when he sobered up.

God was undoubtedly with her. "If you will come talk to us, I know we can help you," she said challengingly.

Jim loves a challenge. In his drunkenness, the more bizarre the challenge, the more likely he was to pursue it. Driving some three hundred miles in the middle of the night just to talk to somebody was just bizarre enough for Jim at that moment. So I tossed some clothes into our station wagon and put in our two girls.

"The dogs," insisted Jim as we left the house. "They're part of the family, and I won't go without them." It was the first dip in a long series of cold-feet barometer readings. So in went the two only partially house-trained puppies. I took the driver's seat and we were off.

On less than half a tank of gas, I knew we'd never make it even halfway to Denver. It was during the gas shortage, too, and I knew we wouldn't find a station open until we reached Cheyenne, a good five-hour drive away. I wasn't sure we'd make it to Cheyenne on a full tank, either, but at least we'd be a long ways down the road, so I turned north out of the driveway to get some gas from Jim's parents' farm. *It would be nice, too,* I thought, *to let them know where we're going and that Jim won't be at work in the morning.*

I had everything under control now, so I grabbed the reins from God again as if to say, *Thanks, Buddy, for saddling the horse. I'll take it from here.*

No sooner did I snatch control of the situation than I began to lose control of myself. I snarled an order at Jim, "Pipe down or you'll wake the girls!"

"Where're you going?" he roared.

"To the farm for some gas."

"No you're not. Turn this car around or I'm getting out."

It was a gentle nudge from the Power above, reminding me of who was really in the driver's seat. I turned the car around and headed for Denver, breathing, "God, help me."

"Pull over," Jim demanded. "I can drive better than you, even if I am drunk." Under another threat of canceling the whole journey, I pulled over reluctantly.

What are you doing! I berated myself. *Letting a drunk take the wheel. He'll kill us all!* I gritted my teeth. Then I relaxed, *I've got to let God handle this.* "Okay," I said, as I opened the door to get out. "If you want to drive, go ahead."

Just as soon as I gave up, Jim gave me back the steering wheel. This time I knew the difference between "driving the car" and "taking over." I took the wheel, but remained God's passenger:

1. God found me a gas pump at an all-night Mini-Mart in Alliance.

2. He showed me the shortest route to the interstate highway and deafened my ears to the escalating stream of insults coming from an enraged drunk who was slowly sobering up after a fitful nap.

3. He removed all evidence of any nearby motels when Jim began to demand that we stop for the night.

4. He got us from Alliance to Cheyenne on one tank of gas, and kept me going that far as well.

In Cheyenne, Jim convinced me that he needed a motel room for a few hours' sleep and a shower and shave before going on to Estes Park. He called Harmony and said we'd be a few hours late for our "talk," but we were still coming.

The counselors met us at the door with such warmth that the overwhelming sense of welcome and well-being almost made me cry. Jim told me later that he knew at that moment that we had come to the right place. He had agreed only to come and talk, but once we got there, he stayed for treatment.

Three weeks later I returned with Jim's parents and brother. We spent Jim's final week at Harmony in counseling together. I was grateful for Jim's new sobriety and for the promise of a healthy family life to come. At the same time, I was fearful that the program wouldn't work for me. What I learned at Harmony was that no program will "work" for anyone. Each individual must do the work himself. The result of that realization was a spiritual awakening that warms me all over just to think of it.

May we all bask in the warmth of God's loving care for ever and ever. Amen. ❧

Is That You, Lord?

Shirley Farmer's story highlights one of the trickier problems related to spiritual discernment: the question of surrender versus persistence.

Situations occur in life that cry out for change. Lousy jobs. Abusive marriages. Bad neighborhoods. If you're stuck in one of these situations, does a point come where you have to accept that the problems are insurmountable? And does acceptance mean you should try to come to peace with conditions as they are, or leave?

Two things are clear: The answers to these questions will vary depending on the situation involved, and prayer is the first step toward figuring out what to do. The famous Serenity Prayer is so popular precisely because it addresses directly this universal human dilemma:

> God, grant me
> The serenity to accept the things I cannot change
> The courage to change the things I can
> And the wisdom to know the difference

In my experience, the question often becomes *how long* should I continue praying for the wisdom to know the difference? I put this question to one of the wisest men I know on this subject, the Reverend Danny Morris, a longtime Methodist minister and the author of *Yearning to Know God's Will*.

"Given that we take God's will to be of ultimate importance," he said, "it follows that we will take as much time as possible in pursuit of knowing what God's will is. But sometimes we're crimped by time or circumstances, and eventually you have to say, 'Well, I've got to make a move, and I'm going to have to go with the light I have. Come on, God, let's go together. I pray for Your blessings to move.'

"But if time or circumstances *aren't* pushing you into a decision just yet, why not continue to pray for discernment? If you go ahead on your own, you're hampered by all the human weaknesses—ignorance, frailty, depravity. By staying the course you have the chance to tap into the infinite resources of God's wisdom. If you have that chance, that's the better thing to do." D.H.

Distracted as we are by all our strivings and frustrations, it's easy to forget the fact that all of us have walked through the most miraculous door of all: Life.

The men and women who have dedicated themselves to preserving lives—doctors, nurses, firefighters, rescue workers—usually have a profound appreciation of life's worth. But sometimes even they can be surprised by the astonishing vitality of the human spirit.

DECISION
—BY KENNETH SWAN, MD—

It's odd, but I hadn't thought about him in years: the soldier whose life I'd saved in Vietnam when my colleagues said he would have been better off dead. Then in spring 1989 I was being interviewed by a writer from *American Medical News* for an article on trauma care. I'm a trauma surgeon, and I told the writer about my experiences in triage—the process of treating first the wounded most likely to survive. That's when I mentioned my decision to save the life of the horribly wounded soldier.

A month later, after the article appeared in print, the writer, Peter MacPherson, called me with questions readers had raised: "Whatever became of the soldier? Do you think you made the right decision—saving him?"

"I don't know," was all I could reply.

The questions brought back the memory of that night in 1968 in vivid detail. Fresh out of surgical residency, I was stationed at the 71st Evacuation Hospital, near Pleiku. I was having supper in my cubicle when a white-faced young medic came barging in. "Doc, come quick!" *Funny, I hadn't heard the helicopters bringing in the wounded . . .*

The soldier was lying on a stretcher—so young, maybe nineteen, with blond hair, a handsome kid, but all torn up and covered with mud, sticks and blood. To my amazement he was conscious, moaning over and over, "Oh, God, I hurt so bad!"

A door gunner, he'd been on a helicopter that had taken a direct hit from a rocket, and he had taken the brunt of the explosion. I looked at his legs, arms, the head injuries and couldn't hold back my tears.

If the triage area had been filled with wounded awaiting medical attention, he would have been one of those shunted aside as least likely to survive. He would never have made it. But now he was the only patient, and it was up to me.

"Start IVs!" I barked. "Get X rays. We'll take him to the OR!"

During seven hours of surgery our medical team managed to save his arms, but we had to amputate both lower limbs and one finger. The neurosurgeon removed a large metal fragment from his brain. The ophthalmologist worked on his eyes, but they were beyond saving.

The next morning in the triage area the chief of professional services put an arm around my shoulder. "Captain," the colonel said gravely, "I think you ought to know, the other surgeons feel you should have let that fellow die last night."

I stiffened. "I was trained to care for the sick and wounded," I replied. "God will decide who lives or dies."

He stared at me for a long moment, then walked off.

I went into intensive care. Ken—I learned we had the same first name—was sitting up, swathed in bandages. He seemed remarkably tolerant of his terrible injuries, almost euphoric; I put it down to the brain injury. I began to wonder if the other surgeons had been right. But still. . .

"Everyone wants him to die," I wrote to my wife. "And yet I know I'll try to keep him alive."

Four days later Ken was evacuated to Japan. A month later I learned from the chaplain's assistant that Ken had made it back home.

Instead of being happy, I was despondent. If Ken had died en route, I could have consoled myself that it was for the best and I had done everything I could. That would have ended it.

But Ken was alive. For months I tormented myself with all sorts of grim scenarios: Ken immured in the back ward of a VA hospital somewhere—crippled, blind, forgotten, more a vegetable than a man. He had come from a poor farm family. Perhaps he was being tended by his widowed mother in a dingy room of a ramshackle farmhouse, trapped within the stump of a body, maybe driven mad by neglect, bedsores and loneliness, maybe wanting to die and not being able to.

Now, twenty-one years later, Peter MacPherson was again raising those old questions, including, "Can you find out what happened to him? If you don't want to, I'll understand."

"No, I'll certainly try," I said.

We began the search for Ken, but with one big disadvantage: I could not remember his last name. MacPherson, who lived in Falls Church, Virginia, searched the National Archives. I tried to find the chaplain's assistant who had told me Ken had made it back to the States. But after six months our search reached a dead end.

It was eighteen months later, in fall 1990, when MacPherson was working on another article, that he was shown a computer file from the Casualty Care Research Center's Wound Data and Munitions Effectiveness Team (WDMET). He wondered: *Could Ken's case be somewhere in that vast computer file?* He called me.

The name rang a bell—the WDMET had been at the 71st Evac. They ran around snapping pictures of our patients for war-wound research.

I called the Casualty Care Research Center. Sure enough, Ken was in their records. *At last!* "Can you tell me his last name?"

"No, sorry. Privacy." He suggested I submit a formal request, which would be forwarded to the Department of Veterans Affairs for processing. I wrote the letter. Then came the Persian Gulf war, and as an Army reservist, I packed my bags—still not knowing Ken's whereabouts—and flew to the Middle East, where I tended the wounded in Kuwait and Iraq, and lectured on trauma care.

Shortly after I returned home in summer 1991, I finally got a call in response to my letter. Ken was indeed alive, the caller said, and living in the South. "His last name is McGarity. He's married and has two children, and he plays the piano and trumpet, and scuba dives."

"You've got the wrong guy," I said. "This man is blind, he has no legs . . ."

"No, this is the right guy. We'll send you more information."

On September 25, 1991—nearly twenty-three years to the day after that fateful surgery—I flew down to Columbus, Georgia, accompanied by Peter MacPherson and a photographer. We were all pretty apprehensive. After our two-and-a-half-year search, this was the big moment. At the Columbus airport we rented a car and drove out to Ken's house in a comfortable suburban neighborhood. It was a lovely fall day. I rang the bell. A woman's voice said, "Coming . . ." Theresa McGarity opened the door.

All these years I had pictured Ken as a slim, handsome young guy with blond hair. The man in the wheelchair behind his wife was stocky and balding. He wheeled right up and in a strong voice said, "Hi, Doc!" He extended his hand. I shook it. His grip, in spite of his missing finger, was strong. He was jocular, even cheerful.

Theresa brought coffee. We talked. That afternoon, I was amazed to discover that not only had Ken learned to play the piano by ear, but he had also changed diapers, baby-sat his two daughters and fixed flat tires (although he couldn't drive the family car). He could even climb up to fix the roof!

"I've cut down trees and done carpentry work," he told us. "Why not? There's a way to do all those things."

Theresa had encouraged Ken to swim—even without legs his body was quite buoyant—and together they learned to scuba dive.

As if all this weren't enough, Ken had also gone back to school and got his high-school equivalency diploma, then he'd completed a year and a half of college. He enjoys history, particularly relating to wars and military strategy.

But what, we wondered, *had motivated him to accomplish all this, given his terrible injuries.*

"When I woke up," he explained, "I was on a surgical flight back to the States. It was October 4, 1968—my twentieth birthday.

"I knew I was hurt—hurt bad. I was blind and had no legs. But I also thought of all the things in the world I wanted to experience—all the adventures I wanted to have, all the things I wanted to learn about.

"I thought, Gee, I can't give all that up just because of this! Then I would have no life at all. That would be crazy! I can still feel the wind blowing on my face, the sun warming my skin, the cold. I can hear sounds, voices, music . . ."

Not everyone was as optimistic as he was. When he got to a VA hospital in Chicago, he overheard a psychiatrist say, "Why did they let this kid live? What am I supposed to do with him?" But those comments only made him determined to prove the doubters wrong.

Ken met Theresa at an annual picnic of citizens band radio enthusiasts in 1970. They had talked a few times on their CBs. Theresa was nineteen, from a churchgoing family and fresh out of high school. She wasn't bothered by Ken's disabilities. Her grandmother was blind, and one of her Sunday school friends had cerebral palsy and was in a wheelchair.

She loved Ken's way of interjecting humor into any situation, even his own. Though blind, Ken insisted he could "see" Theresa's heart—that she was innocent and honest, and from a loving family. They were married just four months after they met.

Theresa looked at me and said, "I always wanted to meet the man who saved Kenneth's life—to thank you for these twenty wonderful years and for our two beautiful daughters. The decision you made that night—how long did it take, fifteen seconds? That one decision is responsible for my whole world—for the life of the man I intend to grow old with."

So I hadn't made a mistake in saving Ken's life. What I said to my superior that morning after Ken's surgery was true: "I was trained to care for the sick and wounded. God will decide who lives or dies."

And Ken McGarity—patriot, hero, husband, father, friend—is living proof of that. ❧

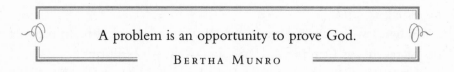

A problem is an opportunity to prove God.

Bertha Munro

Jesus Calls on Peter to Walk on Water
Matthew 14:22-29 (NIV)

Immediately Jesus made the disciples get into the boat and go on ahead of him to the other side, while he dismissed the crowd. After he had dismissed them, he went up on a mountainside by himself to pray. When evening came, he was there alone, but the boat was already a considerable distance from land, buffeted by the waves because the wind was against it.

During the fourth watch of the night Jesus went out to them, walking on the lake. When the disciples saw him walking on the lake, they were terrified.

"It's a ghost," they said, and cried out in fear.

But Jesus immediately said to them: "Take courage! It is I. Don't be afraid."

"Lord, if it's you," Peter replied, "tell me to come to you on the water."

"Come," he said. ❧

~ CHAPTER TEN ~

GOD SPEAKS TO US...
In Our Memories

*A*nyone who's watched a parent die of Alzheimer's disease, as
I have, knows how insubstantial we can be when stripped of
our memories. There was a ghostliness about my father in
the latter days of his illness. It was as if his blood, as well as
his mind, had been drained away.

The opposite is true of people whose memories are robust. They
seem solid. In place. Defined. They know where they're coming from.

We are who we are in large part because we remember who we are.
In our memories we recognize ourselves. The writer William Faulkner
put it well. "The past isn't dead," he said. "It isn't even past."

So often our memories are bittersweet, or simply bitter. If they're
good memories, there's sadness at what we've lost. If they're bad memories, we remember the hurt. Often we carry the hurt. But searching
our memories can also bring us peace. With time we can understand
and accept. We can also see how God has guided us. Moments of grace
become clear. Incidents we had thought little about assume new significance. Actions that seemed inexplicable begin to make sense.

The stories in this chapter show us that the point is not to become lost in our memories, but to become found in them.

Going Home
—By Daniel Schantz—

While I drove across Indiana, I thought the ride seemed endless. I was dreading the visit to my father. The sky was deep blue with wisps of clouds. It reminded me of the white flecks on my grandma's tin kettle. I was taken back to a time before Dad had Alzheimer's, before our roles had been reversed.

One warm spring day when I was a boy, I gazed longingly out the school window. As soon as I saw Dad's blue Chevy, my heart began to race. If my father was picking me up from school it could mean only one thing. The bell rang and I raced outside. Cane fishing rods were sticking out the back window of the car and a sack of sandwiches sat on the backseat. Dad's face wore a sneaky grin.

I hopped into the front seat and hollered, "Let's go!"

We headed toward the river, a small branch of the St. Joe, going to a spot where it widened into a sizable pond. Dad drove off the road and along a ditch to the edge of a wheat field. We bounced over the lumpy dirt, then parked in the tall grass by the oak trees.

"Last one to catch a fish is a toad," Dad announced. I scrambled out of the car and raced ahead of him. After pushing through the thick oak branches, I staked out my territory on the riverbank. I found a tree stump to lean my back against, then propped my pole on a forked branch. That way I would be free to move around while I waited for a fish to make my floater bounce.

Dad was minister of a small church in town, and he could do anything. He could repair a toaster and fix his car, and once he taught me how to find a leak in my bike tire by dipping it in a bucket of water and listening for the sizzle of air coming through. I noticed my line quiver, which Dad had told me meant a fish was biting.

"You got something, Son," he said. Sure enough, I reeled in a good-sized fish. And for the next few hours we pulled them in, one after another, only stopping long enough to eat our deviled-ham sandwiches and bananas.

But as the sun went down, I began to feel uneasy. I was young enough that the darkness still made me nervous. The shadows crept across the pond, and the air began to cool. I edged closer to my dad. Mysterious sounds emanated from the woods and trees. The croaking frogs and buzzing insects were fine, but I was sure there were other creatures lying in wait in the trees and tall weeds—mountain lions or panthers or maybe even some kind of dinosaurs. I slapped quietly at a mosquito so as not to attract the attention of any of those sinister creatures.

All the while Dad seemed unaware of the danger I sensed. Instead he looked at the sky like someone who had stumbled into a beautiful cavern and was admiring the stalactites that seemed to drip from the ceiling.

Let's go home now, I thought.

I wanted to take a bath to wash away the fishy smell, then lie in bed and nibble on cheese crackers as I listened to a baseball game on the radio. But my father didn't look like he was about to budge. Instead, quietly he began to sing an old hymn: "Now the day is over, night is drawing nigh, shadows of the evening steal across the sky . . ."

The frogs grew still. The mosquitoes stopped buzzing. The wild beasts lurking in the woods seemed to vanish.

While Dad sang I looked to the sky like he had, and I saw a thumbnail moon floating amidst feathery clouds that I was sure were angel wings. They were ready to rescue us if need be. Then abruptly, without warning, Dad reached for his rod and stood up.

"Let's go home," he said.

The memory of that day had returned as I was heading home once again. Even though it was more than fifty years later, the late-day Indiana sky brought back the trepidation I'd felt during that childhood fishing trip. Questions, like beasts lurking in the shadows, played in the darkness at the edge of my mind. *How would Dad respond to me? Would he recognize me? What pleasure did he find in life now? Would I be able to make sense of what he said?* Sometimes I wondered why God hadn't taken him after his heart attack two years earlier.

This time I didn't see any angel clouds, and by the time I reached Elkhart, it was night. When I opened Mom and Dad's front door, Dad met me in the hall. He wore a sneaky smile, but it wasn't the one I was used to. He talked gibberish to me and laughed. *He's laughing because he knows he's not making any sense.*

That night I was restless, no crackers or baseball to lull me to sleep. With some anxiety, I took Dad to an antique car museum the next day. He paused at some of the old cars. To my astonishment, he remembered their names.

When we got back to the house that afternoon, I set Dad up in a lawn chair in the driveway, the breeze ruffling his white hair. Mom asked me if I could change a flat tire on her car. As Dad sat there, he whistled a hymn. The melody seemed familiar, but I couldn't place it. I put it out of my mind so I could focus on raising Mom's car with the jack. I took off the old tire. I spun it in my hands, looking for the leak. The next thing I knew Dad was standing at my side with a bucket of water.

"What's that for?" I asked.

Dad looked confused for a moment, and then stared at the tire. *Of course. How could I have forgotten? Water to tell where the tire is flat.*

"Thank you," I said. "Let's find out where we need to put on the patch." Then we poured water on the tire. SSSSSSS. The hissing sound came through. Dad returned to his lawn chair and his soft whistling.

All of a sudden I recognized the song: "Now the day is over, night is drawing nigh, shadows of the evening steal across the sky . . ."

Dad was still Dad. Nothing could change that, even in these twilight years. One day he might not know me at all. Regardless, his soul was filled with sweetness and kindness. I had to be grateful for that small miracle, and trust God with the unknown that lay beyond.

I stood and looked at the sky. I brushed away some tears and saw wispy white clouds coming in. Soon it would look like Grandma's blue tin kettle again. Someday Dad would be going home. But for now, I'd still have the pleasure of his company, even the miracle of it from time to time.

"It's getting a little cold," I said. "Let's go inside." Mom was waiting for us. ❧

> And God shall wipe away all tears from their eyes; and
> there shall be no more death, neither sorrow, nor crying,
> neither shall there be any more pain: for the former
> things are passed away.
>
> REVELATION 21:4 (KJV)

It is said that to understand is to forgive, and I believe it.

Pure evil is rare in human beings; it may even be nonexistent. History, personal as well as collective, plants seeds that bear fruit, healthy or otherwise. Almost always, some sort of logic underlies behavior, however twisted that logic may be.

Our memories hold the secrets of our reasons. Jesus can look into our hearts and know those secrets; think of His conversation with the woman at the well (John 4:1–26). Without that depth of vision, compassion gives way to judgment. Occasionally, though, God grants us the gift of insight, and we see.

MESSAGE IN A MEMORY
—BY LOU DEAN—

"So we'll do the service on Saturday morning, right?" I said to my brother David, as we stood looking down on the Arkansas River. We'd decided to scatter Mama's ashes there because the precious few good memories we had of her were connected to water. The times when she was sober and would join us kids in the rain-swollen creek to catch fish and play with turtles, her contagious giggle rippling over us. Or give us food coloring to put in bottles of water so that we could make rainbows wherever we wanted. Or belt out "Old Man River" right along with the radio.

"Would you say something for Mama, Sissy?" David asked. Instantly I saw my forty-six-year-old brother again as a three-year-old in droopy training pants asking, "Where did Mama go, Sissy? Why did she leave?"

I was nine when Mama first left David and me—as well as our sister Pat, our brother Phil, and Dad—for what she seemed to care about most: drinking. In some ways it came as a relief. No more trips to the Nine-Mile Corner where she'd leave us kids in the car while she went inside to have beers. No more shouting matches between her and Dad, when I'd steal out back quietly with my dog Shorty and a blanket and let the low murmuring of the creek soothe me to sleep.

I lay awake many nights replaying in my mind the image of Mama driving away from our Oklahoma farm in a cloud of red dust. I knew her father had passed away when she was young, and I wondered if she had ached to have him hold her the way I ached to feel her arms around me. Please give me another chance to make her love me, I begged God. But each time Mama returned, it didn't matter how many pictures of a happy family I drew or how many love letters I wrote to her. Her addiction would always draw her away again, to countless bars in countless towns, searching for a peace she never seemed to find.

By the time I was a young adult I was tired of trying to win a place in Mama's heart. I moved out to Colorado and focused my attention on raising my own family. My older brother Phil moved away too, but he succumbed to the same relentless demons Mama had wrestled with, dying as a result of his alcoholism in 1998.

Mama finally stopped denying her drinking problem. But admitting her illness did not make it go away. When David had called me a few weeks earlier, I knew it was taking its final toll. "Sissy, she's not eating—just drinking. Won't let me help her. What should I do?"

It took the police's help to get Mama to let David clean her up and drive her to rehab in Enid, Oklahoma. She died there a few short weeks later.

"I'm sorry I wasn't here to help you with her this time," I said to David, grimacing at the memory of Mama's trailer, littered with empty liquor bottles, rotting food and dirty clothes. We'd packed all her worldly belongings in boxes. Soon they would be all we had left of her. "Yes, I'll try to write something," I said in a low voice. "I'll give it a try."

And I did, but there didn't seem to be any words left when it came to Mama. How many times had I pleaded for her to come back and be part of our family again? Why hadn't it made any difference? Dad had struggled so hard, taking care of our farm and four kids on top of working long hours at the railroad, while Mama poured her love into the bottle. The night before her memorial, I stayed up for hours trying to think of something—anything—to say. But whatever I wrote came out as angry and confused as my feelings. It wasn't working. The crumpled sheets of paper tumbled over the boxes around me like snowballs. *Why should I do this for her now?* I thought. *She doesn't deserve it.*

I gave up and went to bed. I tossed and turned like I had when I was a child whose mother had gone away. Now she was gone forever and I had never really gotten the chance to know her. In many ways, I'd been mourning her loss my entire life.

God, I don't know how to feel anything but bitterness when I think of Mama. You know how much I've wanted to forgive her, but I can't figure out how to begin.

At last I fell asleep. All at once I was a little girl again sitting out back by the creek behind our farm. Mama was beside me. Except she was a little girl too. I'd never seen her look so happy, almost radiant. Together we were mixing food coloring into bottles of water. Then we poured the water into the creek. The streaks of red and blue and green and gold sparkled in the sunlight. Mama let out her bubbly giggle and it too seemed to float on the surface. I awoke with the sound of her laughter still in my ears.

For a moment I kept my eyes closed, trying to hold onto the sense of contentment and peace I'd felt in the dream. Never before had I pictured Mama as an innocent child. She'd never really talked about growing up. I turned on the light and went to a box in the corner containing some books and papers we'd found in Mama's trailer.

I lifted out a photo album and slowly turned the pages. I came to a loose picture with a penciled description. It was Mama as a round-faced toddler nicknamed Chub clinging to an older sibling the way David had clung to me after Mama had left us. I reached back into the box and came up with a small hardbound journal Mama had kept in her youth. I'd never known that Mama wrote!

I read the words hungrily, learning that Mama's father had been an alcoholic too. He'd died early and her mother had to leave five kids at home while she worked to keep the family fed.

So Mama knew what it was like, feeling abandoned. Then why did she put us through it?

I reached into the box once more and came up with a sheaf of yellowing papers. It took me a moment to realize what they were. Letters. The ones my brothers and sisters and I had written her as children. And all those drawings I'd made for her—they were there too. She'd kept them all these years.

Could it be that Mama wanted to love us as much as we wanted to be loved by her? Mama had many demons, there was no question about it. But maybe she had her angels too, nudging her to hold onto these symbols of her family's love.

Early the next morning I stood with David on a fallen cottonwood tree over the Arkansas River. The two of us were silent a few moments before David turned to me. I pulled a piece of paper from my jacket pocket. The wind whipped it about as I unfolded it. I stretched it taut between my trembling hands and began to read.

"Mama, I can envision you now as a six-year-old, so frightened when your father died. I know you suffered when your mother was forced to go off to work. You and your two sisters and two brothers were left by yourselves, to make it on your own the best you could.

"I thank you for your whimsical, childlike sparkle. For teaching me to appreciate music and for helping me see the magic in simple things.

"I know you were probably never free from the guilt of leaving Pat and Phil and David and me when we needed you. I'm sure that guilt fueled your urge to drink and your search for the 'place that would make you happy.'" My voice broke and I had to stop reading. David gave me an encouraging nudge.

"I see you now, a child again, round-faced and innocent, floating away to a home where you will finally forgive yourself, be cleansed of your addiction and be at peace." I refolded the paper and turned to David.

"Good job, Sissy," he said.

My brother opened the urn and let Mama's ashes float up on the wind and gently fall onto the river. As we watched the ashes sparkle on the water, I again pictured those two little girls sitting by a creek. The image from my dream seemed real to me now. I knew a part of me would always be there beside the creek with Mama, washing away the past with magical colored water, our laughter rising up as light and free as the wings of angels. ❦

> He that cannot forgive others breaks the bridge over which he himself must pass if he would ever reach heaven; for every one has need to be forgiven.
>
> — GEORGE HERBERT

As a former sophisticate, I was a bit slow in learning that how I live my life is, at heart, a matter between me and God. Faith from this perspective can be seen as an exciting exploration, a creative act as God helps me discover who I am. Still, as a former sophisticate, I found this hard to swallow. Only later would I come to understand that it is mainly God who does the creating, internally, by His grace and His leading.

Nonetheless I do believe that we contribute, by way of assent or rebellion, to what our lives become. These next two stories, by Roberta Messner and Megan Ballinger, both address the holy collaboration we enter into when we embark upon a life of faith.

What will be my legacy? The memories I leave behind will tell the tale.

THE WEAVER'S PATTERN
—BY ROBERTA MESSNER—

How will I ever make this cockeyed cabin a real home?

That was my thought as I moved into the dilapidated cabin I affectionately dubbed "The Leaning Log." Its walls sagged and its floors were warped. No matter where you stood in it you leaned.

I unpacked only the necessities and stored the remnants of the life I'd left behind in the garage and adjoining breezeway, dreading the long cold winter ahead. As the wind whistled through gaps in the logs, I thought of one of the cabin's former owners, who told me how his father had hung quilts on the walls to try to keep Old Man Winter out.

When summer came, I noticed an abandoned bird's nest tucked under the eaves. Something made me reach for it. In the past, I'd used such treasures of nature for Christmas decorations. But this one was different. Some creative bird had woven the most colorful materials into her nest.

Wait a minute! Isn't this the rosebud wallpaper my friend Carole helped me hang in the guest bedroom at my old house? I'd been reluctant to try wallpapering, but Carole was sure the two of us could figure out plumb lines and trimming around baseboards. The industrious bird had woven that twenty-one-year-old wallpaper into her new home. There had been enough remaining on the roll for a craft project, and I'd never been able to throw it away; all these years later, I'd brought it with me. *And isn't that my red-checked kitchen curtain fabric amidst the mud and twigs?* I'd saved some of the scraps to use in a quilt. *Why, that tenacious mama bird even found my duct tape!*

When I'm the General Contractor, I build on your past, Roberta, Christ seemed to say. *I don't discard it. Just trust Me.* Right then and there, I gave Him the shattered, jagged pieces of my past—failures and fears I'd held on to far too long. It was time for the two of us to rebuild *my* nest, *my* life, *my* relationship with Him. ❧

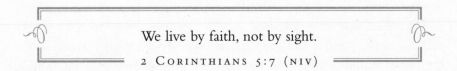

We live by faith, not by sight.

2 Corinthians 5:7 (NIV)

ROSA'S FEAST

—By Megan Ballinger—

At last year's annual Rosa Lee Jackson Thanksgiving dinner, like every year since Rosa died in 1996, Pastor Clarence Warren remembered the woman from his church who had inspired the feast. "Once another pastor and I were over at Rosa's for dinner," Warren said. "You should have seen the spread she laid out. Five or six kinds of salad, five or six meats, five or six vegetables . . . And then, after we were so full we could bust, she brings out her seven-layer chocolate cake."

Rosa got the idea for her Thanksgiving feast thirty years ago while sitting by herself on her front porch in St. Petersburg, Florida, wondering where she would spend the holiday. At forty-nine, she was a young widow, and the last of her children had already grown up and moved out. Images of Novembers past filled her memory. How many turkeys had she stuffed and roasted? How many sweet potato pies had she sliced and served? Would it really be Thanksgiving if she didn't have anyone to cook for? Right then she knew she wanted to spend the holiday at home—but not alone.

Rosa thought of neighbors and friends from church and work who she knew had no place to go for Thanksgiving, and started dialing numbers. She spent days in the kitchen basting turkeys, peeling potatoes, baking cornbread and pies, her memory the only recipe book she used. Thanksgiving Day arrived and with it fifty guests, including some of Rosa's own kids. They scrambled for spots on the couch and folding chairs. But if it was a little crowded, no one seemed to mind. "We laughed and talked and prayed together," Rosa's grandson Darryl Jones, who was ten at the time, remembers. "And we ate. We ate until we couldn't eat any more." With the success of that first dinner, a tradition was born.

The next year one hundred hungry visitors crowded into Rosa's home, and she prepared an even bigger feast. By the third year, she knew her house couldn't hold the throngs any longer. But give up hosting Thanksgiving dinner? Not an option. Neither was trimming the guest list. So Rosa moved the event to the Campbell Park Recreation Center, a few blocks away from her home.

More room meant more people in Rosa's eyes. Rosa opened her heart and her feast to everyone. "No one should be alone on Thanksgiving," she declared. Strangers, even homeless people, came to her feast. And they kept coming back, year after year—families, friends and dozens of elderly singles.

But in 1996, Rosa became ill. She could barely stand, let alone prepare a meal. Her doctors didn't give her much time. "Something came over me when she took sick," grandson Darryl says. "I couldn't let what she'd started die with her. I asked her how she would feel if I took over the dinner, and she said she'd like that."

Just like Rosa, Darryl cooks everything solo, and makes as much of the meal from scratch as he can. "Everybody was crazy about my grandma's dressing," Darryl says. "People would always talk about that. Now, I make a mean dressing myself, but it's still not quite as good as hers." Like his grandma, Darryl donates the leftovers from the dinner to local nursing homes, soup kitchens and the Ronald McDonald House.

Darryl plans to keep up his grandmother's Thanksgiving tradition for "years and years and years." And he has already got a successor in mind. His six-year-old son Jeremiah follows him around the kitchen and has announced his plans to attend culinary school—after he finishes kindergarten, of course.

At this year's holiday dinner, as always, a single candle will burn in front of a frame hanging in the corner of the Campbell Park Recreation Center. Inside it, a photograph of Rosa and a verse from Deuteronomy: "He fed you with manna in the wilderness . . . so that your trust in him would grow."

Rosa's trust in the Lord and in the goodness of other people is part of what made her so remarkable. One Thanksgiving, several men from California who were down on their luck came to her feast. Learning they had no place to stay, Rosa took them into her own home for the night. "We were mad at her because we were so worried," Darryl says. "She just said, 'This is my house and I'm going to be fine.' And she always was. God took care of her because she took care of His."

"Rosa met no strangers," Pastor Warren says. "People from any walk of life, it didn't matter. This Thanksgiving feast was Rosa's way to reach out." Once again this year in St. Petersburg, hundreds of people will give thanks that she did. ❧

 The world and its desires pass away, but the man who does the will of God lives forever.

1 John 2:17 (NIV)

Is That You, Lord?

Life for the person of faith is a journey toward union with God. It stands to reason, then, that we can gain insight into the ways God has directed our steps if we take a look at the way our journey has unfolded. One way to do this is by keeping a prayer journal.

The only hard and fast rule about journal writing is that there are no hard and fast rules. This is an extremely personal exercise, and any suggestions I can make should be taken as just that, suggestions.

Suggestion 1: Aim for consistency. It's awfully easy to fall out of the habit—take it from one who knows. Setting aside a regular time in the day to write is a good idea.

Suggestion 2: Think of your prayer journal as a private correspondence between you and God. You can help establish that mood by setting aside a special notebook for your journal, and by keeping what you write in it to yourself. I start my journal entries with the salutation "Dear Jesus."

Suggestion 3: Don't tell yourself you have to produce a certain amount of pages or paragraphs each time you sit down. Nor should you worry much about the quality of your prose. The idea is to let it flow. Many novice journal-keepers are surprised at the torrent of words that erupts once they get started.

Suggestion 4: In my opinion, the point of a prayer journal is not simply to record what has happened on a given day, but to prayerfully *reflect* on what has happened. That's why memories are an especially rich area for exploration. Try writing down what you remember about different episodes in your life, especially episodes from your childhood. New revelations can emerge from past history. D.H.

Memories and loss are part of the harvest of living. Inevitably our share of both increases as we grow older, but we are not powerless before them. Kathryn Fanning's poignant story testifies to the fact that, with God's help, memories that once possessed us can be transformed.

FAREWELL
—By Kathryn Fanning—

I'd waited seventeen years for the airplane. Glinting in the August sunlight, it glided toward the loading dock of Oklahoma City's Will Rogers Airport.

Don't cry, I told myself. You've cried enough for nearly two decades.

I looked at the television reporter waiting with his cameraman to record my husband's homecoming. I thought of the hundreds of times I'd imagined Hugh's return since October 31, 1967—the day he was listed as missing in action in Vietnam. At first, I'd pictured myself, twenty-four, holding eight-month-old Erin, while two-year-old Michael and three-year-old Kelly clutched my knees and shouted, "Daddy's home! Daddy's home!" Major Hugh Michael Fanning, thin but smiling in his pressed Marine uniform, would step from the airplane for our exuberant welcome.

Each year, I altered the mental scene to adjust for the children's ages. Each year, my fantasy dimmed.

Now, reality was bringing its own images. I concentrated on the men in coveralls sprinting toward the airplane to open the hatch. Perspiration gathered at my neck and the sun felt like a hot iron pressing against my black dress. How could it be so hot outside when my heart felt so cold?

I twisted the ring Hugh had sent from overseas and made a fist around the pearl. It meant more to me than anything else I owned, even the metal MIA/POW bracelet engraved with Hugh's name and date of disappearance. For years, the ring and bracelet had been my closest physical link with him.

Until now. I watched the men unload a wooden crate from the plane. The television cameraman positioned himself for a clear shot. The cold spread through my chest. Remains.

The reporter edged close to me and moistened his pencil with the tip of his tongue, preparing to write on a small notepad.

"How do you feel about your husband's coming home?"

I pressed my lips together to keep from snapping "Stupid question!" I, too, was a writer and I sympathized with his assignment. "Relieved," I answered.

How could I tell the reporter that for seventeen years I'd lived as if holding my breath? Always waiting, always wondering where Hugh was, if he was alive or dead. Every decision, whether to return to college, to buy a house or sell our old car, was made in the light of Hugh's possible return.

The airport employees were now wheeling the wooden crate in front of me. They lifted off the plastic covering to reveal the flag-draped casket.

I wanted to embrace the casket, to hold what had been kept from me for seventeen years. Instead, I twisted my ring, lightly rubbing the pearl.

The cameraman crouched for a close-up, then swung to capture my children, walking arm in arm toward the car.

I watched them, wondering if I had done the right thing, keeping their father's memory alive. On the other hand, I couldn't risk his coming home a stranger. If he had come home. Alive.

I'd put enormous posters of Hugh in their bedrooms. His Air Medals lay on the mantel and his sword rested on the hallstand beside his cover (I remembered his irritation when I forgot and called it a "hat").

The first years after his A-6 Intruder was shot down, I kept his clothes in the closet and told the children stories about our days together at the University of Dallas. My stories made the children laugh and kept him close to me.

When Erin grew older, I held pictures of her father next to her face in the mirror, comparing the kitty-cat eyes, the sculptured nose and long lips. Erin was the female version of her father, I always told her.

Finally, we were home from the airport. I had tied yellow ribbons around the trees in the driveway, welcoming Hugh home. What was left of him.

Inside, a heap of letters lay on the floor, another handful caught in the mail chute. For days I'd answered letters from friends and well-wishers who assured me that now I could "start a new life."

That was easy for them to say. Kelly was already married and the mother of a small boy, Michael was a freshman at Dartmouth College and Erin was soon to graduate from high school. It was too late—for all of us.

I sorted the mail, then revisited every treasured possession of my husband's. The items that had waited for his return had suddenly become relics. The eyes in his photograph followed me around the room as I touched his sword and his cover. I opened the hall closet and buried my face in the dress blues that I'd hung next to the black gown I'd worn to our last Marine Corps Birthday Ball.

I tiptoed to my bedroom and opened the drawer where I kept Hugh's letters. I opened the first of the thin airmail envelopes written in his cramped handwriting, but closed it again and slipped them all back into the drawer. He was free, but I still could not let him go.

The shrill demand of the doorbell startled me. My friend Bette stood on the welcome mat, a covered dish in her hands.

I swung the door open and took the dish from her. "I don't know what I'd do without you," I told her.

She hugged me and followed me into the kitchen where I'd assembled the cakes and cookies that others had brought.

"I'll make tea," Bette said, skipping the usual small talk.

I watched her fill the kettle with water and adjust the flame on the stove. *Would I ever be able to do those simple chores again without the leaden weight inside?* I felt the same way I had after hearing about Hugh in 1967. Somehow, the years were erased and I was beginning the cycle again.

"I want to tell you something that probably will sound awful," I said.

Bette lowered herself slowly onto the kitchen stool and reached for my hand. "Tell me something awful," she said with a smile, as if nothing I could say would surprise her.

"I really wanted a part of Hugh. Something tangible," I whispered. "I thought about taking a little piece of bone." I looked closely at Bette's face to see if she was shocked. She gave another gentle smile.

"I mean, I keep thinking about relics of the saints," I rushed on. "People used to keep locks of their hair, bits of bone. After not having him all this time, except for photographs, I wanted something that was really part of him."

"To add to your collection?" Bette asked.

Her words slapped me like a hard hand. *How could she be so insensitive?* "I thought you'd understand. Waiting for Hugh has been a habit. For seventeen years. I need something solid to hold onto."

Bette dropped tea bags into blue ceramic mugs. "All habits aren't good, Kathryn."

"But I need something real. Something of Hugh," my voice wobbled.

"You have something real—Kelly, Michael and Erin. They're Hugh's blood, his spirit."

I whirled to hide my tears, jamming my hands into my pockets to hide their trembling. "Want sugar?" I asked her, hearing the anger in my voice.

I reached inside the cabinet for the sugar bowl before she could answer, then heard a tiny "ping." Puzzled, I searched the floor, then noticed the cavity in my ring where the pearl once gleamed.

"Hugh!" I spoke his name aloud, as if it were a prayer. "My pearl! I'll die if I've lost it." I scrambled to the floor and searched along the baseboard until I saw it, glowing like a tiny white cloud on the sky blue tile.

"I've only taken it off once," I told Bette. "A nurse made me remove it for an electrocardiogram." I couldn't help laughing at the memory of the nurse's grim determination.

"Maybe you should let it all go." Bette's voice was soft, yet like a threat. "The ring, the bracelet, all of it. You've devoted all of your adult life to Hugh in one way or another. Don't you think the rest of your life should be free?"

How dare she suggest I give up Hugh? His memory was all I had left, especially when my last child would leave home next year.

"You're still grieving, I know," she persisted. "Your grief process was never completed, but you have proof now. You can finally accept that Hugh's gone."

"No!" I pushed my steaming mug of tea away, sloshing a little on the kitchen counter. "I'd rather have what's left of Hugh than have nothing at all."

Snatching up my car keys, I walked to the front door, slamming it behind me. No one could understand how I felt. I was foolish to expect Bette to, no matter how close we'd been.

I drove to the cemetery, feeling guilty about leaving Bette without a word. It served her right. She couldn't understand that Hugh was a part of me that I could never let go.

I spotted the grave that had been dug to receive Hugh's casket. Leaving the car door open. I scuffed through the dry grass and stood in front of the gray granite headstone.

I skirted the hole and traced the words I had chiseled into the headstone; they were Hugh's favorite part of Ecclesiastes—"For everything there is a season, and a time for every matter under heaven . . ." I smiled, remembering how Hugh loved to recite the words in his deep, honeyed voice. ". . . A time to keep, and a time to cast away," I said aloud. I put my hands in my pockets, trying to remember the rest of the verse. I felt the ring and its broken pearl. A time to cast away.

Could Bette be right? The sun sparkled on the polished granite and a slight breeze ruffled the loose sod by my feet. A time to live and a time to die. I tried to swallow. *Was there a reason my pearl had fallen out of my ring? Was God trying to tell me something?*

I remembered more of the verse—a time for war, and a time for peace. The war was over. For Hugh, anyway. He was at peace. Shouldn't I be?

There had to be a way I could begin a new life, even if it didn't seem possible right away.

Minutes later, I was back in my yellow-ribboned driveway, relieved to see Bette's car still at the curb.

"I'm back," I called, as I bolted through the door. "Kids, where are you? There's something I want us to do."

For Hugh, I thought. *And for ourselves.*

Bette was still on the kitchen stool talking to Kelly, Michael and Erin.

"I've been out to the cemetery," I said and smiled at them. "And now I know something I didn't quite know before. It's time to say good-bye." I opened a drawer and picked up a handful of pencils and counted out four of them. "I'm going to write a good-bye letter to Daddy now. If any of you wants to write one, too, I'll ask Major Harmon to place it with mine in the casket tomorrow."

Bette reached over and patted my hand. I knew that she hadn't blamed me for leaving.

Within the hour, I held a packet of four sealed letters, as precious as those in my bedroom drawer. "Good-bye, Hugh," I whispered. "Now we are at peace—all of us." ✌

The healing power of the Holy Spirit can turn all things to our salvation, and memories are no exception. Like Kathryn Fanning, John J. Colligan was imprisoned by agonizing loss. She was freed from her memory. His memory freed him.

FORGIVING THE UNFORGIVABLE
—BY JOHN J. COLLIGAN—

In a hurry to get back down to my basement office, I glanced quickly through the pile of mail on the kitchen table. There was a letter from the district attorney in Colorado who was prosecuting our case. The blood began to pound in my head.

Six months earlier our twenty-one-year-old son Johnny had relocated to Colorado, excited about a new job and eager to explore another part of the country. Nine weeks later he was shot to death.

Tearing open the envelope, I discovered a trial date had been set. The prosecutor wanted Kathy and me to write a letter to the judge telling him what kind of person Johnny had been, how his death had affected our family. The district attorney asked, "What sentence would you recommend for the young woman who killed your son?" For months I had avoided thinking about her. Now I realized the depth of my anger. *No prison term could restore my son's life!*

I remembered that telephone call on Labor Day evening. "John," Kathy had called, "pick up the extension. Johnny's friend Tom is calling from Colorado and wants to talk to both of us."

"Hi, Tom. How is everything?"

For a moment, I thought we had been disconnected. Then a strained voice replied, "I have to tell you that Johnny's been shot."

Shot: "How is he?" I shouted.

"He's dead."

Numbly we listened as Tom shakily spilled out the story. "We were camping and Johnny went to wash his mess kit. Suddenly there was a shot and Johnny fell down." Tom could hardly continue. "There was nothing we could do. The sheriff is going to call you, but I wanted to call first."

After we hung up, Kathy and I clung to each other. "Tom must have got it wrong," I said. "He may be shot, but he has to be okay."

In our bedroom, I reached for the crucifix that hangs on the wall. Clutching Kathy and the cross, I cried, "I don't know what's happening, God, but make it not so. Please heal Johnny and protect our family."

The telephone rang again. It was the sheriff. "Mr. and Mrs. Colligan, I hate to have to tell you this . . ."

Johnny was dead.

A young woman staying at the same campground as Johnny and Tom had awakened that morning "feeling irritable." To vent her frustrations she was shooting a rifle at random targets. When she spotted Johnny washing his utensils at a water spigot, she said to her boyfriend, "Watch me scare that guy." Instead she put a bullet in his heart.

With the support of family and friends Kathy and I got through those first dreadful days. But after the funeral the stillness in our house nearly drove me mad. I walked around like a robot. It seemed the only way to stop the awful pain. I couldn't bear to imagine the campground scene or even think about Johnny's killer. The only way to get through this, I told myself, is to do what I do best—work.

Recently I had resigned an administrative post at a state university so Kathy and I could pursue our dream to develop counseling workshops. Each day I got up at dawn after a fitful sleep and disappeared into my basement office. I stayed until midnight, coming upstairs only for meals.

When I wasn't working I buried myself in football. Johnny had loved being on his high school team, and watching games on television had been our thing. One of our earliest photos of Johnny shows an infant in my arms as we viewed a game from the living room couch.

Now I stared at sports on TV, hoping the images would evoke the good times we'd had together, but they didn't. By midseason I told Kathy, "I don't know if I want to do this. It's no fun anymore." I didn't want to talk to anyone. I didn't want to think.

It was then that the prosecutor's letter arrived. I pushed it aside, I'd answer her questions later. Maybe.

The next day I tried to write about what Johnny had been like. But I kept falling short. For a week I forced myself to relive his life and talk about him with Kathy. Every night we combined our notes. Neither Kathy nor I could stop the tears as we wrote, but slowly the letter took shape.

Finally I came to the DA's last question: What sentence would I recommend?

Sitting in the basement in the pale fluorescent light, I could feel my jaw clench as I suppressed my anger once more. *Lord*, I prayed, *what kind of person have I turned into? Jesus told us, "Love your enemies." I can't, Lord. I can't even pretend to.*

I went up to our bedroom and took down the cross again. Gripping the cold metal so hard my hands ached, I thought of Jesus praying, "Father, forgive them," as he hung in agony. In desperation, I poured out to Jesus all my hurt, anger and bitterness. Exhausted, I finally whispered, "Jesus, help me forgive. I can't do it myself. Help me, please."

At breakfast a few days later Kathy said, "It's strange, but sometimes I feel as if Johnny's about to walk right through our door again. And everything would be the way it used to be."

Except he'd find me a bitter, vengeful man, I thought. I'm no longer the dad he knew. Surely I'm not the kind of father he'd want to have.

As Kathy cleared the dishes, she mused half to herself, "I wonder what Johnny would do if he were in court confronting that young woman?"

"Who knows?" I muttered, heading for the basement. Yet she had set me to thinking. I remembered seven-year-old Johnny listening to the news of the assassination of Martin Luther King Jr. Shortly afterward he came out of his room with his toy guns in his arms. "I don't want to play with these anymore," he said, and threw them in the trash.

He forgave people even when I thought he was being played for a sucker. During his sophomore year, his high school was consolidated with another, a move that caused bitter student resentment. One day Johnny came home upset and puzzled after some boys from the other school had ganged up on him. "Why can't they let it die?" he asked. "I don't like it either, but this is the way things are. Let's just get on with life."

Get on with life. Those were Johnny's words, but now, agonizing over the district attorney's last question, I felt that God was saying them directly to me. Desire for revenge had crowded my heart, leaving no room for the spirit of forgiveness that God wanted me to have. If I clung to my anger, I was as much a victim as Johnny had been. It was time to let go.

Sitting down at my desk, I grabbed a ballpoint pen and formed each word with great deliberation. "Please tell the young woman that I forgive her." As I dug the period into the paper at the end of the sentence, I felt the first glimmer of peace since the day Johnny died. The courts would decide the sentence. That was their responsibility. Mine was to offer the forgiveness I had finally allowed God to place in me. A great weight lifted.

It was time to get on with life. ❧

> If I had cherished sin in my heart,
>
> the Lord would not have listened;
>
> but God has surely listened
>
> and heard my voice in prayer.
>
> PSALM 66:18–19 (NIV)

THE LAST SUPPER
LUKE 22:14–19 (NIV)

When the hour came, Jesus and his apostles reclined at the table. And he said to them, "I have eagerly desired to eat this Passover with you before I suffer. For I tell you, I will not eat it again until it finds fulfillment in the kingdom of God."

After taking the cup, he gave thanks and said, "Take this and divide it among you. For I tell you I will not drink again of the fruit of the vine until the kingdom of God comes."

And he took bread, gave thanks and broke it, and gave it to them, saying, "This is my body given for you; do this in remembrance of me." ❧

~ CHAPTER ELEVEN ~

GOD SPEAKS TO US...
In Our Darkest Hour

*S*ome of the most beautiful passages in the Bible are those in which God assures desperate people that He will stand beside them, no matter what.

"Yea, though I walk through the valley of the shadow of death," reads Psalm 23 (KJV), "I will fear no evil: for thou art with me; thy rod and thy staff they comfort me."

Isaiah 43:1–2 (NRSV) offers comfort to a defeated people in exile. "Do not fear," He tells the Israelites, "for I have redeemed you; I have called you by name, you are mine. When you pass through the waters, I will be with you . . . when you walk through fire you shall not be burned, and the flame shall not consume you."

God has so much to offer us in every part of our lives, but how can we compare the gratitude we feel when He lifts us up in our hour of deepest need, when our own resources are so hopelessly lacking?

The popular poem "Footprints in the Sand" speaks to this. The woman looks back on the path life has taken and sees two sets of foot-prints, one belonging to her, the other to the Lord. Then she notices that, whenever she was going through an especially difficult time, only *one set of footprints appeared. Troubled, she asks the Lord why He would abandon His faithful servant in times of need. "My precious child," the Lord answers, "I love you and I would never leave you. During your times of trial and suffering, when you see only one set of footprints, it was then that I carried you."*

The stories in this chapter all illustrate that God does indeed carry us through our severest trials. We begin with two stories of women with rock-solid faith. When the time of testing arrived, they knew immediately where to turn.

KILLER IN THE HOUSE!
—BY DOROTHYMAE MILLER—

I was drowsing when my daughter Martha's call came at 6:30 AM on a frosty Tuesday morning last December. I'm never surprised when she telephones. I live alone and Martha's always checking on me, thinking I don't take good enough care of myself. "Mom, did you hear the sirens and helicopters last night?"

"I'll say, they—"

"There's a manhunt on for a killer loose in town. I know you don't lock your doors, so go do it now."

She's right, I thought as I swung out of bed. I needed to be careful.

My bedroom is just a few steps from the back door. But at eighty-three I don't move as fast as I used to, and so I was stepping carefully in the dark. I decided to lock the storm door on the enclosed back porch too. When I opened the door a blast of cold air chilled me to the bone.

Suddenly a strong masculine hand caught my wrist. I tried to jerk my arm back, but the grip tightened.

"Oh!" I blurted. Immediately a clammy hand clamped over my mouth. I nearly swooned.

As if from a great distance I heard a voice say, in a kind of crooning whisper, "Don't yell, now. I'm not going to hurt you." My mind reeled. He already was hurting me. In the half-light I could see he was dressed in dark camouflage. He reached for two rifles, glinting in a corner of the porch. *Dear God, this is the killer!*

He backed me inside, cradling his rifles in one arm. "I did something wrong last night. I need a place to stay." His voice was still very low and soft, almost womanly. *Was this the way he talked to the person he'd shot?*

"I need to lie down," I gasped. He looked at me coolly and nodded.

I went back to the bedroom I'd left only moments before. How I longed for things to be the way they had been then. My skin was hot and I couldn't get enough air. The images of those ugly rifles kept playing in my mind. I hate guns. Even the sight of them nauseates me. I tried to breathe more slowly and methodically. Occasionally I'd catch a glimpse of the gunman sliding from room to room. He didn't make a sound.

Oh, Lord, I prayed, *I can't just lie here all day, but what else can I do?*

Gradually I began to breathe easier. I decided to get up and dress. *Well, Lord, if this man wants to kill me, he will anyhow, so I might as well do something, right?*

"Sir," I called out, "I've got to check my blood sugar and take my insulin, and I need to eat something. Would you like something to eat?" My voice was high and piping, but I couldn't control it.

Without a word he sat at my tiny two-place breakfast table in the kitchen. He propped a rifle against the wall, inches from his hand. I put a bowl of cereal before each of us and sat down, my head perhaps two feet from his. He'd taken off his camouflage suit. He was dressed in nondescript gray shirt and pants. His hair was gray, and he had a gray mustache. He looked like any of hundreds of men in our little Missouri town. His azure eyes were calm, unflinching. I'd read about killers who looked like they were singing in a choir as they murdered. *Is that why he's looking at me so calmly?* I shuddered. *Because I'm next?*

He ate slowly, as if he were in a restaurant eating alone. When we'd finished, I told him, "I'm going to wash these dishes." I didn't want to startle him with any sudden moves.

He nodded.

"Now I need to use the bathroom."

Another nod.

"I'm going to the living room now to practice the organ for Sunday. I'm one of the organists for our church."

I sat down in front of my organ. It felt good to put my sweaty fingers on the cool keys. How I love my music! I sing in the church choir and have three organs. I love the old hymns and have a collection of hymnals.

Since it was Christmastime I began with some carols. I was playing terribly, but the deep organ chords soothed me. I mouthed the words quietly: "O little town of Bethlehem, how still we see thee lie . . ." and they soothed me. All the while I played, the intruder again glided from room to room, peering out windows, his expressionless eyes sweeping around as though he were looking for something he'd lost.

Intermittently the man had been listening to the radio in my bedroom. He hadn't wanted me to turn on the television, but when I told him I was upset and nervous and that watching it would help settle me, he relented.

Now the news was coming over the Jefferson City station: "An extensive manhunt has failed to capture a Moniteau County man following a shooting rampage last night. The man, accused of abusing his stepdaughter, shot and killed the teacher who reported the incident. Also dead are two sheriff's deputies who were investigating. A third deputy is in critical condition . . ."

I turned to look for the intruder. There he was right behind me, his eyes unwavering.

"Did you do that?" I asked.

"Yes," he said, as matter-of-factly as if I'd asked him if he thought it would snow.

"You shot four people?"

"I didn't mean to."

Before I could stop myself I blurted, "You've got to turn yourself in! You've got this whole town tied up. It's a terrible thing you're doing!"

The telephone rang. I looked at him; he let me answer. It was my friend Bonnie. Her husband was a highway patrolman in Jefferson City. "Have you heard about the shootings?" she asked.

"Yes," I said, trying to keep my voice even.

"Well, Chris is up near you right now at a roadblock."

"I hope he stays safe," I said.

"You, too, Dorothymae. Stay inside today!"

"I will." She talked a bit more about the manhunt and then we hung up. I hadn't sounded very natural. I wondered if Bonnie had noticed.

Suddenly I glimpsed two policemen outside. They looked to be going door-to-door.

"What should I do if they come here?" I asked the killer. He waved his rifle at me. "Just say you are all right and your doors are locked."

The police approached my house, stopped to stare at it, then turned away and were gone. At that moment a chorus from church came to mind. I began to sing it to myself silently: "Surely the presence of the Lord is in this place . . . I can feel His mighty power and His grace . . ."

It was nearing noon. I fixed two sandwiches, and we sat down again at my kitchen table. "Do you mind if I say a little prayer?" I asked.

He shrugged.

I clasped my hands together and prayed. *Lord, bless this food. Help this man do what is right. And help me to know what to do. Amen.* I looked up into the man's eyes. They no longer chilled me the way they had. My prayer had put things out in the open.

After lunch he asked, "Do you have a car?"

"You're not taking my car," I said. I couldn't believe the firmness in my voice.

"But I may need the car to get away," he protested.

"It's better that you don't."

To my astonishment, he just walked away. *Surely the presence of the Lord is in this place.*

Later in the afternoon I turned to the man and said, "Listen, I'm supposed to go to a Christmas party tonight. My friends are going to wonder if I don't show up."

He looked at me for a long moment, then said, "Okay, you can go to the party. I'm only staying till dark. But you must promise not to tell anyone about me."

I began wrapping Christmas presents for the party while the man watched. The telephone rang. Again the intruder let me answer it. It was Richard Burnett, who reminded me he was driving me to the party. "I'll come to your front door this time, Dorothymae. Someone could be hiding out back."

You're telling me! I thought.

I went and changed for the party. When I came out, I spotted Richard out of my front window, and I rushed out the door. I nearly hollered back good-bye but thought better of it and instead bustled down the walk with my packages. Involuntarily I started humming another hymn. Then I prayed: *Oh, Lord, how good it is to know You and to have had You with me. Thank You for Your presence these past hours.*

Well, if you can believe it, I did go to the Christmas party. Richard sensed that something was up and persuaded me to tell the police, who were able to talk the man into surrendering. My nice neighbors came over the next week and installed a whole new set of locks. And my daughter Martha, bless her, had me install a dusk-to-dawn night-light in the back.

But, you know, it's not the locks and lights that are my comfort. It's the presence of the Lord, who was with me those harrowing ten hours, and who still sends along my beautiful hymns, just when I seem to need them most. ❧

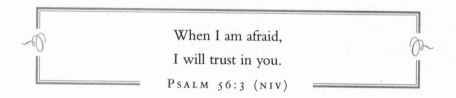

When I am afraid,
I will trust in you.
PSALM 56:3 (NIV)

RESCUE ON THE SUNSET LIMITED
—BY LILLIAN BEECH—

At 2:30 AM on September 22, 1993, I stood on the fog-shrouded train platform at the Mobile, Alabama, Amtrak station, waiting to board the Sunset Limited, a Superliner bound for Miami. I'd never been on a double-decker Superliner before, so I stepped cautiously in the dimly lit passageway as I followed the conductor. He stowed my suitcase, then led me up a flight of stairs.

In the darkened upper passenger compartment I could barely make out the heads of sleeping passengers. I groped toward two empty seats not far from the stairwell. As I settled in, the train eased out of the station with a lazy sway.

I was on my way to Florida to baby-sit my daughter's children. At sixty-seven I was as busy as ever. I'd raised four children, continued to help run the family concrete business, and could still coax a dose of cough syrup down any one of my ten grandchildren. I'd tried to stay extra busy these past six months since my husband died. It helped. But nighttime was when I felt his absence the most; even now, instinctively, I wanted to reach out for his hand.

I said a prayer, as I always do when starting a trip, and pulled a blanket around me. I pray about everything. I knew that when I prayed, God heard my voice. But that past Sunday in church as I listened to the pastor's sermon, I wondered if I listened closely enough for God's voice. After all, listening is a form of prayer too. Now, as the lights outside passed by faster and faster, I listened for God's voice—and dropped off to sleep.

Bam! I was jarred awake by a terrible explosion and the shriek of twisting metal. Then came a tremendous jolt and the sound of people screaming. I clawed my fingers deep into the seat arm and braced my feet on the footrest to resist being thrown forward. Through the window I caught a brilliant flash of flames and smoke shooting into the night. My heart pounded wildly and I thought, *Please, Lord, be with us,* as we lurched and jerked, nosing downward until, with a final sickening shudder, everything was still.

Where were we? The Superliner was dark inside and lodged at a strange angle. There were no lights—only the flickering orange glow of a fire somewhere up ahead. *Lord, don't let me panic.*

I started to stand when a cry went up from the back of the compartment, "We're in water!" More people started yelling. Suddenly I realized I was standing in water nearly up to my knees. The stench of diesel fuel filled my head.

I looked outside again. I noticed water leveling off several inches above the bottom of the window. The rubber seal was holding. But for how long?

"The water's deep back here!" a panicky voice called out. Drenched figures struggled forward in the faint light, pushing and stumbling.

Moans filled the compartment. *How many people were hurt? Were there any dead? Dear God . . .* Then I heard a faint, choking call, "Help! Help!"

No one else seemed to hear. "Help!" the cry came again, fainter this time but still quite distinct. Adrenaline shot through me. "Help!" People were assisting the injured and answering their calls but no one seemed to hear this cry. It was so near! I had to do something.

I scanned the compartment. Through the dimness I saw a spot where there were no seats. Of course, the stairway! The plea came from that black, watery hole! I was sure of it. Amid all the groans and hollering, somehow I knew that spot was the source of the cry.

I grabbed a large man passing by in the aisle. "There's someone down there," I insisted, pointing.

We stumbled over to the stairway and the man probed the water with his foot. Gripping the railing, he took a cautious step down and groped through the water. Nothing. He took another step down. Again he searched the oily water, his arm disappearing fully to his shoulder. I could see the muscles bulge in his neck. Then with a lunging heave he pulled up what looked like a mass of dripping rags from the hole. It was a young girl. He thrust the limp body into my arms.

She started coughing, gagging and shivering violently. *Thank God, she was alive!* I swept away the thick, matted hair from her face. She couldn't have been older than twelve. As I placed her in a seat, word filtered back that someone had got an emergency window open. Then a steady, authoritative voice rang out, "Everybody stay put. We're lodged on some type of piling. Any sudden shift of weight and we might plunge all the way in."

People stayed calm and still. I saw couples holding hands and others comforting the injured. I could hear people praying quietly, and silently I joined in. But the little girl was straining her head and struggling, jerking her arms. "I can't walk," she gasped. "I use a wheelchair."

I stroked and soothed her, wrapping her in my arms to keep her still. She wanted to know where her parents were. I tried to keep her quiet. Finally she put her head down on the tray table, exhausted.

The minutes ticked by. *How much longer before the water came rushing in? Or the fire reached us?* Then the news crackled through the car: "A boat's coming!" I leaned over to look out. A small skiff cutting through the fog, followed by another. Not enough for a major rescue.

"Get the baby on first, the hurt and the elderly," someone ahead ordered. People made way.

"This little girl can't walk," I announced, raising my arm. Quickly a man lifted her up and carried her forward to be put on a boat. *Dear God, keep her safe.* A minute later another announcement came: "If you can swim, you can take your chances in the water."

I can swim a little, I thought. *I might be able to make it.* I climbed forward.

"Are you sure about this?" a man asked, no doubt noticing my age.

I nodded. A pair of strong arms helped me through the window.

I felt the shock of water hitting my face as I went under. I came up saturated with diesel fuel, eyes burning. The taste in my mouth was dreadful. A piece of railroad tie floated by. I grabbed it, pushed away from the Superliner with my feet and began kicking. Now I could see that only the upper compartment was above water level.

God, I don't know which way to go, but when You get me there, I will be sure to give you all the credit.

In a few minutes I spotted powerful beams of light piercing the fog from shore. I kicked toward them. Finally I made it. When I was helped onto land, I glanced at my watch. It had stopped at 4:00 AM.

From newspaper reports the next day I learned that a barge had hit and weakened the bridge over Bayou Canot minutes before the Sunset Limited came roaring through the night. The two engines and first four cars plunged into the bayou, located about twelve miles northeast of Mobile.

I also read about an eleven-year-old survivor named Andrea Chancey who had cerebral palsy. Studying a newspaper's diagram of the Superliner car I had been on, I saw that the lower level had a wheelchair-accessible section for disabled travelers. That's where Andrea and her parents must have been. Tragically, Andrea's parents perished. And though her memories of the crash are scant, she vaguely recalls being pushed upward to safety.

I thought of that small cry for help and what I had felt the Sunday before in church. Yes, we do have to listen carefully for the Lord's voice. Sometimes it comes in a call for help—a call that no one else can hear. ❧

> Those who know your name will trust in you, for you,
> Lord, have never forsaken those who seek you.
>
> PSALM 9:10 (NIV)

I'm a big fan of country music, and this next story reminds me of a song I like a lot, "From Your Knees." Like many country songs, it's told from the point of view of a man whose drinking and cheating has destroyed his happy home. Also like many country songs, its chorus is built on a nifty turn of phrase. "Brother, you would not believe," it goes, "what you can see from your knees."

"From Your Knees" was not one of Ricky Van Shelton's many country hits, but he knows the story it tells. He learned it through personal experience.

D O N ' T O V E R L O O K S A L V A T I O N
— B Y R I C K Y V A N S H E L T O N —

You might not believe part of the story I'm going to tell you. In fact, if it hadn't happened to me, I myself might find it pretty hard to swallow. All I know is my life got turned around when I wasn't sure I wanted to go on living.

In 1991, I was at the height of my career. I had a hit album, had been named The Nashville Network/Music City News Entertainer of the Year and Male Artist of the Year, and had received sixteen other awards in five years. It was a dream come true, one I'd worked hard for. But my life was a mess. I was addicted to alcohol, my marriage was in shambles, and I was so depressed that even music meant nothing to me.

And music had always been the center of my life. I grew up in Grit, Virginia, a small town near Lynchburg, the youngest of the five Shelton children. My daddy worked in a factory, my mama raised us kids.

Faith was important to our family; we went to church more than most people went to work. I started singing when I was so tiny that I couldn't see over the altar rail. My folks would just pick me up, stand me on top of it, hit a few chords on the piano, and I'd let loose with a chorus of "Mansion Over the Hilltop." I knew for certain, with the faith of a child, that God was real and there was a place for me in heaven. My daddy's favorite song was "Don't Overlook Salvation," which I sang loud and strong.

When I became a teenager, my taste broadened to include popular music. By the time I was fourteen, I'd mastered twenty-five chords on the guitar.

Then my older brother Ronnie bought a mandolin. He'd go over to a friend's house, where a group sat around the kitchen table playing the same country songs all night. When Ronnie asked me to come along, I said, "No, thanks." But when he said he'd let me drive his car, that got me interested. I started hanging around with the group, and in the process, I fell in love with country music.

Soon I was hooked on old standards like "Hello Darlin'" and "I'm So Lonesome I Could Cry." While other kids were playing basketball or baseball, I was playing guitar and singing. When my friends went to the junior-senior prom, I played a gig with my brother in some beat-up barn.

The summer I was eighteen I had a real personal relationship with God. But that fall I rebelled and quit going to church. After I got out of high school, I pumped gas and worked as a pipe fitter, plumber—even a car salesman. I always carried my guitar with me, just in case somebody wanted to hear a song after work. If I had a gig out of town and my boss wouldn't let me leave early, I'd quit my job. No contest.

It was in Grit that I met Bettye, the girl who became my wife. Often we talked about how great it would be to move to Nashville, the country-music capital of the world. We could start fresh, and I could try to make something of my music.

In 1984, Bettye was offered a job in Nashville. She said, "Ricky, what have we got to lose? Let's do it."

I said, "Darlin', my bags are packed."

In Nashville I played in the little clubs around town, just like thousands of other hopefuls. After a year and a half I was getting pretty discouraged.

Then the husband of a woman Bettye worked with heard me sing and
said he had the connections to set up an audition with CBS Records. Two
weeks later I was in the studio cutting my first album. It took off and
went platinum—sold a million copies—and five of the songs ended up
number one on the charts.

Suddenly there were managers, band members, and roadies who followed me around. Instead of singing in some dive, I was on national
television. I began touring. In 1988, I was home only twenty days.

Whenever we played, I had a strict rule for the band and the roadies:
If you're wired, you're fired. No drugs or alcohol before a show.

After a show, however, it was anything goes. And eventually alcohol
took control of my life. When I was drinking it was easy to forget Bettye
waiting at home so far away. Even when I was at home I'd do my chores
as quickly as possible so I could pick up a beer. Or two. Or three.

By 1991, I knew I was addicted. Once when Bettye asked me what
was wrong between us, I admitted I'd betrayed our wedding vows—
when I was drunk I had no self-control. Instead of leaving me, Bettye
and one of her friends prayed for me and for our marriage.

I'd come to hate my life, to hate the power that alcohol had over me.
Oh, it never interfered with my professional obligations—I stayed sober
to perform—but it sure made a shambles of my personal relationships
and my self-esteem.

Yet Bettye loved me, and so did my parents. Every time I talked to
Mama and Daddy on the phone, the last thing they always said was,
"We're praying for you, Son."

Their love and the memory of my happy childhood days in church
made me decide to do a gospel album and record all those old-time
favorite gospel songs. It was a present for Daddy and Mama.

Those hymns brought back memories of when God was my companion, my best friend. But my own way to God seemed blocked. The price
of going back to Him seemed too great: I'd have to give up my fun, my
friends, my parties.

I continued my downhill slide, and despair became a way of life.
Seldom did I remember the next morning what I'd done the night
before. I got to the point where I didn't want to be married. I didn't
want to perform. I didn't want to do anything . . . even go on living.

Everything came crashing down one night in California. I woke up in the back of my tour bus, drunk, filled with guilt and shame. Once again I faced the humiliation of knowing I had lost yet another battle. I sat bolt upright, my heart pounding. I felt like I was losing my mind—and maybe I was. If there had been a gun around, I think I'd have shot myself just to stop the misery. "This is it," I said. "I can't handle this anymore."

I picked up the phone and called Murphy, my bus driver, who was sound asleep in a nearby motel. "Ricky, it's the middle of the night," he said. "You sure this can't wait till morning?"

"Murphy," I said, "get over here and take me home." Murphy had been with me for five years, and he could tell from the sound of my voice that I was serious. He showed up, took one look at my face and got behind the wheel of the bus and headed cross-country for Tennessee.

Through three states I lay on my bed in the back of the bus. By the time it was midday we were in Oklahoma and I was stone sober, but I still wanted to die. I kept begging God for help, but frankly I didn't know what He, or anybody else, could do to end my pain.

All of a sudden there seemed to be a cloud floating above me. And then right in front of my eyes appeared what I can only describe as the face of the devil. It sounds unbelievable, but I know what I saw. That face kept coming closer and closer—ugly, overpowering, evil.

I was terrified. The face was smirking, as if to say, "I've got you now, boy. You're mine."

It was true I'd messed up pretty bad. But I would not believe that the devil had me. I started crying and hitting at that horrible face, punching hard like a boxer.

It didn't work. I began to sob as the face came still closer. "You can't beat me," it seemed to say.

And then I heard words coming out of my mouth, strong and sure, as though they had been inside me all along just waiting for the chance to get out. "Maybe I can't beat you," I shouted, "but I know who can. God can beat you."

In an instant that devilish face recoiled with a look of pure terror. It shriveled up right before my eyes and was gone.

I fell back on the bed, gasping for breath. I knew I'd connected with God again. And He had shown me His power, and what His holy name could do.

I haven't had a drop of alcohol since that day. God took my addiction away and gave me back my self-respect. In the months after I got home, I thanked God that His gentle grace and the prayers of my loved ones had kept me going.

Funny thing is, I'd kept hearing that the gospel album I had recorded the year before my life-changing ride in the back of the bus—the one with all the old favorite hymns—was affecting a lot of people's lives. I had called that album "Don't Overlook Salvation." And finally I'd followed my own good advice. ❧

> In my hour of darkness
> In my time of need
> Oh, Lord, grant me vision
> Oh, Lord, grant me speed.
>
> GRAM PARSONS AND EMMYLOU HARRIS
> "IN MY HOUR OF DARKNESS"

I s   T h a t   Y o u ,   L o r d ?

All of us, it's safe to say, find ourselves in crisis at some point in our lives. How can we best seek God's direction when our darkest hour is upon us?

Probably the best insurance you can have is to be spiritually prepared. Our first two stories in this chapter illustrate the point: As women of faith, Dorothymae Miller and Lillian Beech turned immediately to God when crisis came, and with God's help both were able to rise to the occasion.

In order to maintain an ongoing relationship with the Lord, always carry in your heart what the Reverend Billy Graham once called a "Spiritual Survival Kit." Its key elements: prayer, Scripture, and Christian community. Being equipped with those spiritual fundamentals will keep your lines of communication with the Holy Spirit wide open—in times of tranquility as well as in times of turmoil.

Being prepared to walk through darkness with God at our side also means we need not constantly *anticipate* darkness. Jesus affirmed this emphatically during the Sermon on the Mount. "Who of you by worrying can add a single hour to his life?" He asked (Matthew 6:27).

While it is true that bad things do happen to good people, God has assured us that—ultimately—all will be well. As the saying goes, if God brings you to it, He will bring you through it. D.H.

There's a famous poem called "The Hound of Heaven," written in 1893 by Francis Thompson. Perhaps you know it. It tells of a man who spends a good portion of his life running away from God. Nonetheless, every time he looks up, God is there, hand outstretched, offering salvation.

Roger Helle is one of those people who suffered through not one but several darkest hours. The hound of heaven pursued him through all of them.

GETTING TO BE SOMEBODY
—BY ROGER HELLE—

Sometimes you can feel lonely for a very long time—say twenty-eight years.

My twin brother Ron and I were put in an orphanage when we were four because my dad, an abusive man, abandoned us. Mom was fighting an alcohol problem and, overcome with the responsibility of caring for three young children, she just couldn't cope. As a kid you can't understand the terrible problems adults sometimes face. I didn't know Mom didn't want to leave us. Somehow I figured I was just in the way. The loneliness I felt was unbelievable.

In time, Mom came back to take us to live with her. By then we had a stepdad. I was in awe of him. He came from German immigrant stock, hard-working people, and he was always working: at a factory during the day and repairing TVs and electronic equipment at home for extra money. He could fix a busted stereo with a hanger, or a toaster with a bobby pin. I was lucky if I could nail two boards together. I'd follow him around, desperate to help, but it was plain I was only in his way.

It seemed I couldn't do anything right, but I kept trying. One day I spent hours waxing the car. When I proudly took my stepfather out to see my handiwork, the only response I got was, "You missed that big spot on the fender!" And I had.

It didn't help that I wasn't a good student at school, though my brother was. It didn't help that my folks never came to see me play football or any other sport. The point is, by the time the armed services recruiter came around during my senior year, I didn't think very much of myself. And joining the Marines with my brother gave me a chance to get out of the way. Maybe the feeling of loneliness would go away too. Maybe in the Marines I could be somebody.

After basic training I volunteered to go to Vietnam. "Nam" would have shocked anybody, but you can imagine what it was like for an eighteen-year-old who'd never been far from Toledo. Still, I liked being with my buddies in our platoon and I really liked our platoon commander, Sergeant Pruitt. We got along real well. One day he asked for a volunteer to "walk point" with him during a big offensive called Operation New York. "Walking point" means going out in front of the unit to scout for mines and draw enemy fire. "Let me go," I said. Volunteering came easy to me.

The day was sweltering, and by late afternoon, men were dropping from heat exhaustion. Sergeant Pruitt and I were talking, making jokes, when from nowhere came a bullet that tore through his head. I dropped to the ground in shock. One moment the sergeant was alive, and the next moment, in front of my eyes, he was dead!

In an ambush the enemy will pick you off if you're lying in the field, so our superiors gave the command to assault the tree line. There were 650 Vietcong dug in, just waiting for us behind the trees. We couldn't see them, but they opened fire; by the time we got out of that ambush, Danny, my buddy from boot camp, was dead too, and I was covered with the blood of my buddies. I'd really cared for these men, and they'd been blown away—gone from me—in a matter of seconds. The grief and loneliness were awful.

From then on I was pretty reckless. I didn't care about anything but revenge. It was as if danger was a drug and I had to keep increasing the dosage. I volunteered for every dangerous mission I could. I always walked point. I led guerrilla raids into enemy territory. More than once I was the only man to come back. I'd received two Purple Hearts and many other citations by that time. I finished my tour and was sent back to the States, but soon I volunteered to go back again.

One day I heard an "unofficial rumor" that I would be promoted to second lieutenant that afternoon. The morning's task was to go back to a village we'd captured and blow up all the Vietcong weapons we hadn't been able to transport. I sure wanted to get done!

I was carrying two sackfuls of explosives and walking point for my men across an empty field, marking booby traps as I found them, when something slammed into my thigh and thudded at my feet. I didn't have time to be more than surprised before the grenade went off. I was blown backward into the air. I knew I was hurt bad. All I could think of was, *I've got to get out of here!*

Somehow I staggered to my feet, only to have two shots pumped into me from close range. My men opened fire and dragged me out of the field. But a phosphorus grenade I was carrying ruptured, burning through my rifle and flak jacket and into my arm. No one knows what kept the rest of my explosives from going up like fireworks.

They did what they could at the Ninety-fifth Evacuation Hospital in Da Nang, but I had massive shrapnel wounds, stomach wounds, groin wounds, two broken legs, a broken arm and severe burns. My face was so badly swollen that no one could tell if my eyes were open or shut. So no one knew that I was fully awake when my brother Ron, who was also stationed in Vietnam, ran in looking for me.

He caught a doctor at the foot of my bed and said, "Doc, how's Roger Helle?"

No one knew I heard the answer: "Son, he's going to die."

I looked at death. There was nothing to see but a black void. Lying there, unable to move and speak, farther away from life and the living than I'd ever been, I panicked. I didn't want to die! *God,* I cried out into the darkness, *let me live, and I'll do anything You want!* My brother knelt at my bedside, weeping. I had no way of reaching out to him, no words of comfort if I could. Loneliness covered me like a shroud.

I didn't know it then, but God heard my plea. I only knew what the doctors said: If through some miracle I lived, I'd lose my leg, go blind, be crippled, and definitely never be able to have children.

The miracle happened. I lived. I nearly died en route to a hospital in Japan, then gangrene set in. But something was healing my body in ways the doctors couldn't explain. I added my own determination and spent hour after hour in physical therapy at a naval hospital in the States. By the time I was discharged I had another Purple Heart and a Bronze Star, but they didn't make me feel proud of myself. I just felt like a mess.

I found work with the Pinkerton's agency as a private investigator. I guess I was still seeking the "drug" of excitement and danger. Then I got married, to a beautiful young woman named Shirley Metzger, but because of me it wasn't much of a marriage. Just like my stepfather, I worked all the time. Then I started drinking. Before I knew it I was both a workaholic and nearly an alcoholic. For a while I tried to put a good face on our marriage—I even went to church, for instance, but mainly because that's what Shirley wanted.

My job took us to Omaha, and one day Shirley promised our pastor we'd join a Bible study that met during the week. That irked me at first, but I put on a good front there as well. No one at church knew I was a problem drinker, and no one suspected that our marriage was falling apart. When Shirley and I argued—or started to—I was out the door. I never listened when she talked. I rarely came home before midnight, and when I did I went straight to bed. I kept everything inside.

We were sitting around at Bible study one night when the leader stopped and asked us a question.

"Can each of you describe a time when God was very real to you?"

I sat back in my chair, wondering what that had to do with the passage we were studying, when suddenly something very strange happened to me. Slowly everybody in the room faded, and I was looking at a young kid shot to pieces, lying in a hospital bed. I heard the promise he made, and I knew that God was close, very close. Next thing I knew I was back in my chair. For days I felt shook up about that.

Not long after that, I blew up at Shirley once too often, and she left. I couldn't blame her, it was my fault. *Why couldn't I change?* Again the loneliness was so real I could almost touch it.

I begged Shirley to come back, and one morning she did. We faced each other warily. She finally spoke.

"Roger, we have made a mess of our relationship. You know it and I know it and God knows it. I think God is our last chance. I don't think we can fix it by ourselves."

I started to cry. There was no doubt about the truth of her words. Shirley and I knelt together. We prayed simply, "Jesus, we can't do it on our own. Please, please come into our lives. Save Roger. Save Shirley. Save our relationship."

In that moment a whole new awareness came to me. Time after time I'd heard that Jesus loved me enough to die for me. Now I also clearly saw all the times He'd spared my life in Vietnam. I realized that all my life I'd been plagued by a sense of worthlessness that had created my loneliness. But if God loved me as much as He so obviously did, well, I must be worth something!

This assurance changed me. Jesus was in my center, and now He determined my worth. I sure wasn't perfect, but I was willing to change. He took away all the nightmares of Vietnam and gave me peace. Shirley and I slowly pieced together our marriage. Sometimes when we fought I'd still storm out of the room, but something would stop me, and I'd turn around and say I was sorry. Now that I'd learned to value myself, twenty-eight years of loneliness had ended.

Soon it became important for me to help others who might be having some of the same problems with self-worth that I'd had. Shirley and I volunteered to help out at the coffeehouse our church ran for teenagers. Then I felt God wanted me to work with teenagers full time, so I resigned from Pinkerton's and joined Teen Challenge, a national program that offers live-in care for young adults aged seventeen and older who are having trouble with drugs, alcohol or family situations.

On Christmas Eve 1976, Shirley and I brought our newborn son home from the hospital. Not until I'd laid his little basket under the tree did the doctor's words come back: "Roger, of course you can never have children." Hot tears crowded my eyes. At Christmastime God gave the world the miracle of His Son. And now we had been given the miracle of tiny Joshua. As I looked at the sleeping infant at my feet, I felt overwhelmed by God's unconditional love pouring into me, and flowing out.

"I love you, Joshua," I whispered to my son. "I can't tell you how much you're worth." ❧

"God whispers in our pleasure, but He shouts in our pain."

C. S. Lewis

Daniel in the Lion's Den
Daniel 6:11–22 (cev)

The men who had spoken to the king watched Daniel and saw him praying to his God for help. They went back to the king and said, "Didn't you make a law that forbids anyone to pray to any god or human except you for the next thirty days? And doesn't the law say that everyone who disobeys it will be thrown into a pit of lions?"

"Yes, that's the law I made," the king agreed. "And just like all written laws of the Medes and Persians, it cannot be changed."

The men then told the king, "That Jew named Daniel, who was brought here as a captive, refuses to obey you or the law that you ordered to be written. And he still prays to his god three times a day."

The king was really upset to hear about this, and for the rest of the day he tried to think how he could save Daniel. At sunset the men returned and said, "Your Majesty, remember that no written law of the Medes and Persians can be changed, not even by the king."

So Darius ordered Daniel to be brought out and thrown into a pit of lions. But he said to Daniel, "You have been faithful to your God, and I pray that he will rescue you."

A stone was rolled over the pit, and it was sealed. Then Darius and his officials stamped the seal to show that no one should let Daniel out. All night long the king could not sleep. He did not eat anything, and he would not let anyone come in to entertain him.

At daybreak the king got up and ran to the pit. He was anxious and shouted, "Daniel, you were faithful and served your God. Was he able to save you from the lions?"

Daniel answered, "Your Majesty, I hope you live forever! My God knew that I was innocent, and he sent an angel to keep the lions from eating me." ⌁

☙ CHAPTER TWELVE ❧

GOD SPEAKS TO US...
In Miracles

*J*ournalists of a certain age carry in their heads the image of a crusty old copy editor. He wears a green eye shade and a perpetual scowl, and he snorts in disgust whenever he comes across a word or phrase that violates one of the sacred principles of Good Writing.

One of these principles is the Rule of Redundancy. You should never, for example, say that something has been "totally destroyed." Destroyed is destroyed; there is no such thing as "partially destroyed." Nor is there any sense in adding the modifier "very" to the word "unique."

Including a chapter on miracles in a book that consists of one miraculous story after another is a redundancy. Every time God speaks to us, it's a miracle. Every time He chooses to help us, or guide us, or comfort us, or to assure us of His presence and protection, something miraculous has occurred. Still, some miracles seem especially impressive—it's as if every so often God gets a kick out of showing us what He can do. The stories in this chapter are examples of such *occasions. They require no introduction, other than to say that they provide one more opportunity for us to marvel together at blessings received.*

THE HOLY SPIRIT SENT ME
—By Dan Montgomery—

One Friday afternoon I sat in a seminary class gazing out the second-story window at the grassy quadrangle below. My theology professor erased from the blackboard a long list of biblical references to the Holy Spirit.

I felt weary from memorizing a semester's worth of long lists about the Holy Spirit. The divine attributes of the Holy Spirit. The appearances of the Holy Spirit in the Old Testament. The gifts of the Holy Spirit in the New Testament. Today, Dr. Palma had cited all the references to the Holy Spirit in the Book of Acts.

The fire that had spurred me to sign up for the course sputtered out after the first few lectures. Digging up hundreds of historical references about what the Holy Spirit said or did thousands of years before seemed like spiritual archaeology. *History has its place,* I thought, *but can I encounter the Holy Spirit today? What is the Holy Spirit doing in Springfield, Missouri?*

After class I followed Dr. Palma to his office like a lost pup looking for direction. He invited me in.

"Dr. Palma, do you ever hear from the Holy Spirit?" I asked.

"Not directly," he replied. "I don't hear anything personal from the Spirit, such as a conversation would imply. But I do feel comforted now and then. Why are you asking?"

I searched for words. "I want something more from this course. I want to learn how to experience the Holy Spirit and have a real relationship with Him." I shifted in my seat and heard my voice become tense. "I want to know if the Holy Spirit really knows who I am and if He can guide me in specific ways."

Dr. Palma looked out the window and then back at me. "Dan, why don't you ask the Holy Spirit to reveal Himself to you in a personal way and see what happens? Tell Him you want an adventure for today."

I returned to my dorm to get ready for my study date with Gwen, a friendly girl who sat next to me in the Holy Spirit course. I had volunteered to help her get ready for our final exam the following week. We planned to drive over to the Southern Missouri State University library across town.

While in the shower I began to formulate a prayer. Then as I dressed, the prayer finally coalesced in my mind. "Holy Spirit," I prayed out loud, "I'm tired of memorizing all about the good old days. I want to know if you're alive and well in the twentieth century. Can you please speak to me today? In Jesus' name."

When Gwen and I arrived at the SMS campus, I invited her to have a cup of coffee before hitting the books. We strolled over to the building that housed the snack bar, ballroom and student activities center. As we entered, the throbbing beat of music struck my ears. A marquee announced that a rock band was playing in the upstairs ballroom.

I smiled at Gwen and gyrated my body in fun, but we knew we didn't dare go upstairs. The seminary prohibited dancing. Any student caught at a dance could be expelled. We walked to the snack bar, where I bought muffins and coffee and joined Gwen in a booth. No sooner had I sat down than a presence came over me so strongly that I froze. A powerful thought formed inside me and grew into a voice speaking within me.

"What's wrong?" asked Gwen.

"Just a minute," I muttered, staring into space.

The inner voice said matter-of-factly, *Dan, go to the dance.*

My hand trembled as I handed Gwen her coffee and took a sip of mine. "I think the Holy Spirit just spoke to me," I whispered.

"I didn't hear anything," she replied.

"No, I mean inside."

"What did He say?" she asked.

"He said to go to the dance."

"That can't be the Holy Spirit," she said. "It's against the rules."

"I know," I said. "But what if it really is the Holy Spirit? Will you come with me?"

"Okay," she said. "But let's just go in and out."

We finished our coffee and walked upstairs to the ballroom. I felt curious but slightly tense. At the top of the stairs the blaring music hit us full force. The ballroom glowed softly with multicolored track lights.

Now and then a strobe light flashed, making the twisting bodies look like ghosts dancing in slow motion. The voice spoke to me again: *Go stand in front of the band.*

I squeezed Gwen's hand and she followed me across the floor. Suddenly I imagined a scowling dean pointing his finger at me and yelling: *You're out of here!* His mouth would drop wide open when I pleaded, *The Holy Spirit made me do it!*

Just as I thought of abandoning the whole experiment, the inner voice spoke again, this time even more specifically: *Go strike up a conversation with the young man wearing the yellow shirt and blue jeans. His name is Terry. Tell him I love him. I'm sorry for the pain he's gone through. If he wants me back in his life, I will give him new guidance.*

This can't be the Holy Spirit, I thought. *It's got to be my imagination or some kind of wish fulfillment.* I turned to Gwen, not knowing how to explain my perplexity.

"Is He still talking to you?" she asked.

"Yes," I said.

"Well, what are we supposed to do next?"

Gwen had more faith than I did and she wasn't even hearing the voice. I resolved to carry out the strange orders. I had to find out if it was the Holy Spirit leading me. Taking a deep breath, I led Gwen across the dance floor right next to the guy in the yellow shirt. He appeared to be in his early twenties and looked grim. Feeling awkward, I moved into his line of sight.

Gwen peered around my shoulder. I awkwardly introduced us as students from across town.

"My name's Terry," he said.

My heart caught. "Terry, the Holy Spirit just told me to come over here and give you a message," I said.

"Who?" he asked.

"The Holy Spirit!" I shouted as the band hit a loud chord. The strobe light pulsed wildly, highlighting the incredulous look on his face. At that moment the band stopped for a break.

In a normal voice I said, as sincerely as I could, "The Holy Spirit says He's sorry for what happened to you. He says he still loves you very much. He even told me your name."

Terry's mouth dropped open. Then tears flowed down his cheeks.

"I can't believe," said Terry, "that God knows I'm here and sent you to talk to me. I've been so lonely. It's been the worst year of my life."

"Why?" I asked.

Terry told us he had once been a student at the seminary Gwen and I attended. "I was about to graduate," he said. "Some friends talked me into going to a dance. Another student saw me go in and reported me to the dean. I was expelled."

"What have you been doing?" I asked.

"Taking a few courses here. But I don't feel like I belong. This weekend I prayed for the first time in months. I asked God to give me a sign if He still wanted me in the ministry."

I looked at Gwen. She was biting her lip, tears in her eyes. Not caring what people might think, we both hugged Terry. I patted his shoulder and whispered, "The Spirit said to tell you He wants to guide you again. All you have to do is ask Him."

Terry nodded. "Would you pray for me before you go?" he asked.

The three of us made a circle and bowed our heads. "Father," I said, "thank You for giving Terry a sign of Your love. Heal his emotional wounds. Renew Your calling for him and guide him every day into the fullness of Your will. Thank You for bringing us together by the power of the Holy Spirit. In Jesus' name."

Terry rubbed his chest with his hand. "My bitterness is gone," he said with a smile of relief. "Thanks for having the guts to talk to me. I'll never forget tonight." He reached out and shook our hands vigorously.

Later, in the library, Gwen and I cracked the books, a warm glow in our hearts. The Holy Spirit was no longer a remote concept or a list of attributes to memorize. He had revealed himself as a living personality.

I learned that the Holy Spirit not only spoke in days of old, but still speaks to us personally. Since then this Friend has guided me in specific ways for more than twenty-five years. ❧

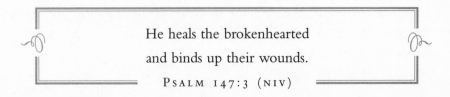

He heals the brokenhearted
and binds up their wounds.

PSALM 147:3 (NIV)

Journal of a Miracle
—By David Philip Clark—

How can I explain it? It's not easy, but maybe these excerpts from my diary will help.

Tuesday, January 26

My cousin Evelyn Wheeler phoned at 8:00 PM. "Phil," she said sadly, "I knew you'd want to know that Sunday night Neva Bertamini had a heart attack. . . ."

Distressing news. How much should one person have to take? First losing her husband to cancer. Then, her only child—a lovely daughter—running off to marry without her consent. Yet Neva kept going with her teaching out at Lakeview High and continued in her Sunday school work. She welcomed her daughter and her daughter's new husband into her home with love and affection. Now this!

Lord Jesus, Neva Bertamini is a fine woman—You know that. And she's Yours. Just let me know any way I can help.

Wednesday, January 27

Off and on during the night I awakened—each time feeling an urge to pray for Neva.

This morning the Lord directed me to James 5:14–15 (KJV). Over and over I read these words: "Is any among you sick? Let him call for the elders of the church, and let them pray over him, anointing him with oil in the name of the Lord; and the prayer of faith shall save the sick, and the Lord shall raise him up; and if he has committed sins, they shall be forgiven him."

"Lord," I murmured at last, aloud. "What would You have me do?"

No immediate answer. I settled down to my writing job for the day —every now and then stopping to study those verses again. By lunchtime, I suspected where the Lord was leading.

After lunch I faced the issue with Him squarely:

"All right, Lord. You know I believe in Your every promise. . . ."

His answer came clearly. Not audible, yet spoken to my heart: "Tonight, I want you to go anoint My daughter Neva—in My name— that she might receive her healing."

". . . Yes, Lord. All right."

I was alone in the house. Putting work aside, I found an empty perfume container. I removed its label, scalded it and poured into it some fresh-smelling baby oil. Then I held it up before the Lord, praying that it might be set apart from a common to a sacred use.

It was 5:00 PM. Looking at the bottle of oil, I said, "Lord, maybe I had better first call the hospital—to see if they'll even permit me to see Neva. . . ."

"No," came the firm command. "Go."

After supper, I drove the fourteen miles to Grove City, praying and praising God all the way.

It was 7:15 PM when I walked through the snow across the hospital parking lot, very conscious of the bottle in my outer coat pocket. I paused. "Look, Lord," I murmured, "I know I could go directly to Neva's room—but tonight I'm not going to. Like Gideon, I've got to put out a fleece. First, I'll check at the main desk. I won't feel sure You are really in all this unless I can officially get past. . . ."

The receptionist reported that nothing in her file indicated that Mrs. Bertamini could not have a visitor.

I climbed the hospital stairs, but hesitated outside her room. The door was slightly ajar and I could see Neva in bed, pale, eyes closed. She was in a semi-private room. In the other bed across from Neva the woman patient was very much awake.

"What do I do now, Lord?"

In the next instant Neva's eyes opened.

I went in, glanced toward the bed beyond. The other woman paid little attention to my arrival.

Neva smiled wanly. I told her about Evelyn's call to me. She nodded a little, said she'd lost three pounds during Sunday's seizure, that she'd even had another attack on Monday.

"And how are you tonight, Neva?"

"Ready for anything," she said in a remarkably calm voice. "Whatever the Lord might have in mind for me, I'm ready."

"You trust Him? Implicitly?"

"Yes, I certainly do."

In the other bed the woman was beginning to doze.

As simply as possible I stated the purpose of my visit. "I guess this is a first for both of us, Neva. I'm only trying, for my part, to obey. As for yourself, however resigned we may be to illness, I'm sure God Himself is never resigned to it. Perfect health is ever His perfect will. I'm convinced that He wants to give you complete healing—body, mind, spirit. I don't think we need to question His wanting to give such a gift."

"Please," she said. "Go right ahead."

I took out my Testament, read aloud the verses from James. I stated that since I was an elder in the Presbyterian church who was seeking to be led by the Holy Spirit, this passage applied to me. "The Lord Jesus Himself," I said, "has told us that if we abide in Him, if His words abide in us, we can ask what we will (in His name) in faith, believing—and know we've already received it. Do you believe that?"

Neva Bertamini nodded.

"Then we'll do just that. Now. Not attempting to predict exactly when you will see your healing—yet expecting it. Thinking of faith as a restoring power coming from Jesus Christ Himself."

The hospital room was utterly still. Neva's roommate went on dozing. Not a visitor, not a nurse came or went.

With fingers that trembled a little I drew out the bottle, applied a few drops of the oil to Neva's forehead, asked for and claimed her perfect wholeness in the briefest of prayers, told her all she had to do now was just thank God for what He already had done. Then I left.

Driving home, I said aloud: "I felt a bit awkward back there, Lord. But I thank You too—now—for everything."

THURSDAY, JANUARY 28

The phone rang at 12:45 PM. It was Neva, calling from the hospital. "Phil," she said in a firm voice, "I've got to tell you what happened. When the doctor came in this morning, I asked him if I could get out of bed. Naturally, he was skeptical and asked if I really felt up to it. I told him I did.

"Well, a while ago I tried it. The minute my feet hit the floor, I began shaking from head to foot, couldn't move my head from side to side— like it's been ever since my first attack. I thought I'd have to call a nurse, but instead I grabbed on to a chair, slid it along the floor ahead of me.

And then it happened. I can't describe the feeling, but all of a sudden the shaking stopped, I could turn my head—I knew I was healed!"

". . . Praise God," I said.

"And when Mrs. Jacobs looked up from her bed and saw me, she cried, 'What happened? You're well.' She could even see it. I told her it was a gift from God. And you should've seen me then! I walked out of that room and down the hall to tell the nurses!"

I was as excited as she was. "We shouldn't be surprised, Neva, should we? We expected this to happen."

FRIDAY, JANUARY 29
Ran into Leah Young, Neva's next-door neighbor, in Safrans' Market this afternoon. Overheard her telling Sarah Safran she'd had a call from Neva saying a miracle had happened, that the doctor had had all sorts of tests taken this morning and found her well enough to go home. "She asked me to come drive her home tomorrow," Leah added, incredulously.

SUNDAY, FEBRUARY 7
Neva was back in church today. Absolutely radiant.

THURSDAY, APRIL 22
Read in the paper today that Neva Bertamini had been chosen "Teacher of the Year" of Lakeview High. So well deserved. The yearbook is being dedicated to her.

MONDAY, MAY 31
Memorial Day holiday. Driving past Neva's house this afternoon, I saw her out front, busily painting her wrought-iron railings. Suddenly I realized that three verbs hold the key to God's top guiding power: Trust . . . obey . . . praise. ❧

> Sometimes a light surprises the Christian while he sings;
> It is the Lord, Who rises with healing in His wings.
>
> WILLIAM COWPER

IS THAT YOU, LORD?

As we near the end of our book on listening to God, I'd like to discuss what may be the most powerful prayer of all: the prayer of no power. The prayer of relinquishment.

To relinquish something is to surrender it. In this case what we surrender is our will, turning it over to God's will. This is the most complete form of asking for, and accepting, God's guidance. We vow to accept whatever the Lord gives us, be it illness, death, poverty . . . *whatever*. We turn it all over to Him. Jesus' prayer in the Garden of Gethsemane is the model of all prayers of relinquishment. "My Father, if it is possible, may this cup be taken from me. Yet not as I will, but as you will" (Matthew 26:39, NIV).

We humans cherish the idea that we command our own destinies, which is why people often surrender to God's will only as a last resort. This is a key concept in Alcoholics Anonymous, which holds that alcoholics must reach an emotional, physical, and spiritual "bottom" before they can finally admit that they are powerless over the drink. Step Three of AA's famous Twelve Steps is an explicit prayer of relinquishment: "[We] made a decision to turn our will and our lives over to the care of God as we understood Him."

For much of her life the beloved spiritual writer Catherine Marshall was a staunch advocate of the prayer of relinquishment. One of her most popular articles for *Guideposts* included some wise words on why surrender is *not* the same as resignation. "The Prayer of Relinquishment must not be interpreted negatively," she wrote. "It does not let us lie down in the dust of a godless universe and steel ourselves just for the worst. Rather it says: 'This is my situation at the moment. I'll face the reality of it. But I'll also accept willingly whatever a loving Father sends.'"

The power of relinquishment embodies one of the great paradoxes, and great miracles, of the Christian faith. We can get what we want if we are willing to obey what God wants. Surrender becomes victory. Amen. D.H.

A Path through the Woods
—By Mary Anne Deer—

We live on a hill in southeastern Vermont, five miles from the nearest town, surrounded by a thickly wooded forest. Even in winter when the leaves have fallen, we can't see any other houses, just the gentle slope of the hill, and silhouettes of trunks and branches. I spend many hours in what I have come to think of as "our woods," observing the minute details of nature. The other day when a nestling fell to the ground, I took out a lawn chair and sat watching the parents care for their baby. Nowhere else on earth do I feel so close to God. But it wasn't always that way.

When we moved here a dozen years ago, my husband Dennis was the one who felt most at home in nature. He had grown up hiking and camping. An Eagle Scout, he knew things I didn't: how to use a compass and how to tell direction by the stars. "Don't you think the house is awfully remote?" I asked him. "You'll get used to it," he replied.

Back then our boys were young: Daniel was three, and Timothy only a baby. I passed my days caring for them. Occasionally I'd glance out the window at the impenetrable forest while I changed a diaper or picked up toys. I took short winter walks around the periphery of the woods, pulling the boys on a sled through the snowmobile tracks. In spring we gathered flowers, and collected acorns and leaves in the fall. Though drawn to the forest, I never liked to venture too far from our deck. The trails were for loggers and snowmobilers, not inexperienced hikers like me.

Then one autumn, after we had been in the house for a year, my mother visited from Florida to enjoy the change of seasons. On a particularly luminous afternoon, Timothy was napping inside and Mom reading in the sunlight. Dennis suggested he and I take Daniel for a walk.

"We can't be gone too long," I said. "I need to be back when Tim wakes up." Mom was not really strong enough to lift him from his crib.

"No problem," Dennis assured me. The rich autumnal light was picking up the brilliant red, gold and copper of the leaves. I figured we had a good hour.

"Enjoy yourselves," Mom said, waving as we headed off.

The leaves crunched under our feet, Daniel kicking them in front of him, forging a deep path. "One, two, three . . ." he counted until he'd used up all his numbers, then he started in on the "ABC" song. Sunlight filtered through the trees, creating patterns on the forest floor like stained-glass windows in a church. *Nature's cathedral*, I thought. I took Dennis's hand and we walked in silence past the main junction of the logging road.

"Do you see any deer?" my husband asked.

"Deer!" Daniel exclaimed. He loved deer. None of us had spotted any, but for some reason I couldn't get over the feeling that deer and all sorts of other animals were watching us. A grouse flew up from behind a bush, startling us all. *They're God's creatures*, I tried to reassure myself. *This is God's home.*

The sunlight slanted lower and lower through the branches. I checked my watch. "We'd better turn back," I said, thinking of the baby.

"We'll find a shortcut home," Dennis said.

With the leaves obscuring the trails, I wasn't so sure, but I decided to trust Dennis. After all, he was the outdoorsman.

We started up a hill. "Come on, sweetie," I said to Daniel. He'd stopped singing and was complaining about being tired. "Look at the squirrels!" I said, hoping to distract him.

I glanced at Dennis. "Have you ever taken this shortcut before?"

"Never," he said. That didn't boost my confidence.

A flock of geese passed overhead and I noticed the sky was turning the dark blue that comes just before dusk. The air was getting cooler too. Why weren't we seeing anything I recognized? By now we should have been out of the woods.

We stopped at a large oak where a hunter had built a tree stand. I was afraid. How would Mom handle the baby when he woke?

"Dennis," I said, "we need to pray." He shrugged and bowed his head. "Dear Lord," I said, "please guide us home."

"Amen," Dennis added without much enthusiasm.

We resumed walking, though we didn't seem to be making any progress. In fact, I was beginning to think we were headed in the wrong direction. By now I was sure baby Timothy was crying for me.

"Are we lost?" Daniel asked.

"No," Dennis insisted, "we're not lost."

"Dennis, we need to pray again," I said. "All of us together, like we really mean it." The shimmering welcome the forest had first given us was fading with the sun. Now the woods felt cold and threatening.

"God," I prayed, "we need to find our way out of here."

Dennis picked up Daniel and took my hand. "Show us the way," he said. And then I remembered my first impression. *Yes, this is God's home.* In the falling dusk as well as the bright sunlight. In all seasons and all times.

We lifted our heads and I noticed a path going in another direction from where we were heading. Lined with trees and edged with grass, it seemed to glow, as though angels had unfurled a carpet of light. I couldn't tell where the illumination was coming from, whether it was the fading sun or a reflection from the clouds, but I knew we needed to take that path. I recalled the soothing line from Psalms, "Thy word is a lamp unto my feet, and a light unto my path."

I turned to Dennis. Our son in his arms, my husband was heading toward it too. The three of us followed the luminescent path, and in a matter of minutes we were back at the main junction of the logging road.

As we reached the paved road I said to Dennis, "You're not going to believe this."

"I couldn't believe it either," he replied.

"Did you see the path?" I asked.

"How could I miss it? It was all lit up. Clear as day."

Walking up the driveway, I couldn't see my mother on the dark porch, but her voice drifted down to us. "I was starting to get worried," she said. Inside the house, Timothy was just stirring from his nap. I lifted him from his crib and hugged him as Dennis helped Daniel with his jacket.

The next day I went bowling with a friend. I couldn't wait to tell her what we had seen. She knew where I lived and how dark the forest sometimes seemed to me. "The whole trail just lit up right after we prayed," I said. "It was as though someone were telling us where to go and how to get there."

My feelings for the woods have never been the same since. As the boys grew, we ventured farther and farther along the trails. When my sons went off to school I walked by myself beneath the oaks, the maples and hemlocks. I've studied the mushrooms, the flowers, the smallest insects found in a handful of rotting leaves. Once I even found myself standing a few feet from a moose and her calf. In all seasons, the forest has dark beauties I'm just beginning to discover. But as long as I remember who made it and who continues to guide my footsteps through it, I know I have no cause to fear. He is a lamp unto my feet, lighting my way. Always. ✺

> Show me your ways, O Lord,
> teach me your paths.
>
> PSALM 25:4 (NIV)

A Calendar for Courage
—By Margaret Hillis—

The gatekeeper at our mission compound limped into the kitchen doorway, bowed crookedly, and announced, "Hsieh si-mu, pastor's wife, here is his excellency, the colonel."

I held my breath. The colonel commanded the troops currently protecting this city of Shenkiu in Central China. It was January 1941; the invading Japanese were only a few miles to the east.

The colonel entered briskly and made his announcement: "The enemy is advancing into Honan Province. We have orders not to defend this city. You should find refuge in one of the villages outside."

I crossed my hands over the sleeves of my wadded e-shang and bowed politely, thanking him for his gracious concern for a "miserable" woman. As the colonel left the room, the icy January blast swept through the doorway. My baby cried. Suddenly the enormity of our danger overwhelmed me.

Our Margaret Anne was scarcely two months old, Johnny just over a year. Yesterday my husband, urgently needing medical care, had been taken by rickshaw to the hospital 115 miles away. I looked at the little Daily Scripture calendar on the wall: January 15. Not until early February would he be back. How would I manage without him? How would I make the myriad decisions that now crowded upon me?

You see, I had not yet experienced the full wonder of God's power to guide us when all other guides fail. Nor did I guess that as His instrument He would use anything as prosaic as a calendar on a kitchen wall.

By mid-afternoon the army garrison in our little city was empty. The departure of the soldiers created panic. Families packed their goods and fled.

The elders of the church called on me before they left. "Come with us," they pleaded. "We will care for you while Pastor Hillis is away."

I looked at the concern in their eyes and I thought of the country homes to which they were headed. My husband and I loved these village homes because we loved the people in them. But they held death for Western babies as too many little graves in our mission compounds showed.

How could I explain to these friends—without offending—that I could not take my children into their homes? Unheated, mud-floored huts, they crowded three and four generations together amid vermin and filth. Just a few weeks ago the six-month-old son of the nearest American family had died of dreaded dysentery. No, my babies were chained to this kitchen where I could boil dishes, milk and water.

But these were not things I could say to Chinese friends. I bowed, I thanked them, I spoke of waiting for my husband's return, of watching the mission property—and went to bed that night shaking with terror. When Johnny woke up whimpering in the cold, I took him into bed with me and lay awake a long time, listening to the wind rattle the waxed-paper window panes and praying that my little boy would live to see his daddy again.

Next morning I was in the kitchen early to start the water boiling for Margaret Anne's bottle. Automatically I reached up to the wall calendar and tore off yesterday's date. The Scripture verse for the new day gleamed like sunlight. "What time I am afraid, I will trust in Thee" (Psalm 56:3, KJV).

Well, I was certainly afraid. I fulfilled that part of it. Now, indeed, was the time to trust God. Somehow the verse sustained me all through the tense day.

The city was being evacuated rapidly. Other church members came to invite me to their family huts. But the Scripture held me. I was not to panic, but to trust.

By mid-morning the next day the city was nearly deserted. Then the gatekeeper came to me, eyes blurred with fear. He must leave, he said, and begged me to find refuge with him in his village beyond the city.

Should I? What could I do without our gatekeeper? The deserted city would be an open invitation to bandits and looters. But the risk to my babies outside was certain; here I still faced only fears. I declined the gatekeeper's offer, and watched him as he sorrowfully took leave.

It was noon before I remembered to pull the page off the little daily calendar on the wall. The tenth verse of the ninth Psalm read, "And they that know Thy name will put their trust in Thee: for Thou, Lord, hast not forsaken them that seek Thee."

As I bowed my head over my noonday meal, my heart poured out its gratitude to God for these particular words at this moment.

My main concern now was food. All the shops in the town were boarded shut. Meat and produce no longer came in daily from farms. I still had the goats for the babies' milk, but the man who milked them had left for his village. Tomorrow I would have to try to milk them myself. I wondered if I could ever make the balky little beasts hold still.

I slept uneasily that night, wondering how I would feed my children, and sure of very little except that we should stay in the city and, some-how, trust God. The sound of distant gunfire woke me.

Before facing the goats I fixed myself a bowl of rice gruel. Then I tore the old page from the calendar and read the new day's message. "I will nourish you, and your little ones," said the God of promise (Genesis 50:21, KJV).

The timeliness of these daily verses was becoming almost uncanny. With some curiosity I examined the back of the calendar pad. It had been put together in England, the year before, but God in His all-knowing had provided the very words I needed a year later, here on the other side of the world.

I was still eating the gruel when a woman stepped into the kitchen. She was carrying a pail of steaming goats' milk. "May I stay and help you?" she asked. "See, I have milked your goats."

Mrs. Lee had been our neighbor for years, but that morning I stared at her as though she had dropped from heaven. She had no family living, she explained, and wished to show her gratitude to the mission.

Late in the day a loud rapping at the gate set our hearts pounding. Braver, Mrs. Lee was the one who went to open it. Her face beaming, she returned leading our caller.

"Gee-tze! Gee-dan!" she cried triumphantly. "Chicken! Eggs!"

A frail, black-robed country woman came in with a live chicken and a basket of eggs. "Peace, peace," she gave the customary Christian greeting as she bobbed to us shyly. Noise of the cannons had not kept her away when she remembered that the missionaries would be hungry.

The calendar promise had come true! God would see to it that our little ones were nourished! That night my heart was full of hope. To the sound of shells bursting in the sky I prayed that somehow God would spare this city and these gentle people whom we loved.

Next morning I rushed down to the little square of paper hanging on its nail and tore off the page. "When I cry unto Thee, then shall mine enemies turn back: this I know; for God is for me," the Scripture declared (Psalm 56:9, KJV).

But this time it was too much to believe! Surely it couldn't be right to take literally a verse chosen just by chance for an English calendar?

As the gunfire drew closer Mrs. Lee and I began to prepare the house for invasion. Any papers that might possibly be construed to have military or political significance needed to be hidden or destroyed. We searched my husband's desk and the church buildings. By nightfall the gunfire sounded from both sides of the city. We went to bed dressed, prepared at any moment to meet the Japanese invaders.

I awoke abruptly in the early dawn and strained my ears for the crunch of military boots on gravel. But only a deep stillness surrounded me. There were no tramping feet, no shrieking shells or pounding guns, only the waking murmur of little Johnny in his crib.

Misgivings warred with excitement as I woke Mrs. Lee and we went to the gatehouse, each carrying a child. She was the first to stick out a cautious head. "There is no one in the street," she told me. "Shall we go out?"

And then, we stepped through the gate and watched as the streets began to fill, not with Japanese soldiers, but with townspeople returning from their country hiding places. *Had the Chinese won?*

As if in answer to our question, we met the colonel. "Pastor's wife!" he greeted me with relief. "I have been concerned about you!"

Then he told us that the Japanese had withdrawn. No, they had not been defeated, nor could anyone arrive at a reasonable conjecture concerning their retreat. The enemy had simply turned back.

I stepped into my kitchen, eyes fixed on a little block of paper pinned to the wall. Oh, you could say it was just a calendar. You could say strangers had chosen those verses without any thought of China, or of the war that would be raging when those dates fell due. But to me it was more than a calendar, and no stranger had picked those lines. To me it was the handwriting of God. ✎

He performs wonders that cannot be fathomed, miracles that cannot be counted.

JOB 5:9 (NIV)

In the chapter on signs and coincidences, I had mentioned that we ought not rely too much on signs and wonders, for faith is the belief in things not seen. A similar caution is warranted here, I think, having to do with the lure of the spectacular.

The grander the miracle, the more likely it is to attract our attention, and the more likely it is to affirm in our minds the sovereignty of our Creator. This is natural. There is something undeniably thrilling—and convincing—when God gives us an unexpected glimpse of His mighty power.

But even as we gaze in astonishment at the Red Sea parted or Lazarus raised, we need to be careful that we don't pay attention only to the spectacular. To do so is to risk missing the quieter miracles that surround us, every minute of every day. When we pause to contemplate them, these everyday miracles reveal themselves to be quite extraordinary indeed. Convincing, too.

Let us conclude with two short reflections that address, eloquently, this important theme.

A Student of Ways
—By Brian Doyle—

Now that I have achieved a certain age, I've learned to listen a little, see small miraculous things and not be such an unadulterated rockhead.

And I've become a student of ways: The way that men's suit pants bunch up at the knees when they stand after kneeling in church; the way that strands of hair work loose from my wife's ponytail when she is working; the way some children sleep with one hand open and legs splayed like scissors; the way a knee is knobby; the way a face curves around a grin in middle age; the way a mouth opens slightly when a man or woman falls asleep in a chair by the fire, and the way they startle gently awake, their eyes wide with amazement.

These are the ways we are, the miracles we swim in, the fingerprints of the Maker. ❧

> If the only prayer you ever say in your entire life is thank you, it will be enough.
>
> Meister Eckhart

News Delivery
—By Shari Smyth—

As I sit on my porch, the world according to the morning paper lying heavy on my lap, grim news fills me with a sense of doom. The world, I think, is spinning out of control. *Lord, where is the hope?*

Across my long porch, a male finch perches on the edge of a hanging fern, warbling his heart out. His tune, I think, also carries news. Grabbing my binoculars, I look inside the fern at the tiny nest cradling three pale blue eggs. The eggs have somehow survived cat-stalking, storms and at least one bird of prey. My newspaper slips to the floor. Through my lenses, I watch the plain, brown female pecking at the eggs. *They're hatching!*

I wait awhile, then I creep closer, climb on a railing and angle the binoculars to peek inside. The hatchlings are twined together, the size of a nickel, naked, helpless and mud brown. They cannot feed themselves and, left alone, their shallow, exuberant breathing would soon cease. But their parents are hovering nearby to nurture their brood, so they can grow up and fly and sing their song and propagate their species all over again.

Here, in this little backyard miracle, I see the hand that holds the world. An event too small, too ordinary to make the morning paper. But, light as a feather, soft as a whisper, its good news lands in my soul.

God is in control. ❧

> The earth is the Lord's, and everything in it, the world, and all who live in it.
>
> PSALM 24:1 (NIV)

JESUS FEEDS THE FOUR THOUSAND
MARK 8:1–8 (NIV)

During those days another large crowd gathered. Since they had nothing to eat, Jesus called his disciples to him and said, "I have compassion for these people; they have already been with me three days and have nothing to eat. If I send them home hungry, they will collapse on the way, because some of them have come a long distance."

His disciples answered, "But where in this remote place can anyone get enough bread to feed them?"

"How many loaves do you have?" Jesus asked.

"Seven," they replied.

He told the crowd to sit down on the ground. When he had taken the seven loaves and given thanks, he broke them and gave them to his disciples to set before the people, and they did so. They had a few small fish as well; he gave thanks for them also and told the disciples to distribute them. The people ate and were satisfied.

Afterward the disciples picked up seven basketfuls of broken pieces that were left over. ❧